Monetary Theory in Retrospect

Monetary theory is much enriched by a study of its history, so argues Filippo Cesarano in this collection of his essays. The inherent complexity of monetary theory invites alternative approaches, thus making the case for the history of the subject all the more compelling.

The book is divided into three parts. The first focuses on the innovative ideas of distinguished economists who anticipated modern theories, elaborating on them along lines that suggest original research programmes. The second examines the impact of expectations on the effectiveness of monetary policy, illustrating how different assumptions within the classical paradigm lead to diverse hypotheses and policy design. The third investigates the role of monetary theory in shaping monetary institutions.

These essays offer a series of suggestive ideas that can be appreciated by a wide audience, from students and researchers engaged with monetary theory and the history of economics to policy-makers seeking to weigh up the assumptions underlying different theories in order to select the models best suited to the problems they face.

Filippo Cesarano, economist at the Bank of Italy, works in the fields of monetary theory, international economics and the history of economic analysis. He is the author of *Monetary Theory and Bretton Woods* (Cambridge University Press, 2006).

Routledge Studies in the History of Economics

1 **Economics as Literature**
Willie Henderson

2 **Socialism and Marginalism in Economics 1870–1930**
Edited by Ian Steedman

3 **Hayek's Political Economy**
The socio-economics of order
Steve Fleetwood

4 **On the Origins of Classical Economics**
Distribution and value from William Petty to Adam Smith
Tony Aspromourgos

5 **The Economics of Joan Robinson**
Edited by Maria Cristina Marcuzzo, Luigi Pasinetti and Alesandro Roncaglia

6 **The Evolutionist Economics of Léon Walras**
Albert Jolink

7 **Keynes and the 'Classics'**
A study in language, epistemology and mistaken identities
Michel Verdon

8 **The History of Game Theory, Vol 1**
From the beginnings to 1945
Robert W. Dimand and Mary Ann Dimand

9 **The Economics of W. S. Jevons**
Sandra Peart

10 **Gandhi's Economic Thought**
Ajit K. Dasgupta

11 **Equilibrium and Economic Theory**
Edited by Giovanni Caravale

12 **Austrian Economics in Debate**
Edited by Willem Keizer, Bert Tieben and Rudy van Zijp

13 **Ancient Economic Thought**
Edited by B. B. Price

14 **The Political Economy of Social Credit and Guild Socialism**
Frances Hutchinson and Brian Burkitt

15 **Economic Careers**
Economics and economists in Britain 1930–1970
Keith Tribe

16 **Understanding 'Classical' Economics**
Studies in the long-period theory
Heinz Kurz and Neri Salvadori

17 **History of Environmental Economic Thought**
E. Kula

18 **Economic Thought in Communist and Post-Communist Europe**
Edited by Hans-Jürgen Wagener

19 **Studies in the History of French Political Economy**
From Bodin to Walras
Edited by Gilbert Faccarello

20 **The Economics of John Rae**
Edited by O. F. Hamouda, C. Lee and D. Mair

21 **Keynes and the Neoclassical Synthesis**
Einsteinian versus Newtonian macroeconomics
Teodoro Dario Togati

22 Historical Perspectives on Macroeconomics
Sixty years after the 'General Theory'
Edited by Philippe Fontaine and Albert Jolink

23 The Founding of Institutional Economics
The leisure class and sovereignty
Edited by Warren J. Samuels

24 Evolution of Austrian Economics
From Menger to Lachmann
Sandye Gloria

25 Marx's Concept of Money: The God of Commodities
Anitra Nelson

26 The Economics of James Steuart
Edited by Ramón Tortajada

27 The Development of Economics in Europe since 1945
Edited by A. W. Bob Coats

28 The Canon in the History of Economics
Critical essays
Edited by Michalis Psalidopoulos

29 Money and Growth
Selected papers of Allyn Abbott Young
Edited by Perry G. Mehrling and Roger J. Sandilands

30 The Social Economics of Jean-Baptiste Say
Markets and virtue
Evelyn L. Forget

31 The Foundations of Laissez-Faire
The economics of Pierre de Boisguilbert
Gilbert Faccarello

32 John Ruskin's Political Economy
Willie Henderson

33 Contributions to the History of Economic Thought
Essays in honour of R. D. C. Black
Edited by Antoin E. Murphy and Renee Prendergast

34 Towards an Unknown Marx
A commentary on the manuscripts of 1861–63
Enrique Dussel

35 Economics and Interdisciplinary Exchange
Edited by Guido Erreygers

36 Economics as the Art of Thought
Essays in memory of G. L. S. Shackle
Edited by Stephen F. Frowen and Peter Earl

37 The Decline of Ricardian Economics
Politics and economics in post-Ricardian theory
Susan Pashkoff

38 Piero Sraffa
His life, thought and cultural heritage
Alessandro Roncaglia

39 Equilibrium and Disequilibrium in Economic Theory
The Marshall-Walras divide
Michel de Vroey

40 The German Historical School
The historical and ethical approach to economics
Edited by Yuichi Shionoya

41 Reflections on the Classical Canon in Economics
Essays in honour of Samuel Hollander
Edited by Sandra Peart and Evelyn Forget

42 Piero Sraffa's Political Economy
A centenary estimate
Edited by Terenzio Cozzi and Roberto Marchionatti

43 The Contribution of Joseph Schumpeter to Economics
Economic development and institutional change
Richard Arena and Cecile Dangel

44 On the Development of Long-run Neo-Classical Theory
Tom Kompas

45 F. A. Hayek as a Political Economist
Economic analysis and values
Edited by Jack Birner, Pierre Garrouste and Thierry Aimar

46 Pareto, Economics and Society
The mechanical analogy
Michael McLure

47 The Cambridge Controversies in Capital Theory
A study in the logic of theory development
Jack Birner

48 Economics Broadly Considered
Essays in honour of Warren J. Samuels
Edited by Steven G. Medema, Jeff Biddle and John B. Davis

49 Physicians and Political Economy
Six studies of the work of doctor-economists
Edited by Peter Groenewegen

50 The Spread of Political Economy and the Professionalisation of Economists
Economic societies in Europe, America and Japan in the nineteenth century
Massimo Augello and Marco Guidi

51 Historians of Economics and Economic Thought
The construction of disciplinary memory Steven G. Medema and Warren J. Samuels

52 Competing Economic Theories
Essays in memory of Giovanni Caravale
Sergio Nisticò and Domenico Tosato

53 Economic Thought and Policy in Less Developed Europe
The nineteenth century
Edited by Michalis Psalidopoulos and Maria-Eugenia Almedia Mata

54 Family Fictions and Family Facts
Harriet Martineau, Adolphe Quetelet and the population question in England 1798–1859
Brian Cooper

55 Eighteeth-Century Economics
Peter Groenewegen

56 The Rise of Political Economy in the Scottish Enlightenment
Edited by Tatsuya Sakamoto and Hideo Tanaka

57 Classics and Moderns in Economics, Volume I
Essays on nineteenth and twentieth century economic thought
Peter Groenewegen

58 Classics and Moderns in Economics, Volume II
Essays on nineteenth and twentieth century economic thought
Peter Groenewegen

59 Marshall's Evolutionary Economics
Tiziano Raffaelli

60 Money, Time and Rationality in Max Weber
Austrian connections
Stephen D. Parsons

61 Classical Macroeconomics
Some modern variations and distortions
James C. W. Ahiakpor

62 The Historical School of Economics in England and Japan
Tamotsu Nishizawa

63 Classical Economics and Modern Theory
Studies in long-period analysis
Heinz D. Kurz and Neri Salvadori

64 A Bibliography of Female Economic Thought to 1940
Kirsten K. Madden, Janet A. Sietz and Michele Pujol

65 Economics, Economists and Expectations
From microfoundations to macroeconomics
Warren Young, Robert Leeson and William Darity Jnr.

66 The Political Economy of Public Finance in Britain, 1767–1873
Takuo Dome

67 Essays in the History of Economics
Warren J. Samuels, Willie Henderson, Kirk D. Johnson and Marianne Johnson

68 History and Political Economy
Essays in honour of P. D. Groenewegen
Edited by Tony Aspromourgos and John Lodewijks

69 The Tradition of Free Trade
Lars Magnusson

70 Evolution of the Market Process
Austrian and Swedish economics
Edited by Michel Bellet, Sandye Gloria-Palermo and Abdallah Zouache

71 Consumption as an Investment
The fear of goods from Hesiod to Adam Smith
Cosimo Perrotta

72 Jean-Baptiste Say and the Classical Canon in Economics
The British connection in French classicism
Samuel Hollander

73 Knut Wicksell on Poverty
No place is too exalted
Knut Wicksell

74 Economists in Cambridge
A study through their correspondence 1907–1946
Edited by M. C. Marcuzzo and A. Rosselli

75 The Experiment in the History of Economics
Edited by Philippe Fontaine and Robert Leonard

76 At the Origins of Mathematical Economics
The Economics of A. N. Isnard (1748–1803)
Richard van den Berg

77 Money and Exchange
Folktales and reality
Sasan Fayazmanesh

78 Economic Development and Social Change
Historical roots and modern perspectives
George Stathakis and Gianni Vaggi

79 Ethical Codes and Income Distribution
A study of John Bates Clark and Thorstein Veblen
Guglielmo Forges Davanzati

80 Evaluating Adam Smith
Creating the wealth of nations
Willie Henderson

81 Civil Happiness
Economics and human flourishing in historical perspective
Luigino Bruni

82 New Voices on Adam Smith
Edited by Leonidas Montes and Eric Schliesser

83 Making Chicago Price Theory
Milton Friedman–George Stigler correspondence, 1945–1957
Edited by J. Daniel Hammond and Claire H. Hammond

84 William Stanley Jevons and the Cutting Edge of Economics
Bert Mosselmans

85 A History of Econometrics in France
From nature to models
Philippe Le Gall

86 Money and Markets
A doctrinal approach
Edited by Alberto Giacomin and Maria Cristina Marcuzzo

87 Considerations on the Fundamental Principles of Pure Political Economy
Vilfredo Pareto (Edited by Roberto Marchionatti and Fiorenzo Mornati)

88 The Years of High Econometrics
A short history of the generation that reinvented economics
Francisco Louçã

89 David Hume's Political Economy
Edited by Carl Wennerlind and Margaret Schabas

90 Keynes's Vision
Why the Great Depression Did Not Return
John Philip Jones

91 Monetary Theory in Retrospect
The selected essays of Filippo Cesarano
Filippo Cesarano

Monetary Theory in Retrospect

The selected essays of Filippo Cesarano

Filippo Cesarano

Routledge
Taylor & Francis Group
LONDON AND NEW YORK

First published 2007
by Routledge
2 Park Square, Milton Park, Abingdon, Oxon OX14 4RN

Simultaneously published in the USA and Canada
by Routledge
270 Madison Ave, New York, NY 10016

Routledge is an imprint of the Taylor & Francis Group, an informa business

Typeset in Sabon by
RefineCatch Limited, Bungay, Suffolk

Printed and bound in Great Britain by
Antony Rowe Ltd, Chippenham, Wiltshire

British Library Cataloguing in Publication Data
A catalogue record for this book is available from the British Library

Library of Congress Cataloging in Publication Data
A catalog record for this book has been requested

ISBN 10: 0–415–42343–0 (hbk)
ISBN 10: 0–203–93936–0 (ebk)

ISBN 13: 978–0–415–42343–4 (hbk)
ISBN 13: 978–0–203–93936–9 (ebk)

Contents

Preface

The history of economic analysis does not appeal to the profession any more and has virtually disappeared from academic curricula. Having long used the tools of the hard sciences, economists feel they have achieved their dream of becoming like physicists, and thus deem the history of the subject to be totally useless. I have always entertained the opposite idea and this collection of papers aims to support it.

My interest in the history of economics dates back to my high school days. Curious about the contribution of theory to assessing opposite models of economic organization like *laissez-faire* and planning, I plunged into a hectic, unsystematic reading of the classics. These readings were most illuminating, but also left me with the misleading idea that economics is simple, perhaps because great economists write clearly about complex issues. As an undergraduate busy with my degree thesis, I revisited the theories of the past simply to survey the literature in a more extensive way. Yet, I found that study of the classics enhanced research in several ways: widening the economist's theoretical background, stimulating novel ideas and suggesting alternative approaches. This sensation was substantiated by my chance encounter with Galiani's treatise on money, which proved to be a mine of insightful analyses and shed light on many aspects of modern monetary theory (Chapter 2).

As a provocative afterthought, that paper posed the general question of the role of the history of economic analysis. The spread of the formalist revolution had progressively diminished interest in the subject, so that making the case for the history of economics was a challenging task (Chapter 1). The argument builds on the absence of cumulativeness or convergence in the growth of knowledge, something that, acknowledged even for the physical sciences, should apply *a fortiori* to the evolution of the social sciences. Convergence does not characterize all fields equally, but is inversely related to the complexity of the subject and, thus, varies along the span of knowledge. This principle is also relevant within economics, which, involving topics of different degrees of complexity, ranging from the simple structure of price theory to the complex structure of growth theory, shows different degrees of cumulativeness.

Owing to the multifaceted nature of money, monetary theory verges on the more complex fields and is therefore suitable for investigating the conjecture of non-monotonic convergence. The papers collected here corroborate this hypothesis, assigning a substantial role to the history of economic analysis. The volume focuses on a variety of issues tackled by several economists (Part 1) and on specific topics relating to monetary policy (Part 2) and monetary systems (Part 3). An overview of the papers is eschewed, however, because it would prevent the reader from discovering their content by himself. Indeed, the pleasant and stimulating side of practising the history of economics is the unveiling of hitherto unnoticed arguments and the links between them, hinting at new research paths. In this respect, historians perform an important signalling activity but, in order to be most productive, theorists must personally pursue this objective. Careful reading of the classics can be suggestive of novel ideas and help to bring about original contributions.

The role of the history of economic analysis in enhancing the progress of economics is the leitmotiv of this collection. The 1983 article (Chapter 1) thus serves as an introduction. Then, when I began to plan the book, my immediate thought was to revisit this topic and write a new paper (Chapter 12), which can be viewed as an epilogue, bringing back the main theme. Both essays focus on the distinctive characteristics of economics as a social science. The complexity of economic phenomena involves a multiplicity of modelling strategies so that, as in other fields, several competing hypotheses may well emerge. But in economics, and to a greater extent in other social sciences, most hypotheses, even if falsified in some circumstances, are non-excludable, witness the centuries-long coexistence of parallel strains of monetary theory, opposing the Currency School to the Banking School, classics to Keynesians, and New Classical to New Keynesian Macroeconomics. The diffusion of formal modelling, by narrowing the focus of analysis, actually heightens this distinguishing feature.

A main implication of non-excludability is that it runs counter to the cumulative character of economics, thus enhancing the role of the history of the subject. By providing useful hints for original approaches, study of the classics can throw a bridge between past and future theories. A paramount example is Michael Woodford's recent book *Interest and Prices* (Princeton, Princeton University Press, 2003), whose title is evocative of the influence of Wicksell, especially with regard to the analysis of a cashless economy.

In fact, one of the many lessons of the history of economics is the importance of revisiting the work of great economists with a view to fostering research. The usefulness of rereading the classics does not fade away because, between the lines, many suggestive hints at novel theoretical models can be detected. This stems from the inherent complexity of economics as a social science, leading to theories that are, for the most part, non-excludable. A graphic testimony is offered by Robert Lucas in the introduction to his *Studies in Business-Cycle Theory* (Cambridge, Mass.,

The MIT Press, 1981, p. 9), in which he stresses the importance of past contributions (that actually go back to Mill, Chapter 4).

> [T]he apparent novelty of the model of 'Expectations and the Neutrality of Money', in combination with the unhappy experience that the substantively original ideas in my own economic thought invariably had proved to be wrong, renewed my interest in the vast pre-Keynesian literature on business-cycle theory. There I found not the obstinate resistance to evident fact described by Keynes, and repeated as 'history' by two or three generations of Keynesians, but a sophisticated literature, however unaided by modern theoretical technology, emphasizing the recurrent character of business cycles, the necessity of viewing these recurrences as mistakes, and attempts to rationalize these mistakes as intelligent responses to movements in nominal 'signals' of movements in the underlying 'real' events we care about and want to react to. If Wesley Mitchell could view agents as 'signal processors' in 1913, then I saw no reason to regard my own adoption of this viewpoint in 1972 as unduly speculative.

These papers span three decades, yet the history of economic analysis was never my main occupation. I considered it a pleasant research activity, to be practised occasionally whenever interesting ideas serendipitously popped up. I benefited from the comments of many people, acknowledged in each article. With some of them, however, I have been in closer touch and my special thanks go to Robert Clower, Benjamin Friedman and David Laidler for their continuous encouragement and stimulating intellectual exchange, which has deepened and extended my knowledge of monetary theory.

Acknowledgements

Chapter 1: Reprinted from *History of Political Economy*, Spring 1983, by kind permission of Duke University Press.
Chapter 2: Reprinted from *History of Political Economy*, Fall 1976, by kind permission of Duke University Press.
Chapter 3: Reprinted from *History of Political Economy*, Spring 1991, by kind permission of Duke University Press.
Chapter 4: Reprinted from *History of Political Economy*, Fall 1996, by kind permission of Duke University Press.
Chapter 5: Reprinted from the *Journal of International Economics*, June 1998, by kind permission of Elsevier.
Chapter 6: Reprinted from *History of Political Economy*, Fall 2003, by kind permission of Duke University Press.
Chapter 7: Reprinted from the *American Economic Review*, March 1983, by kind permission of the American Economic Association.
Chapter 8: Reprinted from the *Manchester School*, September 1998, by kind permission of Blackwell Publishing.
Chapter 9: Reprinted from *History of Political Economy*, Summer 1990, by kind permission of Duke University Press.
Chapter 10: Reprinted from the *Journal of Economic Studies*, no. 5, 2003, by kind permission of MCB University Press.
Chapter 11: Reprinted from *History of Political Economy*, Winter 2006, by kind permission of Duke University Press.

The views expressed in this book are the author's own and not necessarily those of the Bank of Italy.

History of Political Economy 15:1

[1]

On the role of the history of economic analysis

Filippo Cesarano

I

It is a widely held opinion among economists that the history of the subject is of little relevance to the present-day scholar. This opinion is reflected in the sharp decline of interest in the history of economics. Despite the appearance of a professional journal, *History of Political Economy*, dedicated to the discipline, the field is at best regarded as highly specialized and inconspicuous. At present, review articles are the closest equivalent to traditional research by historians of economics. However, such works are based on a more limited analytical perspective and are usually confined to the very recent literature.

In acknowledging these developments, it has been rightly argued that they have been prompted by the failure to specify the nature and significance of the contribution of the history of economics to the further development of economics (Stigler 1969, 229–30; Tarascio 1971, 428). This is no simple task. Several answers have been provided; most of them, however, focus upon enlarging the scope of the historian's work, which is tantamount to avoiding the question altogether. In the following pages an attempt will be made to show the relevance of the history of economic analysis for current research and for the advancement of economic theory.

II

The fading interest in the history of economics[1] sharply contrasts with both the strong growth of other specialized fields and the introduction of new ones fostered by an ever-increasing division of labor. Before the 1940s, the picture looked rather different, and research in the history of economics was clearly of interest to the profession. Furthermore, the history of the discipline was so closely embedded in current theory that continuous reference to classic authors was present in most works of no historical character. In contrast, the last issue of any prominent journal hardly contains any citations of writings dating before the 1940s, which seems to suggest a turning point in the attitude of economists towards the history of

Correspondence for the author may be sent to Filippo Cesarano, Banca d'Italia, Via Nazionale 91, 00184 Roma, Italy.

1. For a summary of the evidence, see Tarascio 1971.

their subject.[2] This is no casual coincidence. In fact, one of the basic factors which has often been pointed out (Bronfenbrenner 1966; Tarascio 1971) to account for the decline of the history of economics is the sharp change in the methodological apparatus and the consequent widening of the economist's 'box of tools' by means of more sophisticated and powerful analytical weapons. This produced two main effects on the development of economics. On one side, it opened a novel and large frontier for research which caught on at once and expanded rapidly. On the other side, the new analytical tools gave the highly misleading impression of a broadening gap between the contributions of past economists and those of modern theorists, overrating the achievements of the latter. In the following paragraphs, it is argued that both these effects helped to establish a climate quite unfavorable to the development of the history of economics.

An important implication of the results brought about by the more efficacious methodological weaponry was the general conviction that economics had acquired the status of a mature or hard science, the development of which seemed to proceed by the accumulation of new and more comprehensive theories. Studies in the history of the discipline had no role in such a context.[3] Historians of economics were not able to propose a ready defense, in part because what had to be justified was not the study of the history of economics (there was nothing to object against this research activity more than to object to the study of the history of mathematics or the history of music), but the relevance of the history of economics to the further development of economic theory.

In his classic tome Schumpeter asked, why do we study the history of economics? (1954, 6), and suggested a three-part answer composed of pedagogical advantages, aid to the search for new ideas, and insights into the ways of the human mind. He maintained that the first two are of foremost importance and saw fit to essentially ignore the third. It is no mere coincidence of timing that in almost all the writings following the publication of Schumpeter's monumental work, these two motivations—the pedagogical and the inspirational—have been either abandoned or considerably played down.[4] Indeed, in that very period, economics came to be

2. Bronfenbrenner 1966 provides empirical evidence for this timing on the basis of the number of articles dealing with the history of economics.

3. Among others, Tarascio makes this point very clearly: " . . . implicit in the use of these methods is the positivistic and/or naturalistic view that since no *logical* distinction exists between the methodologies of the physical and social sciences, economics is a cumulatively progressive science in the same way as, say, physics. By way of analogy then, an economist need not devote his time to outworn theories of the past any more than his counterparts in the physical sciences" (1971, 421; italics in the original).

4. There are a few writers, like Stigler (1969), Boulding (1971), Hollander (1975), and Remenyi (1979), who still repose confidence in the pedagogic value of the history of the discipline. Such a confidence, however, is not complete or unqualified. George Stigler, in the introductory part of his article, has a lot to say in favor of the pedagogical motivation, but he then states that "the real interest of science lies elsewhere" (1969, 222).

characterized as a mature science in which knowledge is acquired in a cumulative fashion, obviating the need to study past accomplishments for teaching purposes and discounting the possibility that new ideas can be found in ancient works. Hence, while economists have sought to find a role for the history of the discipline, most scholars have advanced arguments for the enlargements of the sphere of the subject, as opposed to arguments that ascribe a new importance to traditional forms of history of economic *analysis*. Winch (1962) is a prime example. He noticed that analytic approaches in the Schumpeter-Stigler tradition, by neglecting the influence of philosophical and political values,[5] not only narrowed the scope of the field but also hindered a deeper and more comprehensive interpretation of the works of the past. According to Winch (1962, 200), scholars should examine both *what* an economist wrote and *why* it was written, relating the history of economic thought to other branches of intellectual history. Although this basic theme has been common to several writers,[6] it has been played in different variations, stressing among other things the sociology of science, the relationship of economic theory to economic policy, and the history of specific topics, such as methodology, the international diffusion of economics, and heterodox theories.

It seems, then, that economists have failed to offer convincing arguments in favor of the history of economic *analysis*. There is much to be concerned about regarding this state of affairs. It seems important to find a role for the history of economics *within* economics, i.e., a role that would be relevant to the modern theorist. The aim of this essay is to show that a case for the history of economic theory can still be made.

III

It was argued in Section II that methodological innovations in economics since the 1940s have undermined the study of the history of economics by supporting the notion that economic knowledge progresses in a cumulative fashion.[7] In the following pages, serious doubts are cast on the

5. An early and most forceful exposition of this standpoint is Pantaleoni's (1898); Blaug's treatise (1968) represents a recent statement of the same position.

6. A long but not exhaustive list would include chronologically: Gordon 1965, Nabers 1966, Coats 1969b, Stigler 1969, Tarascio 1971, Goodwin 1972, Samuels 1974, Corry 1975, Remenyi 1979 and Goodwin 1980.

7. A very clear picture of economists' attitudes towards these matters is given by Kenneth Boulding. He first explains the position of the "antihistorical school, summed up in the classic words of an economist, whose name I regret I have not been able to trace, that 'he was not interested in the wrong opinions of dead men.' This presumes that economics is like mathematics in that knowledge about it grows continuously and without loss, so that the moderns contain all that was in the ancients and then some; there is really no point in studying the ancients at all, and therefore, the later the textbook the better" (1971, 229). Boulding, then, identifies the current view of the profession with that of the antihistorical school. The latter "is now common in the United States, where the history of thought is regarded as a slightly depraved entertainment, fit only for people who really like medieval

existence of cumulativity in economics by examining this issue from the general perspective of the history of science. It is suggested that economists have suffered a cultural gap with respect to developments in the philosophy of science and that this explains the naiveté with which the idea that progress in economic theory is cumulative has been accepted.

The notion of cumulativity in scientific development—or the less restrictive one of convergence more widely used by philosophers—is intricate and highly debated. Convergence is a fundamental terminal element to which a given approach to the structure of theories leads, and thus it may or may not result depending upon the approach to epistemology that is followed. A quick glance over the main views of epistemology will show the controversial status of this branch of philosophy and the related discussion about convergence.

The development of logical positivism together with the contemporaneous appearance of works in the different disciplines of historical criticism, symbolic logic, and physics, respectively by Mach, Russell, and Einstein (Toulmin 1974, 600) led in the 1920s to a conception of epistemology which has been concisely called by Putnam the "Received View on theories" (Suppe 1974, 3).[8] In the simplest version of the Received View, theories are axiomatic calculi which connect theoretical terms and specify relationships between them. The axioms of the theory represent formulations of scientific laws regarding phenomenal regularities as described by the observation terms. Correspondence rules link the laws of the theory to the observable phenomena and facilitate the making of predictions which can be evaluated by means of empirical tests. Successful performance in such tests increases the degree of confirmation of a theory. Then, the appearance of new theories (Suppe 1974, 53–56) can be due either to the lack of predictive power of a theory when applied to a wider range of phenomena, or to the enlargement of the scope of the phenomena considered, or, lastly, to the process of reducing several theories to a more general one. The exponents of the Received View, most notably Nagel (1961), argue that scientific progress proceeds mainly through the latter two modes of development which involve two kinds of *theory reduction* and, contrarily to the first one, do not entail the rejection of the precedent theories. "Science thus is a cumulative enterprise, extending and aug-

---

Latin, so that one can become a full-fledged, chartered Ph.D. economist without ever reading anything that was published more than ten years ago" (1971, 232). Explicit references to this standpoint are hard to find, a notable exception being the following statement of a general character by no less an authority than Paul Samuelson: "I believe that knowledge is additive and that the history of economic doctrines suggests that progress comes from unpredictable and varied sources" (1954, 381).

8. For a clear and thorough survey of epistemology in the twentieth century see Suppe 1974, upon which this and the following paragraphs are based. A highly simplified exposition of the Received View has been provided by Margenau 1966, with brief references to economics and other social sciences.

menting old successes with new successes; old theories are not rejected or abandoned once they have been accepted; they are just superseded by more comprehensive theories to which they are reduced" (Suppe 1974, 56).

During its development, the Received View was criticized in several respects, but this eventually helped to produce an improved final version. Beginning in the early 1950s, however, more fundamental criticisms rejected the Received View altogether.[9] Contemporaneously, alternative analytical frameworks were provided along three main lines: descriptive analyses based upon a diffuse skepticism about the feasibility of a rational reconstruction of theories; semantic approaches which focused upon the linguistic formation of a theory; and the so-called *Weltanschauungen* analyses which stressed the influence of sociological and other factors upon the development of theories. The latter approach is the one which has been followed most, with contributions by Toulmin, Kuhn, Hanson, Popper, Feyerabend, Bohm, and others. The variety of the arguments advanced by these authors precludes even a sketchy summary of their views.[10] In this context, the relevant point to emphasize is that, because of its assumptions, theory reduction is incompatible with most of the *Weltanschauungen* analyses. The latter approach stresses the evolving character of the *Weltanschauung*, thus entailing a change in the meaning of theoretical terms following a language shift, in the presumptions determining what are counted as significant facts, and in the standards by which the scientist assesses the fruitfulness of the theory (Suppe 1974, 132). Consequently, this approach rejects convergence as a character of scientific development. Needless to say, various criticisms have also been raised against the *Weltanschauungen* analyses. At present, therefore, there is no commonly accepted analysis of the structure of theories. And if there is no unanimous view about such an analysis, there can hardly be a unanimous view about convergence. Thus, convergence remains a highly controversial issue.

The hypothesis advanced here is that the relevant point for determining the usefulness of studying the history of a discipline is not *whether* the discipline converges but *how* it might converge. The essential issue is not to establish whether the course science takes towards a 'true' theory is that of an upward trend or a stationary path, but how that path behaves relative to the trend. Indeed, even in the presence of convergence, the path of scientific development (the PSD)[11] may be characterized by fluctuations

9. These criticisms were directed to basic features like the observational-theoretical distinction, the role of correspondence rules, and the accent upon axiomatization (Suppe 1974, ch. 4).

10. The interested reader is again referred to Suppe's exhaustive essay (1974, ch. 5).

11. The PSD may be thought of as a time function of the variable 'stock of accumulated knowledge' which can be interpreted in two ways. First, as a sum of theories which are accepted by the community of scientists, not necessarily by all of them, at a given instant;

along the positively inclined trend so that, for some periods, the state of advancement of a discipline may well be at a lower level than the achievements of the past. Only in the extreme case in which the PSD of the discipline is monotonically non-decreasing[12] is it true that at every point in time, any theory T_2 that comes later than theory T_1 does not entail the rejection of T_1 yet is always 'better' than T_1. Hence, the awkward question of the existence of convergence towards a 'true' theory can be neglected, since what is at stake is simply the shape of the PSD and not the presence of a link between convergence (i.e., increase in knowledge) and increase in 'truth content.' A sufficient condition for the usefulness of the history of a subject is the failure to comply with the requirement of a non-decreasing monotonic development path.

It becomes important, then, to analyze the underlying factors which determine the shape of the PSD. It is a main contention of the present study that there is not a unique type of time function which is valid for science at large, but that there exists a whole set of PSDs along the entire range of knowledge. More particularly, the hypothesis advanced here is that it is not possible to single out a given shape of the course of scientific development common to all fields of knowledge; there is, instead, a specific time function for each discipline. Before showing the arguments supporting this hypothesis, it has to be remarked that philosophers of science have always debated the shape of the time function for science in general, arguing either in favor (Received View) or against (*Weltanschauungen* analyses) cumulativity; but there is no suggestion that there are different paths for different disciplines. The rationale of this attitude may be found in the fact that most, if not all, of the philosophers who have looked at epistemology have focused their views upon physical sciences only. Indeed, the bulk of the literature on epistemology identifies 'science' with the so-called hard or mature sciences.[13] The analysis of theories has al-

second, as the accumulated 'truth content' of the theories existing at a given point in time. Various concepts may be used to give an empirical meaning to the notion of 'truth content.' Popper's (1972) conception of verisimilitude of a theory directly derives from his well-known account of scientific advancement in Popper 1968, according to which progress is brought about by theories surviving continuous attempts to falsify them; verisimilitude varies in relation to the set of true entailments of the theory. Alternatively, Hesse's (1974) network model of theories appraises scientific theories according to their predictive content, avoiding the need to make use of the concept of truth. In general, the difficulty of giving an empirical content to both interpretations of the variable 'stock of accumulated knowledge' is not a matter of great concern in the context of this study.

12. This defines cumulativity, which is a more restrictive notion than convergence.

13. This tendency is, however, beginning to change. Mary Hesse (1974, introd.) remarks: "the logic of science is very relevant to two matters of current interest and controversy. Firstly, there are rising doubts about the value of natural science itself as this has been traditionally understood. Far from being the paradigm of all knowledge, its aims to make true discoveries about the natural world and to exploit these discoveries are both being increasingly questioned. And secondly, the question of the character of other modes of

ways yielded a single specification of the path of "science'; therefore, disputes have concerned the interpretation of the PSD, never suggesting, however, that a given analysis of theories could give rise to different development paths for different disciplines.

In the following paragraphs, it is shown that various PSDs relating to various fields of scientific knowledge can result from a particular analysis of theories. The framework of the Received View will be used, despite the criticisms raised against it, simply because it provides a good expository tool. Further, and more important, the Received View admits only a cumulative PSD and is therefore, particularly suitable for the sake of the present study's argument because it makes the most unfavorable case for it.

The principle of the division of labor has been widely applied to science, and scientists do not look at the world from a single point of view. There is instead an *n*-dimensional 'slicing' of the surrounding reality according to the *n* fields of knowledge. This 'slicing' process can be easily shown by considering how a specific event is seen by different scientists. Imagine, for example, that a given quantity of milk, closed in a tetrahedral container, is purchased by an individual at a given point in time. This very single event can be analyzed from several perspectives, posing various kinds of problems. Mathematics will be concerned, say, with the volume of the tetrahedron, physics with the laws according to which the liquid will lie inside the container, biochemistry with the composition of milk and its transformation under various circumstances, economics with the price paid for the milk, anthropology with the influence of milk drinking upon the development of mankind, sociology with the effects of milk availability on the social behavior of ghetto residents, and so on.

According to Margenau 1966 there is a sensory experience upon which the scientist elaborates his 'constructs,' or abstract concepts, and the two are connected by means of 'rules of correspondence.' The logical relationships connecting a complex of constructs, together with the correspondence rules which link the constructs to the protocol experience, is defined as a theory.

Each specific field of sensory experience forms sets related to each branch of scientific knowledge which may be characterized by two basic features: the set's width and its density. Width identifies the extent of the field as defined by the number of different types of sensory elements contained in a set. Density is equal to the absolute number of sensory elements per set. Two important consequences derive from an increase in width and density

knowledge, particularly in history, and the human and social sciences generally, has attained a new importance" (pp. 7–8). Hilary Putnam, in the introduction to the John Locke lectures, goes so far as to claim: "A view of knowledge that acknowledges that the sphere of knowledge is wider than the sphere of 'science' seems to me to be a cultural necessity if we are to arrive at a sane and human view of ourselves *or* of science" (1978, 6; italics in the original).

of a set: on the one hand, the number of alternative theories which may be advanced to explain the sensory experience will be enlarged, since the range of constructs in the set will be larger and more groupings of constructs will be possible; on the other hand, it will be more likely for a given theory to be falsified because it will be more difficult for the theory to capture in its explanations the most hidden sensory elements. Both these consequences play a significant role in accounting for the non-cumulativity of the development path of a scientific field.

Consider for a moment the list of questions raised by the simple event of the milk purchase. It is manifest that both the width and density of the set of sensory experiences increase with the range of sciences considered, and the two consequences just mentioned gradually emerge. As regards the first one, the constructs upon which the mathematician builds his theory in order to answer the problem posed to him is straightforward. The same can be said for the physicist, the biochemist, and perhaps the economist, but certainly not for the other social scientists. In the latter case, the greater width of the set of sensory experiences offers the opportunity of elaborating a larger number of constructs, thereby giving rise to alternative theories. As regards the second one, attempts to falsify the physical scientist's theory are doomed to failure, while similar attempts may be successful with respect to the anthropologist's and sociologist's theories. For them the rules of correspondence may not be able to capture all the relevant sensory facts. Both the larger number of theories and the higher number of ways of falsifying them are inconsistent with a non-decreasing monotonic time function for the PSD.

The arguments developed in this section suggest that neither the view in favor of cumulativity nor the view against it is acceptable. The PSD is not unique; it takes different shapes according to the various fields of knowledge. Indeed, a hierarchy among the sciences can be made, beginning with the most cumulative and sequentially continuing with those disciplines that each display increasingly wide fluctuations about the trend of its PSD.[14] It follows immediately that the usefulness of past theories is greater for those disciplines which display the widest and most frequent fluctuations of the time function. In such disciplines, forgotten theories may contain different constructs or illustrate relationships between constructs which may be highly suggestive for the elaboration of new theories. Finally, it should be noted that, as time proceeds, the shape of the PSD can change; this may even alter the position in the hierarchy, since some fields may face tougher problems while others may experience a steady refinement of theories, thereby determining a larger or a lower degree of variability. Then it is only when a discipline displays a non-

14. It is important to note that a similar hierarchy can be found within a given discipline among the various specialized subfields.

decreasing monotonic PSD that the study of the past bears no relevance to the modern theorist. Section IV asks whether this is the case in economic theory.

IV

The view advanced in the preceding section hinges upon consideration of the overall range of knowledge, not just a small subset called 'science.' As mentioned in note 13 above, philosophers are beginning to adopt a wider perspective, but, so far, the history of science has been studied with strict reference to the subset 'science,' usually identified with the physical sciences. Thus, the mechanical application of the main analytical frameworks to the history of economics suffers from rather serious limitations in that they were designed for a different subject matter (Kunin & Weaver 1971). Nevertheless, there are several examples of economists trying to apply Kuhn's or Lakatos' apparatus.[15] In any case, while it may be feasible to provide such a framework when a hard and fast distinction restricts the subject matter, the same does not seem equally feasible if the object of inquiry is extended to the whole range of knowledge. On the importance of a theory of disciplinary evolution to the writing of the history of economics there can hardly be any doubt (Remenyi 1979, 30–31), but this theory cannot be provided without a prior and deeper understanding of the subject. As suggested in Section III above, the identification of the nature and distinguishing characteristics of economics is the key to the understanding of the shape of the PSD and therefore of the relevance of the history of the discipline. Hence, the remainder of this study examines the nature of economics and comments upon some episodes in the history of economic analysis to support the main conclusion.

The account given in the preceding section of the factors determining the shape of the PSD for the various fields of knowledge does not substantially contrast with a traditional view concerning the distinctive features of the social and physical sciences which can be traced back to John Stuart Mill's *System of logic*. According to such a view (Ryan 1970, 13–15), there is a unity of methodology in scientific inquiry so that there are not two kinds of phenomena, natural and non-natural, but just phenomena which display regular patterns of behavior (and are thus amenable to causal explanation) and others which do not. Thus, the poorer performance of social sciences in explanation and prediction is accounted for by the greater 'complexity' of the questions posed to the social science student. Mill's standpoint with regard to economics can be found in the last of his *Essays* (1844) dealing with the definition and methodology of political economy.

15. An attempt to provide a synthesis of these two approaches can be found in Goodwin 1980.

After illustration of the nature of the distinction between physical and moral sciences (related to the distinction between laws of matter and laws of the human mind) he argues that "most of the moral sciences presuppose physical science; but few of the physical sciences presuppose moral science" (1844, 131); hence, the greater 'complexity' of the moral sciences.[16] According to an alternative view (Ryan 1970, 15ff), the distinction at issue is not a matter of degree but of kind, in that phenomena of human behavior cannot be treated like those relating to inert matter, since the latter do not imply a dimension of 'meaningfulness,' such as the concept of purpose or intention on the part of agents.

It is not the present study's objective to specify which of the two views should be followed; indeed, the point at issue here is not the analysis of the factors which determine the oscillatory character of the PSD for economics, but simply the existence of such a character. The main developments in the philosophy of science since the 1950s have all denied the validity of theory reduction and hence of a monotonic shape for the PSD. This argument, usually advanced with reference to physical sciences, should apply *a fortiori* to economics.[17] What is needed, however, is a direct examination of the PSD of economics in order to provide a tangible case for its permanent oscillatory character. In the next pages, attention will be paid to monetary theory because, as far as the shape of its development path is concerned, it does not occupy an outermost position in economics and has always been in the mainstream of the economist's area of concern. Monetary theory had already reached a high standard of analysis in the eighteenth century, and hence its history spans a long period of time. Two main topics will be examined: the foundations of money and the transmission mechanism of monetary policy.

The 'nature' of money, i.e. its origin and functions, is a fundamental question of monetary theory. Not surprisingly, therefore, the analysis of the functions of money had already arrived at a fairly satisfactory level in early times. What is puzzling is that further development virtually stopped when the whole body of economic theory began to make the most substantive advances.

In fact, the threefold classification of the functions of money (unit of account, medium of exchange, and store of value) can be traced back to Aristotle (Schumpeter 1954, 62–64). The three functions, however, have not always been considered on the same footing. In some periods, the medium of exchange function has been regarded as *the* function of money

16. "The laws of the production of the objects which constitute wealth, are the subject-matter both of Political Economy and of almost all the physical sciences. Such, however, of those laws as are purely laws of matter, belong to physical science, and to that exclusively. Such of them as are laws of the human mind, and no others belong to Political Economy, *which finally sums up the result of both combined*" (Mill 1844, 132; italics added).

17. This point has also been made in Hutchison 1978, 314.

and provided the foundation for the analysis of other topics in monetary theory. Alternatively, the three functions have simply been illustrated without giving prominence to any of them. Even though the treatment of other aspects of monetary economics has provided evidence of an interpretation of the nature of money stressing the store of value function, this has not been explicitly recognized.[18] It is with Keynes that such indirect evidence is embodied in the analysis through the formal split between M_1 and M_2, the transactions motive and the speculative motive. All this is well-known; what it shows is that the study of the nature of money has followed a development path which certainly is not monotonically non-decreasing. This is confirmed by a reading of the recent outpour of literature on the foundations of money,[19] prompted by the acknowledged limitation of Walrasian general equilibrium theory accounting for the roles of money other than as the numéraire. Of the three approaches identified by Barro & Fischer,[20] the latter two make use of assumptions which precisely parallel the medium of exchange and the store of value function so that they merely beg the question and do not shed much light on the properties of money and on the distinctive characteristics of a money as opposed to a barter economy. The first approach, instead, attempts to analyze the mechanics of exchange and manages to attain some interesting results. So far, however, distinct views continue to exist side by side.[21] The phenomenon of money lends itself to several interpretations, and it is no surprise that scholars continually find new or different features to highlight. The basic

18. The leading theorists of the 'indirect mechanism' (Blaug 1968, 158–59) accounting for the effects of variations in the nominal quantity of money—namely, Thornton and Wicksell—did not identify the store of value function as the fundamental one. Indeed, Wicksell clearly takes the position of those who regard the medium of exchange function as the essential function. "The conception of money is involved in its functions and it is usual to distinguish three such functions: as a *measure of value*, as a *store of value*, and as a *medium of exchange*. . . . Of the three main functions, only the last is in a true sense characteristic of money; as a measure of value any commodity whatever might serve. . . . Similarly, the function of acting as a *store of value* is not essentially characteristic of money" (Wicksell 1935, 6–8; italics in the original).

19. An extensive, but by no means complete, survey is the article by Ulph and Ulph (1975).

20. "At the risk—amounting to certainty—of oversimplification, we can distinguish three approaches. The first approach deals with a single period and investigates the possibility and number of exchanges required to attain a competitive equilibrium allocation of goods under various constraints on the exchanges that can be made when all trading is strictly bilateral. . . . The second approach . . . examines single-period exchanges in an economy in which transactions are costly, and determines market equilibrium and the nature of exchanges for that economy. The third approach . . . involves a multiperiod general equilibrium framework in which exchange within periods is with the market, but in which money can be useful in making intertemporal transfers" (Barro & Fischer 1976, 152).

21. A common outcome of this literature is to stress the role of money in providing information, but information is often related to different matters: the quality and availability of goods and their prices, the location and identity of other transactors, the size of the excess demand for and supply of commodities, and so on.

difficulty is, of course, the establishing of sufficient conditions for the emergence of monetary exchange (Clower 1977, 211).

The rather large mass of articles in the last decade has by no means produced a complete theoretical framework on the role of money. What is to be stressed here is that a large part of the recent works gives prominence to the medium-of-exchange function, thereby departing from a basic tenet of Keynesian theory and going back to a classic view. In a work published in the late 1960s, Hicks clearly took this position:

> Any marketable asset which appears on a balance-sheet may be regarded as a store of value; but it does not thereby take on a monetary quality. An insurance policy, even a motor-car, can be a store of value; but it is not money, not even near-money, not even partial money. The other functions, taken by themselves, do confer some monetary quality; the mere capacity of being a store of value does not.
>
> What is it that distinguishes money, regarded as a store of value, from these other assets, which are not money? A preKeynesian economist, confronted with this question, would surely have given the obvious answer. Since the mere capacity of acting as a store of value does not confer monetary quality, it must be the other functions which do so. An asset becomes a money asset if it is not only a store of value, but also a unit of account; or not only a store of value, but also a means of payment. If it has these other functions, and is also storable, it must be reckoned as being money.
>
> This is the obvious answer; and I think I shall be able to show that it is the correct answer. But (since Keynes) it has had a rival. It is commonly said that the essential characteristic of money (regarded as an item in a balance-sheet) is that it does not bear interest; whereas other assets, in some sense or other, do. Thus we are told by Patinkin that what has to be explained is the 'peaceable co-existence' between non-interest-bearing money and interest-bearing bonds. I have myself taken this view in earlier writings, *but I have come to hold that it should not be accepted* [Hicks 1967, 17–18; italics added].

This quotation eminently shows the bivalent character of money which is reflected in all the analyses of the foundations of money. In the development of the theory of monetary policy, this twofold nature can be easily identified from the very beginning of the nineteenth century and relates to the two main approaches to the transmission mechanism, the direct and the indirect (Blaug 1968, 154–59, 619ff). Following the former, along a line of thought going from Cantillon, Galiani, and Hume up to Marshall, an injection of money, given an equilibrium level of cash balances, directly affects expenditure and therefore raises prices. According to the latter, set forth by Thornton and taken up by Ricardo, John Stuart Mill, Wicksell, and Keynes, an increase in the nominal quantity of money raises the supply of loanable funds; hence it lowers the market rate of interest. The discrepancy between the market rate and the rate of return on capital stimulates the demand for loans, thereby raising the market rate, so that the two rates eventually go back to their equilibrium level. It is not difficult to recognize these two currents of thought, or at least their fundamentals, in contemporary monetary theory. The contraposition between direct and indirect mechanisms parallels, with some important qualifications,[22] the present debate between 'monetarists' and 'neo-Keynesians.'

Even though these views of the transmission process cannot simply and uncritically be related to two specific roles of money—as a means of payment and as an asset[23]—still they foreshadow two distinct conceptions of monetary theory that run through the whole history of monetary economics, of which the current debate is the most recent episode. Hence, one should agree with Laidler's remark that, "the nature of the causative links between money and money income—the 'transmission mechanism'—is still controversial" (Laidler 1978, 151). Laidler attributes the emergence of disputes to the extension of research to additional issues on the basis of a common theoretical framework, the IS-LM model.[24] Divergences, how-

22. If one refers to the works by Milton Friedman and James Tobin as representing the two approaches, the following should be noted. In his account of the transmission mechanism, Friedman acknowledges an *initial* impact of an increase in the nominal quantity of money on the asset market as well as the direct effect on expenditures: "The *initial* impact of increasing the quantity of money at a faster rate than it has been increasing is to make interest rates lower for a time than they would otherwise have been. But this is only the beginning of the process, not the end. The more rapid rate of monetary growth will stimulate spending, both through the impact on investment of lower market interest rates and through the impact on other spending and thereby relative prices of higher cash balances than are desired" (M. Friedman 1968, 100; italics in the original). In his 1975 paper, Friedman clearly restates this position stressing his closeness to classical monetary theory: "As I see it, we have advanced beyond Hume in two respects only: first, we now have a more secure grasp on the quantitative magnitudes involved; second, we have gone one derivative beyond Hume" (M. Friedman 1975, 177). As regards Tobin, attention should be given to the extension of the model to other components of net private wealth and to a higher number of assets.

23. It should be pointed out that the often stressed one-to-one correspondence between money as a means of payment and the direct mechanism on the one side, and money as an asset and the indirect mechanism on the other, though justified on grounds of interpretation, does not conform to textual evidence. The following examples taken from two foremost exponents of the different approaches to the transmission mechanism are quite telling. Cantillon, while clearly recognizing the precautionary motive for holding money, and hence the asset function—"Many Landowners, Undertakers and others, always keep some cash in their pockets or safes against unforeseen emergencies and not to be run out of money" (1755, 147)—wholly embraces the direct mechanism. On the other hand, Wicksell does not give prominence to the store of value function (see n. 18 above) but thoroughly develops the indirect mechanism.

24. "Until recently, debates about the transmission mechanism were carried on in terms of a common theoretical structure. . . . It is the contention of this essay that recent research has not so much filled gaps in our knowledge about an agreed theoretical framework, as it has cast doubt upon the usefulness of that framework as a research agenda. In particular, research on price-output interaction, on the consequences of fiscal policy for the behaviour of the money supply, and on questions prompted by the openness of most economies, has emphasized the influence of expectations about price level behaviour on the activities of economic agents" (Laidler 1978, 151–52).

ever, existed also before the tackling of these issues. Friedman, for example (see note 22 above), always recognized the direct effect of an excess supply of money on the goods market and other markets as well.

Even though the topics dealt with in the extension of the theory of the transmission mechanism are too intricate to be analyzed in this context, the following considerations concerning the role of expectations seem in order. The rational-expectations hypothesis, the reference point in current monetary theory and policy debates, has a twofold nature in that it encompasses *both* a 'perfect agent,' i.e., an individual whose information set is sufficiently large (B.M. Friedman 1979, 26), and a 'perfect model.' Most of the criticism against this hypothesis appears to be misdirected because it has focused upon the first part: the 'perfect agent.' However, keeping in mind the content of this section, it can be argued that the weakness of the hypothesis is its second component, the 'perfect model.' Indeed, the assumption of full information on the part of agents is a standard one in economic theory, but the one regarding a 'perfect model' seems rather extreme in the light of the everlasting disputes on monetary dynamics. Furthermore, the main implication of the rational-expectations hypothesis, namely, that only unanticipated changes in the money stock affect the real sector of the system, reflects a basic tenet of classical monetary theory. Classical authors—Hume's celebrated essay "Of money" being the most well-known instance—forcefully maintained that only an unexpected increase in the quantity of money could cause a departure from long-run neutrality by producing an impact on real output and employment during the transition to the new steady state.[25] And this impact would fade away as agents became aware of the change in money supply and hence were able to predict the consequences of such a change. This is precisely the argument upon which the rational-expectations hypothesis rests.

These considerations bring us back to the main argument of this section: i.e., that the development of monetary theory does not follow a non-decreasing monotonic path, but is instead the product of two main currents of thought, each of them, in turn and at different times, prevailing over the other.[26] The rationale for this is related to the 'complexity' of the

25. Changes in the money stock were always assumed to be unexpected by the classics, a 'realistic' assumption in those times: "It is also usually the case that the increase or decrease of actual money in a State is not perceived because it flows abroad, or is brought into the State, by such imperceptible means and proportions that it is impossible to know exactly the quantity which enters or leaves the State" (Cantillon 1755, 163).

Hume was so aware of the crucial importance of the surprise element in implementing a monetary expansion that, while proposing such a measure (taking from every shilling a penny's worth of silver) he purposely noted: "In executing such a project, it would be better to make the new shilling pass for 24 halfpence, *in order to preserve the illusion, and make it be taken for the same*" (1752, 39; italics added).

26. Hicks too identifies this oscillatory feature but, following his relativistic stand, attributes it to the change in the historical context. "Since monetary statistics have long been

phenomenon 'money,' which displays several aspects at once; hence the difficulty in capturing all of them.[27]

This sketchy examination of some aspects of monetary theory gives support to the view according to which there are subfields in economics whose PSDs display an oscillatory character. This, it should again be stressed, does not deny convergence. Indeed, as shown in Section III above, what is important for appraising the usefulness of past theories is not *whether* the PSD converges but *how* it converges.[28] What has been shown for monetary theory can be argued for other subfields as well. The hypothesis of a non-decreasing monotonic PSD for economics appears to be a rather extreme one, so that the burden of the proof must certainly rest with those who hold it.

If the foregoing view is accepted, then the role of the history of economic analysis should be manifest. It is a role which is relevant to the modern theorist. The study of past authors may disclose constructs, and links between constructs, which, though forgotten, may be important for current research. Of course, we should not expect to find, in classic writ-

---

abundant (much more abundant than most other statistics until the present century) monetary economics has always been topical; it has always had a close relation to the circumstances of the time in which it has been written; it has had to change as they have changed" (Hicks 1976, 216).

27. A recent example of this 'complexity' is contained in Friedman's and Tobin's discussion (Stein 1976) of Tobin and Buiter's essay on the effectiveness of fiscal policy. Friedman states: "For the monetarist/non-monetarist dichotomy, I suspect that the simplest litmus test would be the conditioned reflex to the question, "What is the price of money?" The monetarist will answer, "The inverse of the price level"; the non-monetarist (Keynesian or central banker) will answer, "the interest rate." The key difference is whether the stress is on money viewed as an asset with special characteristics, or on credit and credit markets, which leads to the analysis of monetary policy and monetary change operating through organized 'money' i.e., 'credit' markets, rather than through actual and desired cash balances" (Stein 1976, 316). Tobin answers: "Friedman's own litmus paper test, 'What is the price of money?' is fun at cocktail parties. But some of my friends are good enough capital theorists to question the question. They can recognize *both* the purchasing power value of a dollar bill and the per annum opportunity cost of holding a dollar bill rather than some other asset. Others are good enough Marshallians or Walrasians to reject Friedman's favorite money-credit dichotomy. They suspect that 'monetary policy and monetary change' operate *both* through credit markets and through 'actual and desired cash balances'" (Stein 1976, 335; italics in the original).

28. Blaug, for example, is not against the idea of progress in economics, but he rejects a non-decreasing monotonic development path. "The recognition that economic theory has indeed progressed should not be allowed to obscure the highly uneven rate of improvement which has typified the history of analytical progress in economics. General insights into the pure logic of the price system make their appearance embedded in a particular theoretical framework associated with conditions and problems peculiar to the times. As the body of ideas gives way under criticism, much of what is still valuable gets discarded in the enthusiasm over the latest novelty. As a result, the history of economics is not so much the chronicle of a continuous accumulation of theoretical achievements as the story of exaggerated intellectual revolutions in which truths already known are neglected in favor of new revelations. Indeed sometimes it seems as if economics has been propelled forward by a sense of symmetry which demands that every new theory should always be the exact reverse of the old" (1968, 4).

ings, already accomplished results; what we will find is a wealth of hints, suggestions, and ideas broadening the perspective of the modern theorist. The reading of the classics heavily bears upon the creative process by which the formulation of new hypotheses is carried out. In fact, the nature of the contributions by ancient authors spans a wide range going from mere hints to complete models. The latter are likely to be known to the present-day researcher, at least in their essentials; hence, the main benefit to be gained from studying the classics lies at the other end of the range. Stigler (1969, 218–22) has efficaciously illustrated "how to read a book" and points out:

> if a great book such as Smith's *Wealth of Nations* is read repeatedly, on even a fifth or tenth reading one continues to learn new things. I doubt whether anyone will ever fully apprehend all the things that Smith wished to express, and there is even more to learn from an interesting mind than its owner wished to teach us [1969, 218–19].

These advantages obviously decrease as we go back in time because the analytical quality of the works sharply declines. Referring again to monetary theory, the insights that Robert A. Jones got for his article on the origin of money (1976; see especially pp. 757–58) by reading Menger's classic essay (1892) were likely far deeper than the ones any modern quantity theorist may get from Jean Bodin's *Response*.

In the opening essay of his collection of papers, Thomas S. Kuhn has wittily described the task of the historian of science:

> The historian at work is not, I think, unlike the child presented with one of those picture puzzles of which the pieces are square; but the historian is given many extra pieces in the box. He has or can get the data, not all of them (what could that be?) but a very considerable collection. His job is to select from them a set that can be juxtaposed to provide the elements of what, in the child's case, would be a picture of recognizable objects plausibly juxtaposed and of what, for the historian and his reader, is a plausible narrative involving recognizable motives and behaviors [Kuhn 1978, 16–17].

The historian of economics, then, could identify those "extra pieces in the box" and combine them, showing alternative and suggestive patterns of thought. However, it should be stressed that it is the theorist active in a given field, not the historian, who will be able to make use of the classics' insights in order to construct new theories in the specific field. The history of economic analysis is indeed highly relevant for "bringing into attention things which have been only just left out" (Hicks 1976, 209), but this does not stem from forgotten institutional and historical peculiarities, as Hicks's relativistic position would suggest, but rather from the inherent complexity of economic phenomena. Indeed, there is no need to resort to a relativistic approach in order to provide a cogent argument for the history of economic analysis. In the context of this study, the absolutist-relativist distinction appears sterile, diverting attention from the essential issues.

Finally, a judgment can be given on the actually dominant view among economists denying any usefulness to studying early writers, prompted by recent methodological innovations. It can be acknowledged that there is something to this idea: more powerful tools of investigation can certainly shed light upon previously impenetrable issues. It is undeniable that some subdisciplines have benefited by methodological innovations. A most notable example is the theory of consumer behavior which, given the relatively lesser 'complexity' of the relevant set of sensory experiences, has been brought to a high standard of rigor and precision by more refined analytical tools. But the extension of this standpoint to other subfields of economics seems far-fetched. When the phenomenon to be analyzed displays a 'complexity' which is still too great with respect to the advancement of the methodological weaponry, then the latter is of little use. In the sketchy illustrations of this section, money has been identified as such a phenomenon. Capital and growth are other possible candidates.

The many signs of dissatisfaction with the present state of economics may well be due to the decreasing marginal benefit of applying a refined methodological weaponry. Insights and ideas are needed to bring about a change, and the history of economic analysis may contribute to this change.

This article has benefited from the useful comments of Cristina Bicchieri, Mark Blaug, Benjamin M. Friedman, Craufurd D. W. Goodwin, Hilary Putnam, Paul A. Samuelson, George J. Stigler, and two anonymous referees. The usual disclaimers apply.

References

Achinstein, P. 1968. *Concepts of science*. Baltimore.

Allen, W. R. 1965. Discussion of Gordon 1965. *American Economic Review* 55: 143–45.

Barro, R. J., and S. Fischer 1976. "Recent developments in monetary theory." *Journal of Monetary Economics* 2: 133–67.

Blaug, M. 1968. *Economic theory in retrospect*. 2d ed. Homewood, Ill.

———1975. "Kuhn versus Lakatos, or paradigms versus research programmes in the history of economics." *History of Political Economy* 7: 399–433.

Bohm, D. 1965. *The special theory of relativity*. New York.

Boulding, K. E. 1971. "After Samuelson, who needs Adam Smith?" *History of Political Economy* 3: 225–34.

Bronfenbrenner, M. 1966. "Trends, cycles, and fads in economic writing." *American Economic Review* 56: 538–52.

———1971. "The structure of revolutions in economic thought." *History of Political Economy* 3: 136–51.

Cantillon, R. 1755. *Essai sur la nature du commerce en général*, ed. H. Higgs.

Clower, R. W. 1967. "A reconsideration of the microfoundations of monetary theory." *Western Economic Journal* 6:1–9, reprinted in R. W. Clower, ed., *Monetary theory* (Harmondsworth, 1969).

———1971. "Theoretical foundations of monetary policy." In G. Clayton, J. C. Gilbert, and R. Sedgwick, eds. *Monetary theory and monetary policy in the 1970s*. Oxford.

———1977. "The anatomy of monetary theory." *American Economic Review* 67: 206–12.

Coats, A. W. 1969a. "Is there a structure of scientific revolutions in economics?" *Kyklos* 22: 289–96.

———1969b. "Research priorities in the history of economics." *History of Political Economy* 1: 9–18.

Corry, B. A. 1975. "Should economists abandon *HOPE*?" *History of Political Economy* 7: 252–60.

Cunninghan, W. 1892. "The relativity of economic doctrine." *Economic Journal* 2: 1–16.

Dillard, D. 1978. "Revolutions in economic theory." *Southern Economic Journal* 44: 705–24.

Feyerabend, P. K. 1975. *Against method: outline of an anarchistic theory of knowledge*. London.

Friedman, Benjamin M. 1978. "Crowding out or crowding in?: economic consequences of financing government deficits." *Brookings Papers on Economic Activity* (Washington), pp. 593–641.

———1979. "Optimal expectations and the extreme information assumptions of 'rational expectations' macromodels." *Journal of Monetary Economics* 5: 23–41.

Friedman, Milton 1968. "The role of monetary policy." *American Economic Review* 58: 1–17; reprinted in M. Friedman, *The optimum quantity of money and other essays*. Chicago.

———1975. "25 years after the rediscovery of money: what have we learned? Discussion." *American Economic Review* 65: 176–79.

Goodwin, C. D. 1972. "Economic theory and society: a plea for process analysis." *American Economic Review* 62: 409–15.

———1980. "Toward a theory of the history of economics." *History of Political Economy* 12: 610–19.

Gordon, D. F. 1965. "The role of the history of economic thought in the understanding of modern economic theory." *American Economic Review* 55: 119–27.

Harré, R. 1970. *The principles of scientific thinking*. Chicago.

———1972. *The philosophies of science*. Oxford.

Hempel, C. G. 1963. *Aspects of scientific explanation*. New York.

Hesse, M. 1974. *The structure of scientific inference*. London.

———1977. "Truth and the growth of scientific knowledge." Ms. at Cambridge University.

Hicks, J. R. 1967. *Critical essays in monetary theory*. Oxford.

———1976. "'Revolution' in economics." In Latsis 1976.

Hollander, S. 1973. *The economics of Adam Smith*. London.

———1975. "Attack the best defense." *History of Political Economy* 7: 115–22.

Hutchison, T. W. 1978. *On revolutions and progress in economic knowledge*. Cambridge.

Jalladeau, J. 1978. "Research program versus paradigm in the development of economics." *Journal of Economic Issues* 12: 583–608.

Jones, R. A. 1976. "The origin and development of media of exchange." *Journal of Political Economy* 84: 757–75.

Karsten, S. G. 1973. "Dialectics and the evolution of economic thought." *History of Political Economy* 5: 399–419.
Krupp, R. S. 1966. *The structure of economic science: essays on methodology.* Englewood Cliffs, N.J.
Kuhn, T. S. 1970. *The structure of scientific revolutions*, 2d ed. Chicago.
———1977. *The essential tension.* Chicago.
Kunin, L., and F. S. Weaver 1971. "On the structure of scientific revolutions in economics." *History of Political Economy* 3: 391–97.
Laidler, D. 1978. "Money and income: An essay on the 'transmission mechanism.'" *Journal of Monetary Economics* 4: 151–91.
Lakatos, I. 1970. "Falsification and the methodology of scientific research programmes." In Lakatos and Musgrave 1970.
———1978a. *The methodology of scientific research programmes. Philosophical Papers*, vol. 1. Cambridge.
———1978b. *Mathematics, science and epistemology. Philosophical Papers*, vol. 2. Cambridge.
———and A. Musgrave, eds. 1970. *Criticism and the growth of knowledge.* Cambridge.
Latsis, S., ed. 1976. *Method and appraisal in economics.* Cambridge.
Leijonhufvud, A. 1976. "Schools, 'revolutions,' and research programmes in economic theory." In Latsis 1976, 65–108.
Linstromberg, R. C. 1969. "The philosophy of science and alternative approaches to economic thought." *Journal of Economic Issues* 3: 177–91.
Losee, J. 1972. *A historical introduction to the philosophy of science.* Oxford.
Margenau, H. 1966. "What is a theory?" In Krupp 1966.
Menger, C. 1892. "On the origins of money." *Economic Journal* 2: 239–55.
Mill, J. S. 1844. *Essays on some unsettled questions of political economy.* London.
Nabers, L. 1966. "The positive and genetic approaches." In Krupp 1966.
Nagel, E. 1961. *The structure of science.* London.
Niehans, J. 1978. *The theory of money.* Baltimore.
Pantaleoni, M. 1898. "Dei criteri che debbono informare la storia delle dottrine economiche." *Giornale degli Economisti* 17: 407–31.
Popper, K. R. 1968. *The logic of scientific discovery.* New York.
———1972. *Objective knowledge: an evolutionary approach.* Oxford.
Putnam, H. 1978. *Meaning and the moral sciences.* London.
Remenyi, J. V. 1979. "Core demi-core interaction: toward a general theory of disciplinary and subdisciplinary growth." *History of Political Economy* 11: 30–63.
Ryan, A. 1970. *The philosophy of the social sciences.* London.
Samuels, W. J. 1974. "The history of economic thought as intellectual history." *History of Political Economy* 6: 305–23.
Samuelson, P. A. 1949. Review of H. Myint, *Theories of welfare economics. Economica* 15: 371–74.
———1954. "Some psychological aspects of mathematics and economics." *Review of Economics and Statistics* 36: 380–82.
———1977. "A modern theorist's vindication of Adam Smith," *American Economic Review*, 67, 42–49.
Schumpeter, J. A. 1954. *History of economic analysis*, Oxford.
Spengler, J. J. 1968. "Economics: its history, themes, approaches," *Journal of Economic Issues*, 2, 42–49.
Stein, J. L., ed. 1976. *Monetarism.* Amsterdam.
Stigler, G. J. 1955. "The nature and role of originality in scientific progress." *Economica* 22: 293–302; reprinted in Stigler 1965.

———1965. *Essays in the history of economics*. Chicago.
———1969. "Does economics have a useful past?" *History of Political Economy* 1: 217–30.
Suppe, F. 1974. *The structure of scientific theories*. Urbana, Ill.
Tarascio, V. J. 1971. "Some recent developments in the history of economic thought in the United States." *History of Political Economy* 3: 419–31.
Tobin, J. 1969. "A general equilibrium approach to monetary theory." *Journal of Money Credit and Banking* 1: 15–29.
Toulmin, S. 1974. "The structure of scientific theories." In Suppe 1974, 600–614.
Ulph, A. M., and D. T. Ulph 1975. "Transaction costs in general equilibrium." *Economica* 42: 355–72.
Wicksell, K. 1958. "Ends and means in economics" (1904). In E. Lindahl, ed., *Selected papers on economic theory*. London.
———1935. *Lectures on political economy*, vol. 2. London.
Winch, D. N. 1962. "What price the history of economic thought?" *Scottish Journal of Political Economy* 9: 193–204.

Part 1

Classical Monetary Theory

[2]

Monetary theory in Ferdinando Galiani's *Della moneta*

Filippo Cesarano

The theory of money made substantial progress during the eighteenth century and became one of the most advanced fields of economic studies.[1] An important role was played by Italian writers, and particularly by Ferdinando Galiani[2] with his treatise *Della moneta* (Of Money).[3]

FILIPPO CESARANO *is an economist at the Banca d'Italia, Rome.*

1. The early development of monetary thought is examined in detail in Arthur Eli Monroe, *Monetary Theory Before Adam Smith* (Cambridge, Mass., 1923; rpt., New York, 1966).

2. Ferdinando Galiani was born at Chieti on 2 December 1728. At the age of seven, he was sent to Naples where his uncle Celestino Galiani, chief almoner to the king and noted for his reform of the university, looked after his education. The young Galiani came into contact with many personalities of the Neapolitan culture; among these were Bartolomeo Intieri and Alessandro Rinuccini, who introduced him to economics. In 1744 he translated some of John Locke's writings on money as an exercise in English and began his monetary studies, which he concluded eight years later. During this period he took religious orders (1745). In 1748 he lectured on the state of money at the time of the Trojan War at the Accademia degli Emuli and shortly afterward in 1751 published his major work, *Della moneta* (Of Money). Three years later, Bartolomeo Intieri's booklet *Della perfetta conservazione del grano* (Of the Perfect Conservation of Corn) appeared in Naples, but the real author of it was Galiani. In 1759 he was appointed secretary of the Neapolitan embassy in Paris, where he lived, almost without interruption, for ten years. Towards the end of his stay he wrote his other important book, in French, *Dialogues sur le commerce des bleds* (Dialogues on the Corn Trade) (1770). Subsequent to his return to Naples, Galiani published minor works in fields outside economics, such as linguistics and politics, and held several high positions in the civil service until his death in 1787.

The literature on Galiani is rather extensive. A comprehensive account of it can be found in the latest reprint of *Della moneta*, introduced by A. Caracciolo and edited by A. Merola (Milan, 1963), and in G. H. Bousquet's introduction to the French partial translation of *Della moneta* (see n.3 below). Even though no separate study of Galiani has appeared in English, his work has been examined in most treatises in the history of monetary thought—e.g., Monroe's (see n.1 above).

3. First edition, Naples, 1751. The second edition, unaltered in the text but enriched with a foreword, thirty-five notes, and an epilogue, was published in Naples in 1780 and was reprinted as volumes 10 and 11 in the collection *Scrittori Classici*

Despite its title, *Della moneta* does not deal exclusively with topics in monetary theory, but contains outstanding treatments of value theory, public finance, the theory of rent, and human capital, to name a few topics. The subject of this article, however, is restricted to Galiani's monetary analysis, which is examined in the perspective of modern theory. This approach has the disadvantage of leaving aside his valuable treatment of some topics—bimetallism, monetary reform, subsidiary money, and others—which nowadays are relatively inconspicuous. Nevertheless, it brings to the foreground the importance, often overlooked by scholars concerned with the history of monetary thought, of Galiani's theory of money.

After inquiring into the methodological aspects of Galiani's book, his ideas on money will be considered, touching upon the nature of money, the origin of money, the quantity theory and the purchasing power of money, the transmission mechanism of monetary policy, effects of inflation, and international aspects of monetary theory. The final section summarizes the main conclusions.

1. *Galiani's methodology in* Della moneta[4]

The whole text of *Della moneta* is studded with references to the existence of natural laws which regulate the course of economic phenomena.[5] These laws have a universal validity (i: 50–51) and are the exact counterpart of the laws of gravity and of fluids (i: 91). Like physical laws, economic laws can never be violated;[6] both the behavior of the single individual and the economic policy of the prince are constrained by these "general principles"; any action designed in opposition to the "order of nature" will be doomed to failure (i: 169).

Italiani di Economia Politica, edited by Pietro Custodi (Milan, 1803). Citations in this article refer to volumes 10 (i) and 11 (ii) of the Custodi collection, and their pages.

Even though there are no integral translations of the book, a French version of the most interesting chapters of *Della moneta* is available. Ferdinando Galiani, *De la monnaie*, trans. G. H. Bousquet and J. Crisafulli (Paris, 1955).

4. The present essay specifically deals with *Della moneta*, which was published when the author was only twenty-two. In later writings, Galiani's thought underwent substantial modifications, especially with regard to methodology.

5. The most important passages are found in i: 50, 51, 57, 72, 83, 90, 91, 108, 134, 139, 140, 167, 169; ii: 60, 70, 73, 172, 190.

6. In the chapter on the theory of value, Galiani states that "not only the metals composing money, but any other thing in the world, excepting none, derives its natural value from certain, constant, and general principles; that neither whim nor law nor the prince nor any other thing can violate these principles and their effect" (i: 57). These principles "being certain, universal, constant, and established on the order and the nature of earthly things, no arbitrary and casual thing is among us, but everything is order, harmony and necessity" (i: 83).

To prove his argument, Galiani performs the following experiment. A country of Mahometan religion suddenly embraces the Christian faith; drinking wine is now allowed, but, because of the small quantity available, its price will increase. Merchants will carry wine to the country and new producers will be attracted there until profits go back to the equilibrium level. Therefore, two principles are derived:

> First, that initial variations in anything are not to be taken into account but rather permanent and steady states, and in this, order and equality are always found; as when waves are made in a vessel of water, after the confused and irregular movement the water returns to its original level. Second, that it cannot be an accident in nature which brings things to an ultimate limit, but a certain moral gravity which is in everything will never allow them to maintain a straight linear progression, twisting them in a perpetual but finite circle [i: 91].

Translated into the language of the modern theorist, these principles relate simply to comparative statics methodology and to stability of equilibrium.[7] However, while the former effectively defines a tool of analysis, the latter does not; it only reflects Galiani's faith in a harmonious natural order. Despite their contrasting character, these two principles have to be stressed, since Galiani explicitly regards them as the methodological foundation of his entire book[8]. He goes even further. Not only does he successfully employ the tool of comparative statics but in some cases he also attempts to design a dynamic theory of the process through which the new steady state is attained. As regards the stability of equilibrium, he emphasizes the pursuit of self-interest as the driving force of common welfare:

> And this equilibrium [in the market for precious metals] wonderfully suits the right abundance of commodities of life and earthly welfare, although it derives not from human prudence or virtue but from the very vile stimulus of sordid profit: Providence having contrived the order of everything for her infinite love of

7. Even though the passage quoted above may seem rather obscure, Galiani explicitly uses the word *equilibrio* twice in the immediately preceding paragraph (i: 89) and in other chapters of his work, e.g., ii: 192.

8. "What I have said will be applied by me to money a good hundred times; readers should keep this in mind" (i: 91).

men, that our vile passions are often, in spite of us, ordered to the advantage of the whole [i: 89–90].

This argument is used by Galiani in an outstanding discussion of the market as a means of providing information (i: 92–94), to prove that the price of goods determined by the "multitude" is the right one (i: 94–95). The stimulus of profit induces people to enter into the production of a given commodity; if they lose, the industry collapses, and if they exceedingly gain, other producers are attracted, so that everyone always makes a "just profit."

Throughout his treatise, Galiani is continuously concerned with supporting his exposition with "proofs." The analytical quality of these proofs changes sharply from mere historical descriptions to simple but efficacious models, which are used to analyze the effects of exogenously determined changes on a previous equilibrium state. On other occasions, the simplifying assumptions which characterize the model are gradually relaxed in order to obtain a deeper understanding of reality. Galiani does not always state all the assumptions needed in order for the tenets of his model to hold, and he sometimes fails to specify which variables have to be regarded as endogenous. Despite these shortcomings, his theoretical constructions show the application of economic logic. This clearly appears in the model (described above) of production of wine in a formerly Mahometan community, where the concept of long-run equilibrium is utilized.

Continual references in *Della moneta* to natural laws would suggest that this treatise belongs to Physiocratic literature. This interpretation, however, would be highly misleading. Galiani is one of the few writers of the eighteenth century who stresses the use of alternative economic policies in different circumstances.[9] Moreover, he develops the principle of evaluating the costs and benefits of a given policy in order to decide whether it should be carried out.[10] However, the existence of natural laws constrains the implementation of policy actions; the latter can never prevail upon the "unsurpassable force of nature."[11] The economic process is guided by a "Supreme Hand" (i: 92–93), which is the religiously biased (Galiani was an abbot) counterpart of Adam Smith's "invisible hand" a quarter of a century later.

9. See, for example, his discussion of the choice between resorting to inflation and increasing public debt in a situation in which additional taxes could not be levied in order to meet public expenditures (ii: 103–5).

10. E.g., in his analysis of the effects of inflation, section 6 below.

11. See, for example, his discussion "Of Forbidding the Exportation of Money" (Del vietar l'estrazione della moneta) (ii: 183–99).

2. *The nature of money*

The second book of *Della moneta*,[12] entitled "Of the Nature of Money," contains six chapters, but the main arguments can be found in the first two.

Having identified the inconveniences of barter, Galiani inquires about the feasibility of avoiding it completely by "living together" (vivere in comune), as religious communities do (i: 142–51). In a larger society, goods could be deposited in public warehouses at the disposal of everyone. However, the variability in the attitudes of individuals would lead such a system to collapse: lazy people would live at the expense of the active ones, who in turn would tend to work less, since the stimulus of profit would be absent. To overcome these deficiencies, public warehouses should give any producer a "receipt" (bullettino) certifying the quantity of commodities he had deposited, so that he would be entitled to receive an equivalent amount of goods from the same storehouse. Relative prices would be fixed by the prince. To eliminate the danger of counterfeiting, the receipts would all be of the same value and would bear the prince's signature. But the receipts would indeed be money. Money is the means by which everyone's product is represented: it allows the "living together" of a large number of people. The prince, however, might be induced to print an excessive number of receipts; hence, a metallic money is called for.

In his preceding chapter, Galiani makes the distinction between two kinds of money according to their different uses: ideal money (moneta ideale), which is the standard measure of the price of commodities; and actual money (moneta reale), which is effectively transferred in exchange for goods (i: 112–14).[13] To qualify as actual money, a commodity must be easy to carry and to exchange, as well as be universally accepted. Universal acceptability requires that the commodity should satisfy the following "qualities": (1) have an intrinsic value; (2) have a true value easy to calculate; (3) be difficult to debase by fraud; (4) be durable (i: 123–24). Ideal money should not be regarded as the invariable measure of value, because its value varies

12. *Della moneta* is divided into five books: Of Metals (De' metalli); Of the Nature of Money (Della natura della moneta); Of the Value of Money (Del valore della moneta); Of Velocity of Circulation (Del corso della moneta); Of the Rate of Interest (Del frutto della moneta).

13. Long before Galiani's time, frequent alterations in metallic currencies prompted the practice of expressing the price of goods in a hypothetical unit of account of a given weight and quality (ideal money) in order to compute more easily the value of the coins effectively exchanged (actual money).

as the purchasing power of actual money changes; an invariable standard of value cannot exist (i: 152–64).[14]

The immediate implication to be drawn from Galiani's treatment of the nature of money is the classical character of his analysis. Money performs two functions: unit of account (ideal money) and medium of exchange (actual money). Galiani does not identify the store-of-value function of money.[15] More important, there is no theoretical construction in *Della moneta* which bases itself upon the asset function of money. Instead, fundamental models developed by Galiani are founded upon the transactions approach to monetary analysis, stressing therefore the use of money as a means of payment. It is true that Galiani indicates durability as a requisite of actual money, but this cannot be advanced as an argument to prove acknowledgment of the store-of-value function.[16] The same holds for Galiani's statement according to which precious metals have a value before being used as money (i: 72). The statement is of course correct, but it does not entail an understanding of the asset function of money. In *Della moneta* the dominating notion of money is the classical conception.[17]

As shown by the model of "living together," money is seen as the "representation" of the real sector of the economy (i: 148–49). This result sharply contrasts with Galiani's metallist faith. The rejection of a fiduciary currency stems from several parts of the treatise. First, a commodity whose value depends only on "convention and faith" cannot become money; even though "receipts" effectively circulate in some countries, these nations could never pay their debts abroad with such a currency (i: 125–26). Second, the desirability of having a measure of value as stable as possible requires a mechanism for controlling the quantity of money; since only the discovery of new mines (which is a rare event) can substantially alter the supply of precious

14. "Finally, this concept of stable money is a dream, a mania. Every new and richer mine that is discovered immediately changes all measures, without showing any effect on them but changing the price of the goods measured" (i: 160).

15. "Money is of two kinds, *ideal* and *actual*; and it is employed for two different uses, to value things and to buy them" (i: 112; italics in original). "Having explained *every* use of money I will now discuss the nature of metals and chiefly of gold and silver" (i: 114; italics added).

16. Durability is a necessary condition for a commodity to serve as a means of payment. In indirect exchange, the "seller" would never accept something which must be consumed immediately: could electric power be used as money? This remark is not as obvious as it may appear, if an economist of Hicks's caliber fails to recognize it. John R. Hicks, *Critical Essays in Monetary Theory* (Oxford, 1967), p. 17.

17. The classical dichotomy is a recurrent theme in *Della moneta*; see, for example, i: 168, 179–84, 220; ii: 72–73, 135–36.

metals, the latter are "naturally money" (naturalmente moneta) (i: 136–37, 150–51). Third, the possibility of counterfeiting and fraud is far less with a metallic currency (i: 150). Fourth, the use of fiat money in the English colonies of North America has to be regarded as a historical curiosity and can be explained with three arguments: impossibility of counterfeiting, because only "wild people" lived at the borders of the colonies; simple patterns of international trade, since exchanges took place only with England; peculiar character of the inhabitants, the Quakers, whose "fanaticism" made possible the performance of such "extraordinary actions" (ii: 203–6).

The discordance between Galiani's theoretical model, in which the smooth functioning of a fiduciary currency is clearly shown, and his firm metallist belief may be further rationalized with the impression left in Europe by the events associated with the name of John Law which occurred in France during the first quarter of the eighteenth century. An entire chapter of *Della moneta* (book III, chapter 4, pp. 118–31) is dedicated to French monetary history; moreover, John Law's system, "one of the strangest products of the human intellect," is carefully examined (ii: 214–21).[18]

From this point of view it is possible to comprehend Galiani's inconsistency in treating the issue of money and wealth.[19] Precious metals, he claims, are a luxury good; i.e., they are at the very end of the individual's preference scale; but he proceeds, on the basis of untenable arguments, to conclude that gold and silver are *not* wealth (i: 221–23). Galiani fails to distinguish between monetary and nonmonetary uses of precious metals, apparently in an attempt to reconcile his understanding of the role of money in the exchange process with the existence of a commodity standard.[20]

The model of "living together," mentioned above, contains insights into the foundations of monetary theory which go far beyond the classical view of money. Galiani's model contains the basic idea on which the results of current research are based: money is a means

18. References to French monetary events are also found in i: 206, 249, and ii: 24, 56, 111, 229, 269. In the second edition of *Della moneta* (1780) note XXX again discusses John Law's monetary policies (ii: 289–91).

19. He first states "the wealth of a country is land, houses, money" (i: 188); but a few pages later: "money is not wealth but its image and the instrument to circulate it" (i: 220). See also i: 47–48 and ii: 97, 196–97.

20. This is rather puzzling, however, because, in another passage of *Della moneta*, he fully understands the mentioned distinction (see section 4 below). An explanation may be found in the different contexts of the two analyses: the issue of money and wealth in one case (i: 219–24), the price of precious metals in the other (i: 95–104).

to avoid "inconsistent claims" of individuals.[21] However, the way in which the analysis is developed in *Della moneta* basically differs from the approach of the modern theorist. In his conceptual experiment, Galiani is concerned with the inconveniences of barter; accordingly, he elaborates a model of a society in which there would be no need for direct exchange. This is a rather peculiar and somewhat ingenious approach. Instead of the usual analytical step introducing indirect exchange, and hence money, as a remedy to the inconveniences of barter, Galiani inquires about the feasibility of centralizing exchange. In religious communities the "virtue" of people restrains inconsistent claims on the common product; in a larger society, self-interest serves the same function through the use of money. Money is the mechanism, and self-interest is its driving force.[22] The concept of excess demand is not clearly stated in *Della moneta*, but it is implied in Galiani's argument:

> Therefore is should be established that everyone who brings his own works to the warehouse should receive a receipt conceived in these terms: "That this person has remitted such quantity of his things to the public warehouse, let us say for example one hundred pairs of shoes, for the value of which he remains a creditor of society." Then it should be established that no one can touch anything in these warehouses without presenting some receipts for his credits, *and without taking anything more than the value and the quantity of his own credit*, which, when equaled, he should leave or destroy the receipt [i: 144, italics added].

The importance of Galiani's model of "living together" is due not only to the originality of his approach but especially to the results obtained. The latter have great bearing upon other topics of the theory of money and will therefore be reconsidered in later sections.

21. ". . . the essential property of money is to discourage the making of . . . inconsistent claims [in the form of incorrect evaluations of excess demand and supply of commodities] without also discouraging efficient patterns of trade." Joseph M. Ostroy, "The Informational Efficiency of Monetary Exchange," *American Economic Review* 63 (1973): 597–610, at p. 597.

22. "I saw, and everyone can now see, that trade, and money which drives it, from the miserable state of nature in which everyone thinks for himself, have brought us to the very happy one of living together, where everyone thinks and works for everybody else: and in this state not for the principle of virtue and piety alone (which are insufficient in dealing with entire nations), but we earn our living for the purpose of our personal interest and welfare" (i: 148).

3. *The origin of money*

Galiani's theory of the origin of money derives directly from his work regarding the foundations of money, which provides the basis for the proof of his main proposition: the introduction of media of exchange was not due to the will of man; man did not invent money, but became aware of its properties when the use of precious metals as means of payment was already widespread—"the institution of money is without a doubt a very great thing; but it is false that man first thought of money before using it. As I have said, it [money] began to be used without it being realized and without understanding its usefulness" (i: 109).

After brief historical remarks,[23] Galiani tries to prove his argument analytically by identifying the commodity which satisfies the four "qualities" of actual money (i: 123–35), i.e., of the medium of exchange.[24] Precious metals are such a commodity. A fiduciary currency is rejected, since it does not have an intrinsic value and therefore violates the first quality. According to the second, the commodity has to be of uniform quality so that its value varies in proportion to its quantity: only precious metals possess this requisite. Moreover, gold and silver satisfy the third (difficulty to debase by fraud) and the fourth (durability) qualities of the medium of exchange. Hence, man began to exchange goods for those metals not because the latter were understood to be money, but simply because they satisfied all four qualities of the means of payment (i: 137–38).

Even though this analysis is not outstanding, still Galiani's basic insight appears to be quite correct in the light of recent research.[25] Not only does he achieve the correct result, but he identifies the main arguments to reach that result. Galiani explicitly stresses that the easy recognition of its value (second requisite) is the relevant quality a commodity must have for it to be used as a medium of exchange.[26] The rationale of this proposition has to be found in the very function

23. Galiani identifies Phoenicians and Tyrians as the first people to bring precious metals to their Mediterranean colonies in exchange for goods (i: 31). In a later passage, he ridicules those who believe that money was created by an agreement (i: 110).

24. See section 2 above.

25. A paper by Robert A. Jones, forthcoming as an article in the *Journal of Political Economy*, "develops a possible explanation for the emergence of media of exchange through the unconcerted market behaviour of individuals, without decrees, centralized decisions or explicit social agreements." Robert A Jones, "The Origin and Development of Media of Exchange" (University of California, Los Angeles, 1974), p.1.

26. "But the second [requirement] is that which precisely limits metals alone for use as money" (i: 126).

of money as a means of payment: if the purpose of indirect exchange is to save costs in transactions, the commodity chosen as the medium of exchange should not entail the additional costs of supplying information: "Now it is certain that man does not dare make a contract, except one which he can clearly understand and therefore does not fear it to be fraudulent; and since money intervenes in every contract, it is more than necessary that it should be of a material which is readily evaluated" (i: 129).[27] Therefore, the use of coinage was introduced to certify the quality of precious metals, and, hence, to allow an even easier evaluation of the means of payment (i: 129–30).

Galiani's analysis appears to be founded upon a principle which has been demonstrated again in recent work:[28] the property of easy recognition of value may be regarded as the market characteristic which determines the adoption of a given commodity as the medium of exchange.

4. *The quantity theory and the purchasing power of money*

There is no detailed treatment of the quantity theory in *Della moneta*. Indeed, the scientific reputation of the quantity theory was well established in Galiani's time. Therefore, his contributions concern issues related mainly to the specification and application of the theory.

The important property of precious metals is their relative stability of supply (i: 89) and hence of value. However, not only gold and silver coins but also "the notes representing money" (le carte rappresentanti il danaro) must be included in the quantity of money. The latter, moreover, is not the only relevant variable, since it is the velocity of circulation which makes the quantity of money appear scarce or abundant (i: 98–99).[29] Nevertheless, Galiani firmly opposes sharp changes in the supply of precious metals. A whole chapter (book IV, chapter 2, ii: 163–82) is devoted to refuting the supposed benefits of a positive variation in the quantity of gold and silver. Similarly, increases in velocity of circulation may stimulate economic

27. A closely related approach is presently found in Karl Brunner and Allan H. Meltzer, "The Uses of Money: Money in the Theory of an Exchange Economy," *American Economic Review* 61 (1971): 784–805.

28. Concluding his paper, Jones states that "the approach suggests that a very common good would emerge as a first commodity money in a barter economy. The important point is that this 'commonness' is *a market characteristic of goods* rather than an intrinsic physical characteristic such as portability, divisibility or cognizability" (pp. 25–26; italics added).

29. ". . . it is the velocity of circulation of money, not the quantity of metals, which makes money appear more or less abundant" (i: 99).

activity but not generate wealth: velocity of circulation is an effect, not a cause, of changes in wealth (ii: 135–36):

> Hence there are those reprehensible writers who, having left themselves vulnerable to the voice of the crowd and confusing the effects with the causes, wholeheartedly propose to their prince to increase the quantity of money and wish an increase in velocity; while they do not take into account either agriculture, manufacturing, or population, from which alone useful and true velocity comes. The quantity of money should not be increased except when it seems that there is not enough of it to initiate trade without stopping commerce and leaving it dry [ii: 137].

Even though in some passages (i: 41–44, 170, 176–80, 189) Galiani associates abundance and scarcity of money respectively with prosperity and poverty, he opposes sharp and continuous changes in the quantity of money. The conception of an optimal money supply is particularly stressed in *Della moneta*.[30] Yet Galiani fails to work out a procedure for the determination of such an optimum. In his attempt (ii: 137–45), however, he provides an empirical estimation of the quantity of money and of the income velocity of circulation in the Kingdom of Naples.

Galiani's discussion of the purchasing power of money is worthy of attention. The value of gold and silver, he argues, is to be determined by following the principles of value theory (i: 53).[31] Precious metals are valued as commodities before being used as money (i: 72). He then makes an empirical evaluation of the amount of silver existing in the Kingdom of Naples for both monetary and nonmonetary purposes and states:

> First I shall say that noncoined silver metal being four times greater than minted silver, following the principles I laid out in the preceding chapter [on value], one must have no doubt that the value of silver depends four times more on its use as metal than as money; otherwise either mines would not be worked after

30. In the introduction to book IV, for example, he refers to "a competent quantity of money" (una competente quantità di moneta) (ii: 134). And in a later passage he states: "it is concluded that money, very useful as the blood is in the body of the state, has to be there maintained within certain limits which should be proportioned to the veins through which it runs; beyond which, increasing or diminishing, it becomes deadly to the body which it sustained" (i: 229).

31. Galiani's treatment of the theory of value (i: 54–91) is outstanding. According to Schumpeter, he "carried this analysis to its eighteenth century peak." Joseph A. Schumpeter, *History of Economic Analysis* (New York, 1954), pp. 300–302.

> the state was replenished with sufficient money for its trade, or the price of money would change at great speed [i: 101].

Moreover, the value of the metallic currency does not depend on its weight, but on the quantity of commodities it can buy. Therefore, to inquire about the purchasing power of money in ancient times, historians have to look at the "standard of living" (costumi di vivere) in those periods (i: 51–53). This is indeed a very lucid account of the basic principles underlying the working of a commodity standard.[32]

In the conceptual experiments developed in *Della moneta*, the price level always changes proportionally to the variation in money supply. Galiani does not specifically state all of the assumptions needed for the validity of this result; the latter is, in any case, consistent with his theoretical framework, which refers to once-and-for-all increases in the quantity of money and disregards the influence of expectations.[33] His comparative statics experiments invariably confirm the principle of neutrality of money. Hence, he is a strong opponent of mercantilistic policies aiming at the continuous accumulation of precious metals: when adjustment is completed, a higher price level cancels out all effects of the increase in the quantity of money (ii: 165–66).

Galiani clearly separates real from monetary aspects in his analysis. In *Della moneta* the classical dichotomy is immanent. The clearness of the distinction between real and monetary causes of price changes is rather striking in the following passage about the cost of goods during famine and prosperity:

> High prices caused by famine are of short duration and are followed by very low prices: the high prices during prosperity are forever increasing. *The reason for this is that in the years in which war or plague or the inclement weather spoils the harvest, the number of sellers decreases with respect to that of the buyers*; hence prices increase and many people become impoverished. . . . *But with prosperity the higher velocity of money*

32. Exactly two hundred years later Milton Friedman writes: "Under a strict commodity standard the supply of currency and the supply of other goods in terms of the currency commodity are determined entirely in the market by the demand for the commodity for monetary and other uses and by the supply of the commodity, which is ultimately governed by costs of production." "Commodity-Reserve Currency," *Journal of Political Economy* 59 (1951): 203–32; reprinted in Milton Friedman, *Essays in Positive Economics* (Chicago, 1953), p. 206.

33. The likely effects of the "expectation of an augmentation" (aspettazione d'un alzamento) are rejected in the only passage found in *Della moneta* (ii: 99) which refers to this issue.

produces the increase in prices . . . and prices increase so much more because of the abundance of money [i: 179–80, italics added].

It may have appeared from the above discussion that Galiani's treatment of monetary equilibrium is founded only upon the supply side. This is, however, not entirely correct. He stresses the role of the public's behavior in determining the equilibrium relative price of precious metals (ii: 22–23). Furthermore, in his experiments on doubling the quantity of money, Galiani explicitly describes the attainment of the new equilibrium position through the disposal of the excess supply of money in the commodity market, thereby revealing his understanding of the role of demand in the determination of monetary equilibrium.

5. *The transmission mechanism of monetary policy*

Galiani went beyond an analysis of the comparative statics of changes in the quantity of money. The result of neutrality of money is verified when a new steady state is reached; there is, however, a dynamic process through which equilibrium is attained. Galiani attempted to formulate a theory about such a process.

A model of an open economy (ii: 85–88) analyzes the dynamics of variations in money supply. After an increase[34] all debts of the prince decrease, since he pays his creditors with a debased currency; civil servants are the first to experience this initial impact. If the economy were closed, the dynamics of inflation would develop very slowly. But in an open economy the exchange rate will vary;[35] merchants find foreign goods more expensive, and consequently they increase the price of domestic goods. The latter effect, however, is not felt by foreigners, given the revaluation of their currency, but by those citizens who have a fixed nominal income, e.g., civil servants. They will ask the prince for an increase in wages and the process is completed.

34. In the terminology of the time, "augmentation" or "raising" (alzamento) referred to what would today be called a once-and-for-all increase in the nominal quantity of money. Galiani defines three ways of implementing a "raising": by cutting a hole in the middle of the coins; by decree, giving a new face value to the coins without altering their metallic content; by melting and coining again the same quantity of metal, but lowering either the weight or the titer of each coin (ii: 112–14; the latter two ways are mentioned also on ii: 67). He also discusses advantages and disadvantages of each of them.

35. Galiani is well aware that if fixed exchange rates are assumed, adjustment is accomplished by an outflow of money from the inflating country: "and if this [the exchange rate] did not change, one state would absorb the money of the other" (ii: 85).

Galiani's model is more a contribution to the theory of the balance of payments adjustment than to the dynamics of monetary policy. The important concept here is that the effects of inflationary policies are related to the slowness of the mechanism through which changes in the quantity of money are transmitted to the economy. The same argument was advanced in a celebrated passage by David Hume[36] one year after the publication of *Della moneta*.[37] Galiani attempts to go even further than Hume by providing a theoretical explanation of the slow response of the economy to monetary stimuli. He formulates the hypothesis according to which individuals have a given "connection of ideas" about the prices of commodities and do not quickly change it. More particularly: "truth" is the basis from which people conceive their "ideas"; to the latter, they associate the "sound of names" (ii: 69–70). The prince, by affecting the "names," can secure a gain; hence, inflation is peculiarly defined in terms of its effect:

> Augmentation of money is a profit that the prince and the state make from the slowness with which the multitude changes the connection of ideas about the prices of goods and money [ii: 68–69].

The lack of instantaneous adjustment in the price level is the sole source of the effects produced by changes in money supply. An increase in money supply

> does not produce any change in things, but in names; thus in order for the prices of things to remain the same, they have also to change with regard to their names. If this happened on the

36. ". . . we must consider, that though the high price of commodities be a necessary consequence of the encrease of gold and silver, yet it follows not immediately upon that encrease; but some time is required before the money circulates through the whole state, and makes its effect be felt on all ranks of people. At first, no alteration is perceived; by degrees the price rises, first of one commodity, then of another; till the whole at last reaches a just proportion with the new quantity of specie which is in the kingdom. In my opinion, it is only in this interval or intermediate situation, between the acquisition of money and rise of prices, that the encreasing quantity of gold and silver is favourable to industry." David Hume, "Of Money," in *Political Discourses* (1752; rpt. in David Hume, *Writings on Economics*, ed. Eugene Rotwein, Madison, Wis., 1955), pp. 37–38.

37. Among eighteenth-century writers, the most profound treatment of the transmission mechanism of monetary policy is found in Richard Cantillon. In particular, the analysis of the latter shows two important propositions not contained in Galiani's *Della moneta*: first, that an increase in the quantity of money affects *both* the goods and the loanable funds market; second, that the variation in the price level is not necessarily proportional to the change in money supply. *Essai sur la nature du commerce en général* (1755; ed. Henry Higgs, London, 1931), pp. 159–99.

same day in which the increase was installed and happened entirely, and entirely in proportion, then the increase would have no consequences; just as a law which established that money, instead of being called by Italian names, should be called by Latin or Greek or Hebrew names would have no consequences [ii: 70].

Galiani's analysis implicitly assumes the real sector of the economy as essentially stable (i: 83).[38] Monetary policy can produce effects only because individuals hold completely static expectations about the prices of goods, thereby slowing the adjustment of the economic system. However, if the prince abuses his power, the "connection of ideas" collapses, and people no longer refer to a given set of prices (ii: 70). This latter argument entails a basic contribution: expected inflation is completely inefficacious. In Galiani's own words, "Finally, a prince who, abusing augmentation, practiced it every month, destroying every connection of ideas between prices and commodities, would render it quite useless and inefficacious; and only with other policies would obtain what today is obtained with augmentation" (ii: 71).

6. *Effects of inflation*

In *Della moneta*, Galiani is concerned only with unexpected inflation deriving from a given increase in the supply of money. He discusses the benefits (utilità) and the costs (danni) of augmentation occurring before adjustment is completed, in order to evaluate its net effect (ii: 68, 75). The analysis is one of the poorest of the book. He deals first with the "false" effects of inflation, advanced by other authors, and then with the "true" costs and benefits.

Galiani rejects the argument according to which the prince's revenues increase; only his expenditures decrease (ii: 74). Public revenues, in fact, will not diminish, because higher prices will make the payment of taxes easier for the peasants; total tax revenue will increase, since agriculture accounts for the largest share in national income (ii: 80–81). The only true effect of an increase in the money supply is that debtors are better off (ii: 83); however, the prince, who is the largest debtor, does not greatly benefit from it because tax revenue *decreases*.[39] The prince can benefit from augmentation be-

38. In another passage of *Della moneta*, Galiani gives only cursory attention to economic fluctuations and regards their occurrence as in the "order of nature" (ii: 190).

39. This is but one of many examples of the contradictions which are found in

cause of the time required to reach a new equilibrium: once the price level has increased, no further gain can be expected (ii: 87–88).

Dealing with the "true" effects of inflation, Galiani argues that in times of prosperity a redistribution of income occurs between poor and rich people. The former are debtors of their labor, while the latter are debtors of their money: hence, while the worker (the poor) will supply the same amount of labor, the employer (the rich) will pay a lower real wage. Hence, in a difficult moment, the prince can take advantage of increasing the money supply, the burden falling on civil servants who are his employees. The prince should resort to augmentation only in case of temporary difficulty in the economy; otherwise, higher public expenditures should be financed by public debt. Finally, the true benefits of augmentation are to meet emergencies, to save expenditures, to pay debts (ii: 105).

Though marred by frequent inconsistencies, Galiani's analysis still contains valuable contributions, especially from the viewpoint of economic policy. The principle which guides his treatment of inflation is the evaluation of costs and benefits of an inflationary policy in order to know whether augmentation should be practiced or not (ii: 68, 75). His discussion, however, is always focused upon a single effect of inflation. For example, augmentation makes debtors better off, but does not change the welfare of the country, since a loss of the same amount is borne by another group of citizens (ii: 83). He does not attempt to carry out a global analysis.

Galiani does not regard inflation as a policy tool to be used in normal times, since, in the long run, its effect on the real sector of the economy is nil. Nevertheless, the clear understanding that inflation is a concealed way of levying taxes (ii: 74, 76, 88–89, 96–98) prompts his call for inflationary policies whenever a country confronts an emergency and yet taxes cannot be increased (ii: 76). In such a critical situation, there should be no fear to inflate, because either the economy recovers and it is then possible to levy higher taxes, or it definitely collapses (ii: 88). Augmentation is an extraordinary instrument of economic policy to be used only when the benefits to be gained will more than offset the eventual costs (ii: 103–4, 117). Galiani favors inflation as a policy to be resorted to in critical times and compares it with "repudiation" (fallimento). While the latter has a

---

Galiani's discussion of the effects of inflation. While attempting to criticize the views held by other writers, Galiani often confuses real with monetary variables and violates his own assumption, i.e., to study the effects of inflation only before the attainment of a new steady state.

sudden effect on a few and powerful people, the impact of the former is slow and affects everybody (ii: 111–12). Furthermore, Galiani is not against the redistributive effects of inflation.[40] Since the burden of taxes should be borne by the rich, augmentation is "just" because it hits those classes of wealthy people which are also unproductive:

> Those who rent are not only well off but are idle and slothful, and should pay more because without increasing the wealth of the state they consume not only their own but also foreign goods. Nor do we have to fear the tender voices of orphans, widows, virgins, and children; because these are very few. The real orphan, the real poor man is the hard-working farmer, the craftsman, the sailor, and the merchant. We must have pity on these people, since they are accustomed to hiring and therefore gain during augmentation [ii: 109].

The contrast between this and an earlier passage (ii: 100–1) in which Galiani calls inflation unjust, because income is redistributed between the poor (the worker) and the rich (the entrepreneur), is due to the different kinds of individuals identified under those names.

7. *International aspects of monetary theory*

Contributions to international monetary economics are found throughout *Della moneta*. Apart from the third chapter of the fourth book, which deals with balance-of-payments deficit, there is no organic treatment of the topic in Galiani's work. Yet, the few passages in *Della moneta* which deal with an open economy contain the basic principles of the theory of the balance-of-payments adjustment: "When industry develops in a country, the latter becomes more a creditor than a debtor to neighboring countries; hence, after being provided with the goods of the others, it will still draw money because of the surplus [in its balance of payments]. With an increase in money and a change in proportions, everything appears more expensive" (i: 176).

In an earlier passage, Galiani further elaborates the mechanics of the adjustment process: the purchasing power of money in a given country does not diminish by the same proportion as the inflow of money from abroad, if part of this inflow is spent on foreign commodities. Huge outflows of precious metals from the American continent did not proportionally increase the price level in Europe, be-

40. Galiani postulates that redistribution between the poor and the rich is "unjust" (ii: 92–94, 100–101).

cause a large part of gold and silver was given to India in exchange for commodities (i: 46–47).

A different adjustment process occurs when flexible exchange rates are assumed.[41] The pursuit of inflationary policies results in variations in the exchange rate (ii: 84–86); foreigners, however, are not affected by this course of events, since the worsening in their terms of trade is exactly offset by the revaluation of their currency (i: 168, ii: 86, 123–24, 127).

Money flows occurring after the process of adjustment should not be tampered with by laws or regulations. The latter would be useless because no one would observe them; moreover, in case such a law was effectively enforced, it would be best for the prince to violate it. A balance-of-payments deficit always occurs subsequent to either great prosperity or calamity. In the former case, an outflow of money, deriving from the high level of income, cannot be a cause of poverty; in the latter case, the outflow of precious metals is the effect, not the cause, of impoverishment. It is in the "order of nature" to experience alternating periods of abundance and famine, and money flows are the medicine to cure the disease (ii: 183–92).

Galiani clearly understood the adjustment mechanism of the balance of payments, both in the case of fixed and in that of flexible exchange rates. His elaboration of the gold standard process of adjustment is explained by the peculiar character of the currency used at that time: precious metals were a medium of exchange for both domestic and international transactions. Therefore, the application of the transactions approach to an open economy follows directly: excess supply of money in a given country does not proportionally increase the price level, because it is partly spent on foreign goods. Galiani views the balance of payments as an essentially monetary phenomenon: flows of money originating from payment imbalances are the driving force of the equilibrium mechanism. It is not difficult to recognize similarities between this conception and recent trends in research in this field.[42]

In Galiani's analysis, there may be found the embryo of a purchasing power parity theory. Such an interpretation may be given to his continual reference to the invariability of the welfare position of foreigners after the pursuit of an inflationary policy.

41. See the discussion of the model describing the transmission process of monetary policy in section 5 above.

42. Harry G. Johnson, "The Monetary Approach to Balance-of-Payments Theory," in *Further Essays in Monetary Economics* (Cambridge, Mass., 1973), pp. 229–49.

His discussion of international monetary theory is dominated by the classical background of his thought. Man should never oppose the "order of nature": any law designed with this aim will worsen the welfare of the country. Hence, long-run capital movements are not a cause of impoverishment: capital is always directed towards the investments with the highest rate of return. Therefore, if money is invested abroad, this is beneficial to the whole nation (ii: 192–99). Galiani's main concern is to refute mercantilistic doctrines: the only effect of increasing the supply of money is a higher price level (ii: 168). Finally, he reaffirms once more the classical conception of monetary theory: "Therefore, concluding, the basis of every good government . . . is . . . that one has to swim in the abundance of foodstuffs and not of gold" (ii: 170).

8. *Conclusions*

Historians of economic thought have often pointed out the difficulty of classifying Ferdinando Galiani as a follower of a specific doctrinal current, given the variety and abundance of ideas found in all of his writings.[43] However, as far as the treatment of monetary theory in *Della moneta* is concerned, he definitely appears as an outstanding exponent of the classical tradition. The unit of account and the medium of exchange functions are the only "uses" of money. Money is just a "representation" of the real sector of the economy; it is a mechanism which saves transaction costs inherent in direct exchange. Once-and-for-all changes in the quantity of money result in proportional variations in the price level. The latter, however, do not occur instantaneously; therefore, variations in money supply produce several effects before a new steady state is attained. Money flows enhance the adjustment of the balance of payments; a different adjustment mechanism will operate if exchange rates are flexible. These principles distinctly represent the main building blocks of that coherent structure which is classical monetary theory. Hence, with regard to the theory of money, *Della moneta* can be unambiguously identified as one of the earliest and most profound works in the classical tradition.

In spite of the prominence of Galiani's contributions, his writings did not have a major influence on the historical development of economic analysis. This was mainly due to the absence of a transla-

43. This point is stressed in Luigi Einaudi, "Galiani economista," in *Saggi bibliografici e storici intorno alle dottrine economiche* (Rome, 1953), pp. 269–305; first published in German with the title "Galiani als Nationalökonom," *Schweizerische Zeitschrift für Volkswirtschaft und Statistik* vol. 81, no. 1 (1945).

tion of *Della moneta*.[44] How momentous the impact of Galiani's treatise might have been stems from the following judgment about Galiani's theory of value by Schumpeter, who says of Galiani that "he displayed sure-footed mastery of analytic procedure and, in particular, neatness in his carefully defined conceptual constructions to a degree that would have rendered superfluous all the nineteenth-century squabbles—and misunderstandings—on the subject of value had the parties to these squabbles first studied his text, *Della moneta*, 1751."[45]

As regards monetary theory, the real significance of Galiani's work emerges from the reading of the recent literature on the subject; some of his analyses reflect the very principles on which current research is founded. The merits of Galiani's contributions are to be found in the large number of his correct insights rather than in the rigor of his analysis. Yet, his simple models show a quite penetrating application of economic logic. In fact, despite some confusion in the treatment of the money and wealth issue and of distributional effects of inflation, *Della moneta* displays a consistent body of economic knowledge. Indeed, when Galiani's main assumptions are taken into account, i.e., stability of equilibrium, completely static expectations, and a metallic standard, today's economists can add little, except rigor and precision of analysis, to what he showed more than two centuries ago.

44. As mentioned by G. H. Bousquet in his "Introduction" (see n.3 above), it appears from Galiani's correspondence that the Abbé Morellet made a French translation of *Della moneta*, but no trace of it has been found.

45. Schumpeter, pp. 300–301.

Financial support from the Ente per gli Studi Monetari Bancari e Finanziari "Luigi Einaudi," Rome, is gratefully acknowledged. Thanks are due to William R. Allen, Federico Caffè, Robert W. Clower, Robert A. Jones, Joseph M. Ostroy, and two anonymous referees, for their useful suggestions; to Christine Stone for help with my English. Needless to say, responsibility for this article solely remains with the author.

History of Political Economy 23:1
© 1991 by Duke University Press
CCC 0018–2702/91/$1.50

[3]

De Viti de Marco as a Monetary Economist

Filippo Cesarano

Antonio de Viti de Marco's contributions to public finance have been momentous in developing the theory of a public economy.[1] The path-breaking character of his writings on several topics—public goods, the incidence and distribution of taxation, and public debt—has been widely recognized, establishing him as one of the leading figures who laid the foundations of the field.[2] Apart from these celebrated achievements, however, his work on other subjects is virtually unknown. Besides the language barrier, this is also accounted for by the nature of his many articles, published in the *Giornale degli economisti,* in that most of them are not theory-oriented but focus on a wide range of actual policy issues, such as tariffs and international trade, labor relations, and regional and agricultural policies.[3] By contrast his studies on money are chiefly theoretical and, excepting public finance, make up the main part of his overall scientific production. Indeed his very first publication was

Correspondence may be addressed to the author, Banca d'Italia, Servizio Studi, Via Nazionale 91, 00184 Rome, Italy.

1. Antonio de Viti de Marco was born at Casamassella, near Lecce, on 30 September 1858. In 1881 he graduated in law at the Università di Roma and then taught at Camerino, Macerata, and Pavia. In 1887 he was appointed to the chair of public finance in Rome, which he held until 1931, when he resigned upon refusing to take an oath endorsing the educational precepts of the Fascist government. Three years later he also resigned from the Accademia dei Lincei for the same reasons. Besides his academic occupations—he was on the board of editors of the *Giornale degli economisti* from 1890 to 1913—he was actively involved in politics as well. An unyielding defender of liberalism, he founded the Antiprotectionist League and was a member of parliament almost uninterruptedly from 1900 to 1921. His main political writings are collected in two volumes (1918, 1930). He had a many-faceted personality with tight links to Anglo-American culture (he married Harriett Lathrop Dunham, the daughter of a U.S. banker) and was a man of wide-ranging interests, including the management of a large estate in his native town, where he experimented with new agricultural technology. He died in Rome on 1 December 1943. See also Einaudi's introduction to de Viti de Marco 1934a; Gangemi 1945, 1972; Stammati 1945; Ricci 1946; Rossi 1948; Papa 1965; Morgenstern 1968; Cardini 1985; Caffè 1987.

2. The main reference here is Buchanan's classic study (1960), which thoroughly analyzes the scope and originality of de Viti's approach to public economics. The importance of the latter is recognized by several authors (Musgrave and Peacock 1958, x; Musgrave 1959, 69–73; 1985, 8–9, 51). See also the references at the end of note 1 above and some of the essays published in d'Albergo 1972. For an enthusiastic review of his *First Principles of Public Finance* (1934a) see Benham 1934; for a critical one, see Simons 1937.

3. Comprehensive bibliographies can be found in Gangemi 1972 and Cardini 1986.

a volume on the quantity theory (1885), and his last one was a booklet on banking (1934b).

There are compelling reasons for an examination of de Viti's monetary economics, not merely to fill a gap in the appraisal of his work but because these writings, although not up to the standard of his public finance contributions, display a good deal of originality and, as regards economic fluctuations and banking, anticipate various ideas characterizing the most recent advancements. This essay, it should be stressed, is exclusively concerned with de Viti's writings relevant to the *theory* of money, which principally consist of the two books mentioned above. Thus his articles commenting on current affairs (e.g., 1891, 1892, 1893a, 1893b, 1893c), are considered only insofar as they have analytical relevance. After a discussion of his approach to methodology, subsequent sections inquire into the quantity theory and international adjustment, the business cycle, and the theory of banking and monetary policy. The concluding pages evaluate the significance of de Viti's monetary economics.

I. *Methodology*

Although de Viti dedicates only short passages to it, methodology bears heavily upon his writings. His methodological stance was influenced by Cairnes, whose major publication on the subject (1875) looms large with him (1885, 6, 12; 1934a, 36–37). In line with the classical approach (see Blaug 1980, ch. 3), de Viti viewed economics as a deductive science which, though adopting realistic assumptions, arrives at the formulation of laws by strictly adhering to the *ceteris paribus* clause. Economic laws may well be at odds with observed events, as perturbing factors are always at work, but this does not impair their validity: methodological consistency dictates that we appraise economic analysis within the bounds set by the assumptions. Thus any criticism directed at the predictive failure of a theory is misplaced (1885, 14–15). In fact the role of empirical research in this approach is at odds with an approach featuring Friedmanian positivism. According to de Viti, the only purpose of analyzing data is to filter out findings that violate the *ceteris paribus* clause in order to isolate a "depurated" reality satisfying the assumptions of the theory (1885, 11–13).[4]

4. Mark Blaug clearly describes this classical view: "Over and over again, in Senior, in Mill, in Cairnes, and even in Jevons, we have found the notion that 'verification' is not a testing of economic theories to see whether they are true or false, but only a method of establishing the boundaries of application of theories deemed to be obviously true: one verifies in order to discover whether 'disturbing causes' can account for the discrepancies between stubborn facts and theoretically valid reasons; if they do, the theory has been wrongly applied, but the theory itself is still true. The question of whether there is any way of showing a theory to be false is never even contemplated" (1980, 81).

He departs from classical apriorism in the study of public finance considered as "a concrete science that . . . must be brought down finally to real phenomena" (1934a, 36) in contrast with economics, which is an abstract science. Thus "public finance cannot use logical abstraction to the same extent as does general economics" (1934a, 37).[5] Nonetheless, in our context here, his position on method is closely related to the classical tradition as embodied mainly in Cairnes's writings.

II. *The Quantity Theory and International Adjustment*

The bulk of *Moneta e prezzi* (1885, chs. 3–7) is concerned with the monetary analysis of an open economy. (Chapters 1 and 2 deal instead with the quantity theory.) Given the strong influence of British classical economists on de Viti's work, this is hardly surprising.[6] Although his performance on these topics does not rank high, it nevertheless deserves to be considered because it contains some original insights which are central in his treatment of other subjects, such as banking. Furthermore, the structure of his model is of interest in that it builds on elements pertaining to contrasting strains of classical monetary economics.

De Viti is a firm supporter of the "quantity principle." Although following the classics,[7] he faults them for failing to distinguish metallic from fiduciary money and to discern the differential effectiveness of changes in these variables (1885, 8–9). Contrasting the medium-of-

5. This statement should be taken with some care, since the prevalent methodological attitude of the Italian finance authors has been fundamentally different from the problem-solving and predictive approach of Marshallian economics. According to Buchanan: "In many respects, 'la scienza delle finanze' resembles philosophy more than it does Marshallian economics. The goal of Italian fiscal theorists has been that of providing generalized or philosophical explanations of the fiscal process. Research has been concerned with the 'nature of things' rather than with finding operational propositions in the modern scientific sense. Italian scholars have been interested, by and large, in constructing complete, integrated systems, and the criterion for success has been logical consistency rather than usefulness for making predictions, actual or conceptual" (1960, 37–38).

6. As Laidler points out: "Nowadays monetary theory usually starts with the assumption of a closed economy, but this characteristic is a relatively recent innovation, stemming from two sources: Keynes' use of the closed economy assumption in the *General Theory,* and the growing dominance of American writers in the macroeconomics literature since the Second World War. It will already be apparent that English Classical economists took an open economy for granted: a theory of the balance of payments was an integral part of their monetary economics, and had been since the days of Cantillon and Hume, whose price-specie-flow mechanism, so called, formed the starting point for virtually all subsequent work on this matter" (1988, 92).

7. In his overall work on money he continuously refers to the teachings of the "teoria classica" or "scuola economica" and particularly to Hume, Ricardo, J. S. Mill, Cairnes, and Jevons. De Viti shows a thorough and up-to-date knowledge of the literature and quotes quite a few publications in English, French, German, and Italian, even by minor authors.

exchange with the unit-of-account function, he stresses the related distinction between effecting transactions by means of metallic money and doing so by other payment or credit instruments and limits the validity of the quantity theory to the former assumption. On the contrary, "credit"—checks, discountable bills, and bilateral accounts that permit offsetting debts and credits—may or may not affect the purchasing power of money depending on the type of disturbance. On the one hand, a proportional increase in the production of every commodity, contrary to Cairnes's contention, leaves both relative and "nominal" prices constant, because transactions are settled without resort to metallic money. In this case, de Viti argues, pressure on bank reserves is ruled out, since the very growth of output brings about debts and credits which balance exactly. Banks, then, do not alter their reserves, as these depend on the difference between assets and liabilities. On the other hand, when the stimulus to trade is not due to a change in production but to a speculative wave, prices can temporarily increase sustained by the issue of bills. But discounting bills will now produce a drain on reserves, and eventually price-level stabilization, because banks grant credit considering both the volume of business and the "goodness of the bills issued" (1885, 34–40).

De Viti blends propositions that belong to conflicting approaches to classical monetary economics, namely the Hume-Ricardo theoretical framework followed by the currency school and the Adam Smith analysis taken up by Tooke and other banking school exponents.[8] First and foremost, despite his adherence to the quantity theory, he firmly upholds the real-bills doctrine without ever noticing any strictures upon the latter or the incompatibility of the two hypotheses. The rationale of this singular standpoint lies in his conception of money, carrying metallism to extremes.[9] His hard and fast distinction between money and "credit" as payment media, underlying an equally strict separation of the functions of money, leads him to a narrower definition of money—confined to metals—than the definitions selected by the currency and banking schools, which also include notes, and notes and deposits respectively.[10] This distinction is reflected in the different principles he

8. Detailed accounts of the development of monetary theory can be found in Viner 1937; Wood 1939; Mints 1945; Corry 1962; Fetter 1965; and O'Brien 1975. Recent articles on the same topic are Laidler 1988 and Santiago-Valiente 1988.

9. In one of his articles commenting on the messy banking situation in Italy during the 1890s, he labels as "false money" the issue of inconvertible notes (1892, 444). He stuck to a metallist view throughout his life. See, for example, his book on banking (1934b, 58, 66, 72–74), published half a century after *Moneta e prezzi*. On theoretical metallism and classical economics see Schumpeter 1954, 698–701.

10. This matter had been hotly debated throughout the nineteenth century, but by the time of the publication of de Viti's book (1885) Mill's authoritative account ([1848] 1909, book 3, chapter 12) favoring a most extended aggregate was generally accepted (Mints

adopts for accounting for the effects of changes in these variables as described just above. While the quantity theory exclusively applies to money, whose variations are the necessary and sufficient condition for price-level movements (1885, 41–42), the banking principle regulates the volume of fiduciary media, which do not affect prices except at the beginning of a speculative wave. Being the only instrument allowed to settle balances, money provides both the unit of account and the control variable of the standard (1885, 47). In this analytical structure the financial sector is conceived as a veil, wrapping the real economy but designed to leave its basic relationships unaffected.[11] The unit of account is divorced from the medium of exchange and enables people to execute transactions without the intervention of money (1885, 87–89, 117–18).[12]

De Viti's eclectic viewpoint cannot be classified within a specific school. In fact he refers to classical monetary economics as a single current of thought, seemingly unaware of its two-sided nature. He often takes an original view of a subject. In particular his analysis contrasts with the standard account of the foundations of money—which stresses the primacy of the medium-of-exchange function and its tight connection with the unit of account—from Adam Smith[13] to the present (see

1945, chs. 6 and 10; Laidler 1988, 80–82). Anna J. Schwartz, in her *New Palgrave* article "Banking School, Currency School, Free Banking School," diverges from this common interpretation and attributes to the banking school a more restricted definition comprising metallic and government paper money. De Viti's heterodoxy, then, can be easily appreciated. In this respect he even rejects the interpretation, widely held by metallists (Schumpeter 1954, 318–20), of fiduciary payments media as instruments increasing velocity, thus maintaining a sharp separation between money and "credit" (1885, 36–37). Reference to velocity is found in his treatise on public finance—published, however, fifty years later (1934a, 414 n. 1).

11. Santiago-Valiente has recently provided a similar interpretation of Adam Smith: "credit is, in principle, a passive element in the final price formation process of the economy while money regulates the level of prices in agreement with the laws ruling either barter or a pure commodity money economy. In this perspective the 'real-bills' doctrine is one ingredient in Smith's effort to bridge the gap between the theory of value and the theory of money by devising a 'neutral' monetary and banking system" (1988, 61). However, de Viti patently differs from Smith with respect to the theory of the price level (see below).

12. Discussing the evolution of monetary arrangements, de Viti likens an advanced credit organization to the medieval barter economy, thus stressing the idea of a payment system functioning without metallic money: "Accordingly, in the early Middle Ages payments in kind were resorted to when, after the fall of the Western Empire, Rome ceased to be the center to which the gold of the world flowed, and Italy found itself without a stock of metal. Likewise, and for the same reasons, though in a much more advanced way, payments in kind were resorted to later, and today resort is made to a perfectible credit organization, which can be considered as a development of the medieval idea, in that it generalizes and impresses a great rapidity to payments in kind and exchanges of commodities, leaving to metallic money the supreme task of settling the balances" (1885, 152).

13. In the fifth chapter of *The Wealth of Nations* a penetrating passage explains the assignment of the unit-of-account function to the very commodity which emerges as the

Jevons 1875, 13–14; Pantaleoni [1894] 1957, 224–25; Wicksell [1906] 1935, 7; Niehans 1978, ch. 7). This enduring proposition of received monetary theory has recently been disregarded by the "new monetary economics."[14] This literature builds on the distinction between tangible money and an abstract unit of account, the latter providing the basis of an accounting system of exchange. Such a system entails a different explanatory model from the one relating to tangible money. Therefore, although starting from quite opposite hypotheses rooted in extreme versions of metallism and cartalism respectively, de Viti's approach and the contemporary one hinge on similar general principles insofar as the relationship between the functions of money is concerned, and the implications thereof.

While de Viti's conception of money is of some interest, especially from the perspective of contemporary theory, his discussion of the open economy, despite its length (1885, chs. 3–7), displays no originality and is worth but little attention. Concerning the Hume-Ricardo adjustment mechanism, he describes the effects of gold discoveries, drawing largely on Cairnes's writings (1873, 1874). Although he recognizes (1885, 58ff.) the direct effect on the balance of payments that results from changes in money incomes (Viner 1937, ch. 6), he does not assign this factor a significant role in the equilibrating process, which essentially rests on

means of payment: "But when barter ceases, and money has become the common instrument of commerce, every particular commodity is more frequently exchanged for money than for any other commodity. The butcher seldom carries his beef or his mutton to the baker, or the brewer, in order to exchange them for bread or for beer; but he carries them to the market, where he exchanges them for money, and afterwards exchanges that money for bread and for beer. The quantity of money which he gets for them regulates too the quantity of bread and beer which he can afterwards purchase. It is more natural and obvious to him, therefore, to estimate their value by the quantity of money, the commodity for which he immediately exchanges them, than by that of bread and beer, the commodities for which he can exchange them only by the intervention of another commodity; and rather to say that his butcher's meat is worth threepence or fourpence a pound, than that it is worth three or four pounds of bread, or three or four quarts of small beer. Hence it comes to pass, that the exchangeable value of every commodity is more frequently estimated by the quantity of money, than by the quantity either of labour or of any other commodity which can be had in exchange for it" ([1776] 1976, 36). It should be emphasized that in *The Wealth of Nations* Smith reversed his previous opinion on the primacy of the medium-of-exchange function. As Cannan recalls in his introduction to the 1976 edition, in the *Lectures on Justice, Police, Revenue and Arms*—reported by a student in 1763—Smith considers money "first as the measure of value and then as the medium of permutation or exchange" (1976, 32 n. 3), this view being borrowed from Francis Hutcheson's *System of Moral Philosophy* (Cannan in Smith 1976, xvii–iii; xlii–iii).

14. Although the expression is due to Hall (1982b), the new monetary economics originates with Black (1970). Other important references are Hall 1982a and Greenfield and Yeager 1983, 1986. For a critical appraisal see White 1984, 1986, and McCallum 1985. Cowen and Kroszner (1987) examine this literature from a history of economics viewpoint.

the price-level differential. Aside from considering the role of capital mobility in shortening the adjustment mechanism (1885, 116), he does not make any substantial progress.

III. *The Business Cycle*

In the course of the nineteenth century, business-cycle theory began to take shape, attempting first to identify the main causes of crises. These included most elements of the explanations advanced in subsequent periods—such as overproduction, psychological factors, the influence of investment, the role of money and credit—but at this early stage a more comprehensive theoretical framework was still lacking.[15] De Viti is no exception; in the main he follows the "orthodox theory of business fluctuations" (Wood 1939, 157) wherein speculative bursts are propelled by cheap credit and followed by a "curative" depression. However, his analysis of the process underlying the development of cycles goes further and emphasizes some elements of the modern treatment of the topic.

In the final chapter of *Moneta e prezzi* (1885) he puts forward a real hypothesis of fluctuations and takes to task fellow economists who assign a causal role to monetary phenomena and do not consider them as mere symptoms or consequences of disturbances. Disturbances consist in a loss of wealth and do occur in a world without money (a barter economy) or even without exchange (a "use economy").[16] Money and credit, then, are important in propagating business cycles and quickening their effects but not in initiating them; hence they do not provide an explanation. Perturbations of the commodity market are the "economic and sufficient cause of crises" (1885, 201).

De Viti distinguishes between "passive" and "active" crises (1885, 203). The former are set off by exogenous causes which sharply reduce production or consumption—such as a bad harvest or the outbreak of a war—entailing a net loss for society. The latter arise from endogenous factors, chiefly an anticipated increase in consumption leading to overproduction of goods. It is in the discussion of "active crises" that his most interesting insights can be found (1885, 210–32), stressing imper-

15. See Mitchell 1927, 1–11; Hansen 1951, part 3; Schumpeter 1954, 738–50. The contributions of the first half of the nineteenth century are examined in detail by Link (1959), and Haberler ([1937] 1964) provides a thorough and accurate survey of the post-1900 literature.

16. The main difference between the two concerns the distribution of the wealth loss. In the second one, the loss exclusively falls on producers; in the first, it may be shifted to consumers through the exchange mechanism. For example, when an epizootic develops in the flocks of a shepherd tribe, every member of the community suffers a welfare reduction. Instead, if exchange takes place, producers will sell their goods at higher prices, thus wholly or partly compensating the loss (1885, 195–96).

fect information in accounting for the dynamics of the cycle.[17] Following a rise in observed or expected prices, which is indicative of a growth in consumption, firms decide to expand production and demand more labor and capital, under the assumption that they are not fully employed (1885, 219 n. 1). As wages and profits go up, workers and capitalists purchase more goods, thus reinforcing the upward variation in output. The shift in the commodities supply curve is then much larger relative to the initial displacement of demand, because of the entrepreneur's confusion between the increase in demand for the whole industry and that for the single firm.[18] The consequent rise in input and commodity prices generates a further confusion between an increase in absolute and in relative prices. Referring to an example dealing with hat production, de Viti states:

> The general price increase can arrive at the limit that every single producer, in view of the expected gain, thinks convenient. And this limit will be high, because every hat producer counts on the sale of 100 hats more than his previous production, and furthermore believes that he will sell at today's prices, which are rising, but which instead must go down when the new demand is satisfied. This too is a computation mistake, like the previous one; and although it seems very glaring, it is a rather general fact in industrial life that the producer who enlarges his production in view of high prices hardly ever thinks that with the mere increase in supply he himself contributes to the decrease in prices. (1885, 219)

This sequence of events is made possible by the development of credit. By contrast, in a purely monetary economy firms can purchase inputs not by promises of payment but only by hard cash, and thus overproduction cannot occur. The whole process comes to a stop when the attempt to discount an excessive volume of bills puts pressure on bank reserves and the quantity theory works out its effects. In the end

17. "Active or speculative crises occur instead, when it is anticipated or there are clues that consumption is not yet satisfied; and then it is attempted to push production to the level of consumption. So we are in a period of dynamics, whose static result should be the adjustment of the new supply to the new demand for commodities. This is the first base of an active crisis; which will burst only when and to the extent that the static result is not attained *for an error of anticipations*" (1885, 210, emphasis mine).

18. "In fact, as said at the beginning, every producer, pushed by the keenness of today's competition, thinks to be the only one, or to arrive before others to satisfy the higher demand manifesting itself on the market by the initial price rise. Thus he increases his production, without considering that other producers act in the same direction. Here we have a computation mistake, stemming from the struggle between the economy of the single producer and the economy of his industrial group" (1885, 216–17). Attention had earlier been called to price movements as a guide to the firm's decision process by Sismondi in his *Nouveaux principes d'économie politique* (1st ed., 1819; 2d ed., 1827) (Mitchell 1927, 5–6).

the excess supply of goods leads to a fall in prices, and entrepreneurs suffer a loss.[19]

De Viti's final aim is to show that variations in the money stock do not account for economic fluctuations, in order to corroborate his real hypothesis of the business cycle. There are, however, serious gaps in his analysis, and consequently his conclusions are rather farfetched.[20]

The main elements of this analytical framework—the initial speculative increase in prices, the consequent expansion of input demand, the key role of credit, and the final "revulsion"—are essentially those present in John Stuart Mill's approach. In particular the notion of the entrepreneur's miscalculations of the relevant variables had provided the main argument of Mill's attack on Attwood's inflationary policy proposals as early as in 1833 (Humphrey 1977) and can again be found in both the *Essays* (1844, 67–68) and the *Principles* ([1848], 1909, 526–28, 550–51). De Viti puts even more emphasis on this concept. Economic agents' mistakes in interpreting market signals are at the very center of his approach to economic fluctuations. In the last pages of his book, analyzing the effects of a continuous increase in the money stock, he links the eventual rise in prices to his hypothesis of the business cycle and arrives at suggestive results hinging on entrepreneurs' confusion between absolute and relative prices.

> We have shown that an active crisis bursts when producers infer from the increase in prices a larger demand for consumption, but exceed in estimating its degree and measure of absorption.
>
> Now a partial increase in prices is a clue of an increased demand for consumption, when the quantity of money has remained the same and a deviation in the direction of demand has occurred. But the increase can be due simply to the circumstance that the cir-

19. "In conclusion, it should be said that the fall in prices ushers in the moment at which the rule of the fiduciary economy ends and the full metallic economy falls to a point where the quantity principle operates in all its efficacy. The difference between fiduciary prices and the corresponding metallic prices represents the net loss of producers. The theory of crises is a case of price dynamics" (1885, 226).

20. This note attempts to give a sketchy account of his weak, albeit articulated, view. On the basis of his definition of crisis as a loss in wealth, as contrasted with wealth redistribution, he distinguishes between a once-and-for-all and a continuous decrease in money supply. In the first case a change in relative prices is postulated, producing wealth redistribution. The occurrence of a crisis then depends on whether the gainers save the extra wealth or consume it. Only in the latter instance, the capital stock being affected, does a depression follow, but its cause is the increase in consumption, not the initial fall in money. On the other hand, a gradual and continuous decrease in money supply is assumed to leave relative prices unaltered and to bring about a wealth redistribution from producers to lenders following the temporary reduction of the profit rate and the increase in the interest rate. Hence there can be no contraction in economic activity unless lenders make a "computing error" and divert capital to consumption (1885, 232–44).

> culating money stock has gone up. Then the growth of demand does not represent increased consumption.
>
> The producers' computation in this case is false from the first moment, and an expansion in production must, if all other conditions remain the same, bring on a crisis because consumption cannot absorb a new supply; prices fall and the invested capital is not replenished. . . .
>
> Investors have not considered that such a remarkable partial increase in prices was a transitional phenomenon of monetary dynamics, and that when the new gold will have penetrated into the country's total circulation, those prices will have to fall as much as the prices of the commodities, which had not been affected by the action of the new gold, proportionally have to increase. (1885, 254–56)

Like Mill and other authors belonging to both the currency and the banking schools, de Viti offers no recipe for dampening business fluctuations. Indeed the prevailing hypotheses concerning cycles, which stressed real factors, led him to conceive disturbances as an unavoidable feature of the economy, thus leaving little or no room for policy. He departs from Mill, however, in one important respect concerning the "general superabundance" of goods. In his essay "Of the Influence of Consumption on Production" Mill, though excluding the possibility of "an excess of all commodities" in a barter economy, admits such a temporary eventuality in a monetary economy following an increase in the demand for money (1844, 68–74). De Viti, however, considers the barter and the money economy alike and, in both cases, denies the occurrence of superabundance, which instead requires the existence of credit (1885, 220–21). This rather peculiar stance is coherent with his overall approach to monetary theory, which is based on a theoretical metallism that sharply distinguishes money from credit. Thus he does not follow Mill's momentous insight on the possible failure of Say's Law in a monetary economy, which was founded on the different nature of money and commodities.

Though it fails to provide a general and coherent framework, de Viti's theory of economic fluctuations evokes Mill's analysis of disturbances by recurring to the notion of imperfect information along exactly the same lines pursued by recent authors. An essential element of Robert Lucas's equilibrium model of the business cycle is just this: "information is *imperfect,* not only in the sense that the future is unknown, but also in the sense that no agent is perfectly informed as to the current state of the economy" (1981, 179–80, emphasis his). While the starting point of the modern theory consists of an unexpected monetary shock, the prime mover of de Viti's apparatus is an exogenous increase in consumption. It is this different source of initial disturbance which explains his continuous reference to a *real* theory of economic fluctuations. But the nature of the behavioral hypothesis is in fact the same. This tight similarity also concerns the main characteristics of the structure of the model, namely the response on the part of producers to price changes which are regarded as permanent, the effects of such signals on capital accumulation, and the rapid adjustment of investment. All these features, put forward by Lucas,[21] are present in de Viti's work.

IV. *The Theory of Banking and Monetary Policy*

De Viti's approach to banking and monetary policy is closely intertwined with his conception of money. In his metallist theoretical framework the eventual development of "credit" instruments falls into place somewhat separately or subordinately with respect to money, in that the latter performs the key functions of settling balances and anchoring the price level. This stance goes back to the late scholastics and has a longstanding tradition running through Cantillon, Galiani, and Turgot well up to the First World War (Schumpeter 1954, 317–22).

After his first publication on the quantity theory (1885) de Viti's interest in monetary economics focused more on the applied than on the abstract aspects of the subject (see, e.g., 1891, 1892, 1893a, 1893b, 1893c). His last work, *La funzione della banca* (1934b), however, was again of a theoretical nature. The main objective of this booklet, which is an expanded version of an earlier paper (1898),[22] is to discover a "general organic function" of banks, thereby providing a hypothesis explaining bank behavior and its relation to money and credit. Following an evolutionary approach,[23] he identifies such a function with the payment function, or the provision of payment services, and aims to demonstrate that all banking activities can be reduced to this very role.

21. See especially his "Understanding Business Cycles" (Lucas 1981, 215–39). Mentioning mostly Lucas's views here does not mean that I disregard other important contributors to modern business-cycle literature or ignore Lucas's own intellectual indebtedness to Friedman and Phelps, but is simply dictated by the necessity of keeping the length of this paper within reasonable limits.

22. The content of the 1898 article is fully incorporated in the 1934 volume. Thus, although the quotations supplied here mainly refer to the latter, it should be emphasized that the basic ideas date back to the end of the 1890s. In the preface de Viti critically remarks that "the oddities that one reads in the 'modernist' monetary literature originated from the World War and from the long practice of paper money inflation" (1934b, 13).

23. In contemporary literature White (1984) and Selgin and White (1987) adhere to the evolutionary approach to monetary and banking arrangements. Both works by de Viti (1898, 1934b) examine several interesting issues in banking history, such as the origin and implications of government control, the role of public debt in the founding process of credit institutions, and the nature of the oldest banks. Despite their attractiveness these topics are peripheral to de Viti's contribution, as his aim is purely theoretical. In fact his analysis of major events was instrumental in framing his theory of banking (1898, 7; 1934b, 17–18).

A recurrent feature of his work—namely, to hold to a specific hypothesis inflexibly, trying to bring complex phenomena under the same explanation—appears in his theory of banking as well.[24] In order to maintain the uniqueness of the payment function, he adroitly considers loans as a way of developing the payment system, in that the bank merely transfers "the *temporary use* of money" (1934b, 42, emphasis his) from customers who do not have to make payments to those who do. Furthermore, the introduction of bills-discounting gives rise to "credit deposits," as contrasted to specie deposits, and thus the bank still is solely concerned with the payments industry.[25] Elaborating this theory, he argues that there is no limit to the expansion of bank credit: as long as balancing is carried out, "credit payments" can grow without bounds, the banker's main concern being the "goodness of each single bill" (1934b, 49). In this theoretical framework the metallist principle assigns to cash the fundamental function of balancing net debt positions, while the real-bills doctrine assures sound bank management. Bank solvency, then, depends on the quality of the portfolio and not on the quantity of deposits; moreover, the level of reserves is irrelevant to the bank's solidity, the latter being only related to the characteristics of the loans (1934b, 41–52).

De Viti manifestly owes much to Adam Smith. His support of the real-bills doctrine hinges on a conception of credit strictly distinguished from money and designed to provide a "neutral" financial sector (see note 11 above). Likewise, the different role of bank reserves in deposit and in commercial banking (Santiago-Valiente 1988, 50–51) and the separation of commercial and investment banking also follow the message of *The*

24. He describes four stages of development in which the nature of deposits changes from the mere safekeeping of money to the sophisticated medium of payment of a clearing system. In this process merchants, money-changers, and goldsmiths begin to employ the sums entrusted to them in their own business, therefore acting as "investment intermediaries." In the second stage, in consequence of management abuses leading to the impossibility of paying back depositors, the bank refrains from making loans and becomes a "payment intermediary." In the third stage, however, the restrictive legislation enacted for the purpose of assuring solvency is eluded, since market forces strongly induce banks to lend their deposits and to keep just the reserves necessary to settle the balance of their customers' transactions. When a multiplicity of banks is considered, the fourth and final stage of development is reached, and the clearing house performs the balancing role (1934b, ch. 1).

25. Explaining the implications of the transition from "monetary banks," which receive deposits in specie, to "credit banks," which grant loans, de Viti states: "The first [consequence of notable importance] is that now the bank grants credit on its own account, no longer as an intermediary between payer and payee, or between borrower and lender. It has so become an autonomous industry, which negotiates its own credit; in doing so it is not subject to the limitations of monetary banks, whose credit capacity was limited by the existing quantity of money. Instead, developing as the 'organ of credit payments,' it is able to closely follow business activity, which is the source of bills issue" (1934b, 46).

Wealth of Nations.[26] De Viti's model, however, does not show the same internal coherence, for while Smith consistently accounts for the value of commodity money by its cost of production (Laidler 1981, 186–89; Santiago-Valiente 1988, 45–47), de Viti upholds the quantity theory.

De Viti's theoretical structure foreshadows some elements of the "new monetary economics" (see note 14 above). In his approach banks play a major role in effecting transactions through balancing but not in the determination of prices, as the monetary base anchors the price level. Besides, like Adam Smith, he regards the real-bills doctrine as a principle of sound bank management and not as a sufficient condition for price-level determinacy. On the other hand, the modern theory neglects the real-bills doctrine and related attention to the short-term character of loans, banks' portfolio management activities being pure financing decisions à la Modigliani and Miller (Fama 1980).

Probing further into the evolution of banks, de Viti envisions a "complete banking organism" (1934b, 57) where all payments are made by check. Having recognized the obstacles to its realization,[27] he shows how, through the issue of banknotes, this complete system can be approached as closely as possible. However, abiding by a firm metallist standpoint, he draws from this analysis implications quite different from those of Wicksell. In fact, whereas Wicksell had pointed towards eliminating the monetary role of precious metals altogether ([1906] 1935, 126), de Viti gives gold a pivotal place and closely follows the real-bills doctrine. Thus the control of the monetary system rests upon the main-

26. He contrasts banks with other credit institutions as they pertain to the payments and loans industry respectively: "Now, in fact, the one [the bank] and the others [credit institutions] make loans *in money;* but for the bank, money, considered as a means of payment, is by itself the ultimate end of its industry; while for credit institutions, money intervenes as a measure of *capitals,* that is, of instrumental goods, which are lent or borrowed. . . . In conclusion, *money* and thus the presence of a payer and a payee are the necessary and sufficient premises of the bank, without credit being a theoretically essential or historically permanent element of the phenomenon. Instead, the existence of available capitals and the presence of a lender and a borrower are the necessary and sufficient premises of credit institutions" (1934b, 91–92, emphasis his). This proposition is also advanced by Adam Smith ([1776] 1976, 326–27).

27. Wicksell ([1906] 1935, 87–126) extensively discusses the same topic, identifying three obstacles to the establishment of the "ideal bank": (1) small payments, (2) international payments, and (3) the industrial use of precious metals. De Viti includes the first two and further adds the unfeasible task of extending branch-banking to the whole country, but he does not discuss problems relating to precious metals, following his metallist position (1934b, 57–58, 76). Nevertheless he emphasizes the "neutrality" of money in its role of unit of account in a payments system managed by banks: "The modern banking organism, seen as a whole of banks of deposit and banks of issue, brings us back to the natural barter economy, after having eliminated all obstacles which made its development impossible. Money now serves to give value to goods which are exchanged. All the delicate building of payments which are made through banks is founded on the principle of 'balancing' " (71).

tenance of convertibility and the monitoring of portfolio quality on the part of banks.[28]

De Viti's firm support of the "monetary theory of credit"—based on "a sharp distinction between money as the only genuine and ultimate means of payment and the credit instrument that embodied a claim to money" (Schumpeter 1954, 717)—has important implications for his conception of monetary policy. Banks of issue have followed precisely that path of development from deposit to commercial banking. But the long-time government practice of having recourse to them in order to finance budget deficits has made banknotes just a form of public debt—a perpetuity bearing no interest.[29] Then, when notes are issued not against a deposit in specie but following bills-discounting, the money held by the bank is simply a reserve, and the main principle governing sound bank management is again the real-bills doctrine.

Monetary policy, as it is conceived nowadays, obviously finds no place in de Viti's overall analytical framework.[30] Rejecting any infringement of the rules of a metallic standard, he approaches this topic from a public finance perspective. In his *First Principles* the issue of irredeemable paper money is viewed as "a case of *ultra-extraordinary* finance" ([1934a] 1936, 399, emphasis his) giving rise to distribution problems, to be resorted to only in critical conditions, such as in times of war, when bonds cannot be easily sold.[31] Eventually inflation occurs because of a

28. References to convertibility and the real-bills doctrine abound in de Viti's writings. On convertibility see 1892, 452, 455, 461–65; 1893a, x, xv; 1893b, viii, x. On the real-bills doctrine see 1891, 4, 9–10; 1892, 444, 450–52; 1893a, xii; 1893b, vii–viii.

29. Referring to the scholastics' view of credit founded on the metallist theory of money, Schumpeter emphasizes its lasting influence: "The clear perception of the truth that a bank note and a checking deposit are fundamentally the same thing is in fact one of the strong points of this theory. Thus money remains very strictly defined. Credit, particularly bank credit, is merely a method of using it more efficiently. I cannot stop to show, but the reader may easily see for himself, that most phenomena that go under the heading of credit *can* be described in this way. Government paper money may then either be included with full-weight coin in the total of the quantity of money or else construed as a government debt—that is, as a promise to pay in coin at some time or other. The latter view predominated, and throughout the nineteenth century there are instances of governments issuing notes with the legend: 'This note is part of the government's floating debt,' suggesting an analogy with treasury bills, especially when the notes carried interest, as they not infrequently did" (1954, 319, emphasis his). De Viti also recognizes that the quantity of notes which is permanently in the hands of the public—corresponding to the modern notion of transactions demand for money—"is a form of 'collective property' " (1934b, 66).

30. Discussing theoretical developments in the twentieth century, Mints states: "On the subjects of monetary and banking policy there has been something more nearly resembling an evolution of ideas. To be sure, this could not come from the adherents of the real-bills doctrine, for they in effect excused themselves from all responsibility in this matter by prescribing merely that banks should maintain convertibility of their obligations and discount only bona fide, self-liquidating commercial bills" (1945, 11).

31. "To sum up: the issue of temporarily irredeemable paper money presents itself to

violation of convertibility and of the real-bills doctrine (403–4), generally following fiscal mismanagement by the government. De Viti's solution consists in balancing the budget, thus stopping the flow of paper money. After an interesting discussion of the distributional effects of different stabilization policies, he analyzes the advantages of a gradual action as opposed to a shock therapy. Though not clearly taking sides,[32] he refers to the latter as having "the advantage of accelerating the liquidation of the crisis through the disappearance of ailing industries" (424). In the next paragraph, however, he arrives at several elements still current in debate on rational expectations and the related implications of deflationary policy.

> Such [a] policy may be carried out with more or less speed, according to a whole set of factual circumstances, which vary, necessarily, from country to country, and whose absolute and relative evaluation goes beyond the competence of pure economic theory. Speaking generally, it may be said, in the first place, that the plan for revaluation adopted must be public and that it must be put into execution some time—for example, a year—after its approval, so that (a) no one is taken by surprise and all the agents of production are prepared for a nominal and temporary reduction of their remuneration in view of the increasing purchasing power of money; (b) some entrepreneurs may be able to adapt their conditions of supply to decreasing prices in the future; and (c) . . . the deflation should not affect current contracts in process of execution. (424)

V. *Conclusions*

During the first half of the nineteenth century, monetary economics was in a state of flux that gave rise to conflicting theoretical frameworks. De Viti did not espouse any specific approach. Indeed, his analysis encompasses elements pertaining to opposite strains of the classical theory of money, whose bivalent nature he failed to notice. In the main he draws much from Adam Smith's view of money and banking, aiming at designing a neutral financial sector. In this connection his stance is quite

---

the State for the moment as a fiscal device which is quicker and less costly in comparison with an extraordinary tax on property. From a purely fiscal point of view, it represents the path of least resistance; and on that account every State sees itself forced to follow it when the other sources of public revenue—both ordinary and extraordinary—are exhausted or are held to be exhausted" (1934a, 406). In a recent article Friedman states: "Government, of course, stepped in at an early stage in the introduction of fiduciary elements, both to regulate private issuers of fractional reserve promises to pay and to take advantage of the possibility of obtaining real resources by introducing fiat elements into promises to pay the monetary commodity" (1986, 642).

32. In earlier writings he favors a policy of quick adjustment (1892, 447, 456–58).

extreme and does not look in the same direction as the banking school, which, together with the antibullionist movement, represents the immediate development of Smith's analysis. In fact de Viti further accentuates the contrast between money and credit, the latter entailing a payment medium of a different nature which does not affect the price level. His theory is so eclectic that his model does not always show overall coherence. Nor does he propound any of the main ideas that characterized the advance of the field in the last decades of the nineteenth century, namely those due to Menger, Walras, Wicksell, and Fisher. Thus his writings on money do not share the pathbreaking character of his work on public finance. His contributions here consist rather in a wealth of suggestive insights, some of them anticipating contemporary theory. The distinctions between tangible and fiduciary media of payment—most particularly regarding the separation of the functions of money—and an emphasis on imperfect information provide the foundations of his approach to money and business cycles respectively, bearing heavily upon modern analyses.

The incisive comments of two anonymous referees led to a substantial improvement of this paper. This acknowledgment falls short of doing justice to their essential contribution. The usual caveat applies.

References

Benham, F. 1934. Review of *Principii di economia finanziaria,* by A. de Viti de Marco. *Economica* 1 (August): 364–67.

Black, Fischer. 1970. Banking and Interest Rates in a World without Money: The Effects of Uncontrolled Banking. *Journal of Bank Research* 1 (Autumn): 9–20.

Blaug, Mark. 1980. *The Methodology of Economics, or How Economists Explain.* Cambridge: Cambridge University Press.

Bordo, Michael David. 1975. John E. Cairnes on the Effects of the Australian Gold Discoveries, 1851–73: An Early Application of the Methodology of Positive Economics. *HOPE* 7 (Fall): 337–59.

Buchanan, James M. 1960. "La scienza delle finanze": The Italian Tradition in Fiscal Theory. In *Fiscal Theory and Political Economy: Selected Essays.* Chapel Hill: University of North Carolina Press.

Caffè, Federico. 1987. Antonio de Viti de Marco. In *The New Palgrave: A Dictionary of Economics,* edited by John Eatwell, Murray Milgate, and Peter Newman, vol. 4. London: Macmillan.

Cairnes, J. E. 1873. *Essays in Political Economy, Theoretical and Applied.* London: Macmillan.

———. 1874. *Some Leading Principles of Political Economy Newly Expounded.* London: Macmillan.

———. 1875. *The Character and Logical Method of Political Economy.* London: Macmillan.

Cardini, A. 1985. *Antonio de Viti de Marco.* Bari: Laterza.

———. 1986. *Guida bibliografica agli scritti di Antonio de Viti de Marco.* Rome: Jacelli.

Corry, B. A. 1962. *Money, Saving and Investment in English Economics 1800–1850.* London: Macmillan.

Cowen, Tyler, and Randall Kroszner. 1987. The Development of the New Monetary Economics. *Journal of Political Economy* 95 (June): 567–90.

d'Albergo, Ernesto, ed. 1972. *Scritti "in memoria" di Antonio de Viti de Marco.* 2 vols. Bari: Cacucci.

De Cecco, Marcello. 1984. *The International Gold Standard: Money and Empire.* 2d ed. London: Frances Pinter.

Dehove, Gérard. 1946. L'oeuvre financière d'Antonio de Viti de Marco. *Revue d'économie politique* 56 (July–September): 249–91, (October–December): 436–56.

de Viti de Marco, Antonio. 1885. *Moneta e prezzi, ossia il principio quantitativo in rapporto alla questione monetaria.* Città di Castello: Lapi.

———. 1888. *Il carattere teorico dell'economia finanziaria.* Rome: Pasqualucci.

———. 1891. Proroga o corso forzoso? *Giornale degli economisti,* ser. 2, 3 (July): 1–16.

———. 1892. Il riordinamento della circolazione fiduciaria. *Giornale degli economisti,* ser. 2, 4 (May): 442–65.

———. 1893a. La questione delle banche d'emissione. *Giornale degli economisti,* ser. 2, 6 (February): vii–xix.

———. 1893b. L'ordinamento delle banche d'emissione in Italia. *Giornale degli economisti,* ser. 2, 6 (April): vii–xl.

———. 1893c. Gli spezzati d'argento. *Giornale degli economisti,* ser. 2, 7 (September): 185–205.

———. 1898a. La funzione della banca. In *Rendiconti della Regia Accademia dei Lincei,* 7, fasc. 1. Rome.

———. 1898b. *Saggi di economia e finanza.* Rome: Giornale degli economisti.

———. 1901. Angelo Messedaglia, commemorazione. *Giornale degli economisti,* ser. 2, 22 (May): 432–61.

———. 1918. *La guerra europea.* Rome: Edizione dell'Unità.

———. 1925. Maffeo Pantaleoni. *Giornale degli economisti,* ser. 2, 66 (April): 165–77.

———. 1930. *Un trentennio di lotte politiche (1894–1922).* Rome: Collezione Meridionale Editrice.

———. [1934a] 1936. *First Principles of Public Finance.* Translation of the definitive Italian edition of *I primi principii di economia finanziaria.* (Torino: Einaudi). London: Cape.

———. 1934b. *La funzione della banca: introduzione allo studio dei problemi monetari e bancari contemporanei.* Torino: Einaudi.

Fama, Eugene F. 1980. Banking in the Theory of Finance. *Journal of Monetary Economics* 6 (January): 39–57.

Fetter, Frank W. 1965. *Development of British Monetary Orthodoxy.* Cambridge: Harvard University Press.

Frenkel, Jacob A. 1976. Adjustment Mechanisms and the Monetary Approach to the Balance of Payments: A Doctrinal Perspective. In *Recent Issues in International Monetary Economics,* edited by E. Claassen and P. Salin. Amsterdam: North-Holland.

Frenkel, Jacob A., and Michael L. Mussa. 1985. Asset Markets, Exchange

Rates, and the Balance of Payments. In *Handbook of International Economics,* edited by R. W. Jones and P. B. Kenen. Amsterdam: North-Holland.
Friedman, Milton. 1986. The Resource Cost of Irredeemable Paper Money. *Journal of Political Economy* 94 (June): 642–47.
Gangemi, Lello. 1945. *Anteguerra e dopoguerra nel pensiero di Antonio de Viti de Marco.* Naples: Morano.
———. 1972. Bibliografia degli scritti di Antonio de Viti de Marco. In d'Albergo 1972.
Greenfield, Robert L., and Leland B. Yeager. 1983. A Laissez Faire Approach to Monetary Stability. *Journal of Money, Credit, and Banking* 15 (August): 302–15.
———. 1986. Competitive Payments Systems: Comment. *American Economic Review* 76 (September): 848–49.
Haberler, Gottfried. [1937] 1964. *Prosperity and Depression.* 6th ed. London: Allen & Unwin.
Hall, Robert E. 1982a. Explorations in the Gold Standard and Related Policies for Stabilizing the Dollar. In *Inflation: Causes and Effects,* edited by R. E. Hall. Chicago: University of Chicago Press.
———. 1982b. *Monetary Trends in the United States and the United Kingdom:* A Review from the Perspective of New Developments in Monetary Economics. *Journal of Economic Literature* 20 (December): 1552–56.
Hansen, Alvin M. [1951] 1964. *Business Cycles and National Income.* Expanded edition. New York: Norton.
Humphrey, Thomas M. 1977. Two Views of Monetary Policy: The Attwood-Mill Debate Revisited. Federal Reserve Bank of Richmond, *Economic Review* 63 (September–October): 14–22.
Jevons, Stanley. 1875. *Money and the Mechanism of Exchange.* London: Kegan Paul.
Laidler, David W. 1981. Adam Smith as a Monetary Economist. *Canadian Journal of Economics* 14 (May): 185–200.
———. 1984. Misconceptions about the Real-Bills Doctrine: A Comment on Sargent and Wallace. *Journal of Political Economy* 92 (February): 149–55.
———. 1988. British Monetary Orthodoxy in the 1870s. *Oxford Economic Papers* 40 (March): 74–109.
Link, Robert G. 1959. *English Theories of Economic Fluctuations, 1815–1848.* New York: Columbia University Press.
Lucas, Robert E. 1981. *Studies in Business-Cycle Theory.* Cambridge: MIT Press.
McCallum, Bennett T. 1985. Bank Deregulation, Accounting Systems of Exchange, and the Unit of Account: A Critical Review. *Carnegie-Rochester Conference Series on Public Policy* 23:13–46.
Mill, John Stuart. 1844. *Essays on Some Unsettled Questions of Political Economy.* London: Parker.
———. [1848] 1909. *Principles of Political Economy.* Edited by W. J. Ashley. London: Longmans Green.
Mints, Lloyd W. 1945. *A History of Banking Theory in Great Britain and the United States.* Chicago: University of Chicago Press.
Mitchell, Wesley C. 1927. *Business Cycles.* New York: National Bureau of Economic Research.
Morgenstern, Oskar. 1968. Antonio de Viti de Marco. In *International Encyclopedia of the Social Sciences,* edited by David Sills, vol. 4. New York: Macmillan. Reprinted in d'Albergo 1972, vol. 2.

Musgrave, Richard A. 1959. *The Theory of Public Finance: A Study in Public Economy.* New York: McGraw-Hill.
———. 1985. A Brief History of Fiscal Doctrine. In *Handbook of Public Economics,* edited by A. J. Auerbach and M. Feldstein, vol. 1. Amsterdam: North-Holland.
Musgrave, Richard A., and Alan T. Peacock, eds. 1958. *Classics in the Theory of Public Finance.* London: Macmillan.
Niehans, Jürg. 1978. *The Theory of Money.* Baltimore: The Johns Hopkins University Press.
O'Brien, Denis P. 1975. *The Classical Economists.* London: Oxford University Press.
Pantaleoni, Maffeo. [1889] 1957. *Pure Economics.* Translated from the 2d Italian ed., 1894. New York: Kelly & Millman.
Papa, Antonio. 1965. Antonio de Viti de Marco. *Belfagor,* no. 2 (31 March): 188–209.
Patinkin, Don. 1961. Financial Intermediaries and the Logical Structure of Monetary Theory. *American Economic Review* 50 (March): 95–116.
Ricci, Umberto. 1946. In memoria di Antonio de Viti de Marco. *Studi economici* 1 (January–March): 81–86.
Rossi, Ernesto. 1948. *A. de Viti de Marco: uomo civile.* Bari: Laterza.
Santiago-Valiente, Wilfredo. 1988. Historical Background of the Classical Monetary Theory and the "Real-Bills" Banking Tradition. *HOPE* 20 (Spring): 43–63.
Sargent, Thomas. 1979. *Macroeconomic Theory.* New York: Academic Press.
Sargent, Thomas, and Neil Wallace. 1982. The Real-Bills Doctrine versus the Quantity Theory: A Reconsideration. *Journal of Political Economy* 90 (December): 1212–36.
Schumpeter, Joseph A. 1954. *History of Economic Analysis.* Oxford: Oxford University Press.
Selgin, George A., and Lawrence H. White. 1987. The Evolution of a Free Banking System. *Economic Inquiry* 25 (July): 439–57.
Sidgwick, Henry. 1883. *The Principles of Political Economy.* London: Macmillan.
Simons, Henry C. 1937. Review of *First Principles of Public Finance,* by A. de Viti de Marco. *Journal of Political Economy* 45 (October): 712–17.
Smith, Adam. [1776] 1976. *An Inquiry into the Nature and Causes of the Wealth of Nations.* Edited by Edwin Cannan. Chicago: University of Chicago Press.
Stammati, Gaetano. 1945. In memoria di un maestro: Antonio de Viti de Marco. *Economia e commercio* 1.4 (November–December): 41–46.
Viner, Jacob. 1937. *Studies in the Theory of International Trade.* New York: Harper.
White, Lawrence H. 1984. Competitive Payments Systems and the Unit of Account. *American Economic Review* 74 (September): 699–712.
———. 1986. Competitive Payments Systems: Reply. *American Economic Review* 76 (September): 850–53.
Wicksell, Knut. [1906] 1935. *Lectures on Political Economy,* vol. 2. London: Routledge.
Wood, Elmer. 1939. *English Theories of Central Banking Control, 1819–1858.* Cambridge: Harvard University Press.

[4]

On the Effectiveness of Changes in Money Supply: The Puzzle of Mill's View

Filippo Cesarano

The conduct of monetary policy, a most controversial subject in economics, is as yet unsettled. The rules-versus-discretion debate between monetarists and Keynesians in the 1960s, and between new classicals and new Keynesians nowadays, is but the latest instance of an academic argument that goes back to the Currency-versus-Banking School controversy and beyond. At the center of this discussion are the main features of the model analyzing the transmission and effects of variations in the money stock on output and the price level.

In an early dispute on this issue Thomas Attwood opposed John Stuart Mill. In several papers and pamphlets, as well as in parliamentary speeches and testimony, Attwood argued for the pursuit of full employment through the active management of an inconvertible paper money. Mill strongly criticized this approach on various grounds and rejected the possibility of stimulating output through monetary impulses. This controversy is well known, yet it is worth revisiting for several reasons. First, economists are divided on their assessment of Mill's view, which indeed poses a puzzle since, while in the early essay "Of the Influence of Consumption upon Production" (1844; but written around 1830) he admits the effectiveness of money supply changes, he does not in the *Principles* (1848). Second, a closer look at Mill's arguments clarifies the different approaches to money within the classical school. Third, this

Correspondence may be addressed to Mr. Filippo Cesarano, Banca d'Italia, Ufficio Ricerche Storiche, Via Milano 64, 00184, Roma, Italy. Thanks are due to Samuel Hollander, David Laidler, Neil Skaggs, and a referee for their useful comments. The usual caveat applies.

History of Political Economy 28:3 © 1996 by Duke University Press.

analysis sheds light also on contemporary discussions of monetary policy. This article addresses these points and puts forward an interpretation of Mill's puzzling position.

I

Two opposite strands in the development of classical monetary theory are usually distinguished. The first, mainly associated with David Ricardo and the Currency School, advocates a set of rules governing the monetary system while the second, related to Henry Thornton and the Banking School, argues for flexibility in monetary management.[1] Of course, behind each policy recommendation a distinct theoretical framework analyzes the channels through which variations in the money stock are transmitted, as well as the effects of those variations. Although Mill is most often classified with the Banking School, opposing assessments of his argument do exist. On one side, Joseph Schumpeter (1954, 710–11), albeit recognizing Mill's eclecticism, finds his contributions to be in line with Ricardo; Pedro Schwartz (1972) shares this judgment. On the other side, John Hicks (1967) emphasizes the advance represented by Mill's treatment of the influence of credit on business cycles and puts him in the opposing camp.[2] Samuel Hollander (1985, 581) approvingly

1. In the preface to his *Critical Essays*, Hicks states: "It is useful to recognize that pre-Keynesian monetary economics was not monolithic, in order to understand how it is that in our day monetary economics is not monolithic either. Some of our present differences echo much older differences. There is one in particular, that came to the surface in the Currency School-Banking School controversy of the eighteen-forties (but is older than that), and which persists to this day. We still have a Currency School, seeking in vain—but one sees why—for a monetary system that shall be automatic. It is represented, over its long history, not only by Lord Overstone and his friends, but by Ricardo himself; not only by Mises and Hayek and Friedman, but also by Pigou. The Banking School (or Credit School, as I wish they had called it) has a history of almost equal antiquity. It has greater names upon its roll than that of Tooke: Mill and Bagehot among the Victorians; Hawtrey and Robertson, as well as Keynes, in the twentieth century" (1967, vii–viii). The literature on this topic is extensive. Reference can be made to Jacob Viner (1937), Lloyd Mints (1945), B. A. Corry (1962), Frank Fetter (1965), D. P. O'Brien (1975), and David Laidler (1991).

2. Schwartz remarks: "Authors usually misunderstand Mill's position and praise him for his anti-Ricardianism in monetary matters, assuming that he moved towards a more 'Keynesian' position, but they are wrong. Mill, once a metallic standard obtained, recommended a more passive attitude to monetary phenomena than that held by Ricardo and his disciples, let alone the Attwoods and other Birmingham reflationists, the true 'Keynesians' in this plot" (1972, 35). On the contrary, Hicks states, "Mill is unable to follow Ricardo in looking for mechanical rules by which credit is to be controlled; it can only be controlled by quite subtle appreciation of the

cites Hicks but also finds "a paradoxical flavour [in] the story of Mill on money and banking" (598). Indeed, Mill's multifaceted approach—"a blend between Ricardo's and Tooke's" (Schumpeter 1954, 710)—poses problems of interpretation in several respects, which have been thoroughly considered in Hollander's monumental study.[3] This paper, however, focuses only on the effectiveness of variations in the money supply.

The 1844 essay has often been considered to conflict with other works, especially the *Principles*, because it dwells upon short-run analysis and shows that, in a monetary economy, Say's law can be violated.[4] Yet, when closely examined, its content is coherent with the rest of Mill's writings. The 1844 essay, a comprehensive critique of the theories of overproduction, opens with a firm rejection of the need to stimulate consumption since "there will never . . . be a greater quantity produced, of commodities in general, than there are consumers for [it]" (1844, 49). Hence, there is no need for government intervention because, as long as no obstacles hinder the agents' behavior, the economy will quickly return to a stable equilibrium. Mill's momentous contribution is the treatment of economic fluctuations, which anticipates modern business cycle theory and, in turn, introduces many elements of his analysis of changes in the money stock. The basic hypothesis is analogous to the natural rate hypothesis. During expansion, factors of production are fully employed. But this is *not* an equilibrium position because it stems from an information failure on the part of producers who mistake a variation in the general price level for a change in relative prices. In this equilibrium model of the

'feel' of the market, by monetary *policy*. In all this Mill is on the same side as Thornton; he believes in monetary management" (1967, 166).

3. In a recent study, Neil Skaggs (1994) shows the originality of Mill's contributions to Banking School principles since his early essays. He also notes the controversial nature of Mill's work: "Mill adhered to the long-run implications of the quantity theory throughout his life. He began his career as a rigid Ricardian and ended it as a flexible one. The presentation of the quantity theory in the *Principles* is sophisticated. It is noteworthy, however, that in 1844 and after, Mill showed considerable sympathy for Tooke's income theory of prices, clearly espousing it in his 1857 parliamentary testimony. Thus, the charge made by Laughlin that Mill simultaneously maintained two inconsistent theories appears to have merit" (1994, 562).

4. Corry observes, "This article ('On the Influence of Consumption upon Production') is remarkable for its discussion of the effects of changes in the demand for money, but the puzzle is its timing, for both before and after it, Mill produced unquestioning support for the unqualified Classical position. In his article 'The Currency Juggle' (1833), and later in the *Principles* he was particularly severe on all forms of monetary unorthodoxy" (1962, 101).

economy, an adjustment process is set in motion that necessarily brings about recession.

> Periods of "brisk demand" are also the periods of greatest production: the national capital is never called into full employment but at those periods. This, however, is no reason for desiring such times; it is not desirable that the whole capital of the country should be in full employment. For, the calculations of producers and traders being of necessity imperfect, there are always some commodities which are more or less in excess, as there are always some which are in deficiency. If, therefore, the whole truth were known, there would always be some classes of producers contracting, not extending, their operations. If *all* are endeavouring to extend them, it is a certain proof that some general delusion is afloat. The commonest cause of such delusion is some general, or very extensive, rise of prices (whether caused by speculation or by the currency) which persuades all dealers that they are growing rich. And hence, an increase of production really takes place during the progress of depreciation, as long as the existence of depreciation is not suspected; and it is this which gives to the fallacies of the currency school, principally represented by Mr. Attwood, all the little plausibility they possess. But when the delusion vanishes and the truth is disclosed, those whose commodities are relatively in excess must diminish their production or be ruined: and if during the high prices they have built mills and erected machinery, they will be likely to repent at leisure. (1844, 67–68)

The closeness of this analysis to contemporary business cycle theory is both self-evident and striking. The economy departs from equilibrium because agents do not correctly perceive market signals. The scant understanding of the causes of price variations (1844, 68) distorts the agents' behavior and causes fluctuations in economic activity. This theoretical framework provides the basis of Mill's critique of Attwood's active monetary management. An engineered change in the quantity of money may at first raise real income as long as the impact on prices "is not suspected" (1844, 68). However, this expansionary effect is eventually reversed when individuals become aware of inflation. Therefore, a variation in the money stock is a source of disequilibrium; it increases the variability of output without permanently raising its level. Truly, the violation of Say's law is brilliantly shown in a monetary economy, where an excess supply of commodities counterbalances an excess demand for money (1844, 69–70). But, owing to the equilibrium hypothesis, this phenomenon is deemed to be only temporary so that a permanent "general over-production" is impossible (1844, 71–74).

These arguments are reiterated in Mill's subsequent paper, "The Currency Juggle" ([1833] 1967), specifically directed against Attwood's expansionist views, and characterized more by polemical overtones than analytical depth. Currency depreciation is a tax and is tantamount to a "gigantic plan of confiscation" (184) with strong redistributive effects. The hypothesis is again that full employment is a disequilibrium state because the lack of information makes it impossible to equate consumption and production precisely. Therefore, an increase in money supply induces entrepreneurs to miscalculate relative prices and "the effectual demand" for their products. The eventual disequilibrium is then corrected by a costly adjustment.[5] In "The Currency Juggle" ([1833] 1967), emphasis is placed on the endogeneity of the money stock which expands and contracts during the cycle mainly driven by speculation. An injection of liquidity in the middle of the crisis would only enable "debtors to cheat their creditors" without raising output since Say's law applies (191). The role of money and credit is central to, and is intertwined with, Mill's theory of economic fluctuations. In fact, monetary theory and business cycle theory are both part of a coherent analytical framework introduced in the early essays (1844; [1833] 1967) and developed in later works with scarcely any break (see also Skaggs 1994, 542).

In the *Principles*, the equilibrium model of the economy is extended through the explicit introduction of expectations,[6] which were only implied in the previous writings (see the quotation above). Furthermore, the conventional character of the money object and the role of credit are recognized. Although the treatment of the nature of money is quite standard along the lines laid down by Adam Smith ([1776] 1976, 26–52), Mill likens pounds and shillings to "a sort of tickets or orders which he [the income-earner] can present for payment at any shop he pleases" ([1848] 1909, 487). The ticket analogy notwithstanding, he does not depart from

5. "Mr. Attwood's error is that of supposing that a depreciation of the currency *really* increases the demand for all articles, and consequently their production, because, under some circumstances, it may create a *false opinion* of an increase of demand, which false opinion leads, as the reality would do, to an increase of production, followed, however, by a fatal revulsion as soon as the delusion ceases" ([1833] 1967, 191).

6. The role of expectations in Mill's work has been examined by Evelyn Forget (1989) in relation to the microeconomic issues of natural value and market adjustment.

theoretical metallism,[7] and Schumpeter (1954, 699) rightly classifies him as a metallist together with all the leading economists of the time. In fact, on the next page, Mill plainly states: "Money is a commodity, and its value is determined like that of other commodities, temporarily by demand and supply, permanently and on the average by cost of production" ([1848] 1909, 488). In chapter 12 on the influence of credit on prices, however, Mill goes rather far in the analysis of the role of banks in monetary arrangements and suggests the smooth operation of a system in which all payments are made by checks and in which money does not circulate at all. This is described as an "ideal case" ([1848] 1909, 524) and is a clear anticipation of Wickell's "ideal banking system" ([1906] 1935, 79–126), although he does not identify the main problem underlying such a system, namely, Wicksellian price-level indeterminacy.[8] These analytical deficiencies disappear in the treatment of inconvertible paper money ([1848] 1909, chap. 13), which can circulate and perform all monetary functions well on the sole basis of convention: each individual accepts it because others will accept it. On purely abstract grounds, Mill has no doubt about the operation of fiat money, the value of which depends on the quantity fixed by the issuer ([1848] 1909, 542–43) but fiercely opposes it on welfare and policy grounds.

> Such a power [of issuing inconvertible currency], in whomsoever vested, is an intolerable evil. All variations in the value of the cir-

7. Schumpeter gives the following definitions for metallism: "By Theoretical Metallism we denote the *theory* that it is logically essential for money to consist of, or to be 'covered' by, some commodity so that the logical source of the exchange value or purchasing power of money is the exchange value or purchasing power of that commodity, considered independently of its monetary role. . . . By Practical Metallism we shall denote sponsorship of a principle of monetary policy, namely, the principle that the monetary unit 'should' be kept firmly linked to, and freely interchangeable with, a given quantity of some commodity. Theoretical and Practical Cartalism may best be defined by the corresponding negatives" (1954, 288).

8. "We just now made the imaginary supposition that all persons dealt with a bank, and all with the same bank, payments being universally made by cheques. In this ideal case, there would be no money anywhere except in the hands of the banker: who might then safely part with all of it, by selling it as bullion, or lending it, to be sent out of the country in exchange for goods or foreign securities. But though there would then be no money in possession, or ultimately perhaps even in existence, money would be offered, and commodities bought with it, just as at present. People would continue to reckon their incomes and their capitals in money, and to make their usual purchases with orders for the receipt of a thing which would have literally ceased to exist. There would be in all this nothing to complain of, so long as the money, in disappearing, left an equivalent value in other things, applicable when required to the reimbursement of those to whom the money originally belonged" (Mill [1848] 1909, 524–25).

In the 1980s, a growing body of literature, the so-called new monetary economics, began to analyze the workings of a payments system devoid of tangible money and managed by banks.

> culating medium are mischievous: *they disturb existing contracts and expectations*, and the liability to such changes renders every pecuniary engagement of long date entirely precarious. . . . Not to add, that the issuers may have, and in the case of a government paper, always have, a direct interest in lowering the value of the currency, because it is the medium in which their own debts are computed. ([1848] 1909, 544; emphasis added)

Mill's apparently puzzling approach begins to clear up. His advance on credit and the monetary system comes up against the limit of the equilibrium hypothesis,[9] unsurpassable except in the very short run, and the role of expectations. Therefore, active monetary management fails to affect output while it meddles with the price system, increases uncertainty, and has undesired redistributive effects. Attwood's full employment monetary scheme is, then, criticized by dwelling on the significance of expectations. After a monetary injection, output would grow only if people anticipated an increase in their real income. But this argument ultimately rests on a failure by agents to revise expectations as prices go up, which Mill excludes.

> I presume, however, that the inducement which, according to Mr. Attwood, excited this unusual ardour in all persons engaged in production, must have been the expectation of getting more commodities generally, more real wealth, in exchange for the produce of their labour, and not merely more pieces of paper. This expectation, however, must have been, by the very terms of the supposition, disappointed, since, all prices being supposed to rise equally, no one was really better paid for his goods than before. Those who agree with Mr. Attwood could only succeed in winning people on to these unwonted exertions by a prolongation of what would in fact be a delusion; contriving matters so, that by a progressive rise of money prices, every producer shall always seem to be in the very act of obtaining an increased remuneration which he never, in reality, does obtain. It is unnecessary to

9. In the first chapter on money in the *Principles*, Mill emphasizes neutrality and makes no reference to possible violations of Say's law. "The introduction of money does not interfere with the operation of any of the Laws of Value laid down in the preceding chapters. The reasons which make the temporary or market value of things depend on the demand and supply, and their average and permanent values upon their cost of production, are as applicable to a money system as to a system of barter. Things which by barter would exchange for one another, will, if sold for money, sell for an equal amount of it, and so will exchange for one another still, though the process of exchanging them will consist of two operations instead of only one" (Mill [1848] 1909, 488).

> advert to any other of the objections to this plan than that of its total impracticability. It calculates on finding the whole world persisting for ever in the belief that more pieces of paper are more riches, and never discovering that, with all their paper, they cannot buy more of anything than they could before. ([1848] 1909, 550)

The modernity of this passage is impressive. Nowhere does the word "rational" appear, yet this analysis underlines the effects of the flow of information about market prices on the agents' behavior and on equilibrium. With regard to David Hume's ([1752] 1970) more subtle expansionist hypothesis—based on a different price adjustment speed for different commodities, which would allow the producers of the goods whose price rises first to gain—Mill objects that such a gain must necessarily be balanced by the loss of those whose product is the last to increase in price. And again, this can occur only if agents do not exploit the available information; otherwise the losers, perceiving the change in prices, will raise their prices too, thus stopping the expansionary process from the very beginning ([1848] 1909, 551). In Mill's model, departures from equilibrium are due to the impact of incomplete information on expectations and can be only temporary. The role of information is central in his analysis of the effects of changes in money and of economic fluctuations. There is nothing inherent in the functioning of the economy that causes instability, which, instead, stems from the agents' misinterpretation of market signals. This is a recurrent theme in Mill's work, and, in the 1844 essay, he reaffirms the validity of Say's law in the long run if "every increase in production [is] distributed *without miscalculation* among all kinds of produce in the proportion which private interest would dictate" (1844, 73; emphasis added).

In the *Principles*, money and credit play a fundamental role in business cycle theory.[10] Three cases are distinguished: barter, a monetary economy, and a credit economy ([1848] 1909, 525–27). In the first one, Say's law fully applies and an oversupply of commodities is entirely ruled out. In a monetary economy, instead, Say's law can be violated but only up to the limit set by the existing money stock and by a possible

10. Chapter 14, "Of Excess Supply," begins: "After the elementary exposition of the theory of money contained in the last few chapters, we shall return to a question in the general theory of Value, which could not be satisfactorily discussed until the nature and operations of Money were in some measure understood, because the errors against which we have to contend mainly originate in a misunderstanding of those operations" (Mill [1848] 1909, 556).

increase in velocity. Finally, in the presence of credit, such a limit is waived and speculation can much amplify cyclical fluctuations. In any case, the agent's misreading of market signals sets off output expansion, which is eventually followed by a strong downturn in economic activity. In this process, an excess supply of commodities may well occur and is reflected in an excess demand for money. But this phenomenon is temporary, inasmuch as "the theory of general overproduction implies an absurdity" ([1848] 1909, 560).

> I have already described the state of the markets for commodities which accompanies what is termed a commercial crisis. At such times there is really an excess of all commodities above the money demand: in other words, there is an under-supply of money. From the sudden annihilation of a great mass of credit, every one dislikes to part with ready money, and many are anxious to procure it at any sacrifice. Almost everybody therefore is a seller, and there are scarcely any buyers; so that there may really be, though only while the crisis lasts, an extreme depression of general prices, from what may be indiscriminately called a glut of commodities or a dearth of money. But it is a great error to suppose, with Sismondi, that a commercial crisis is the effect of a general excess of production. It is simply the consequence of an excess of speculative purchases. It is not a gradual advent of low prices, but a sudden recoil from prices extravagantly high: its immediate cause is a contraction of credit, and the remedy is, not a diminution of supply, but the restoration of confidence. ([1848] 1909, 561)[11]

II

Mill's analysis centers upon the equilibrium hypothesis, the significance of expectations, and the role of information. These are the elements of his theoretical apparatus that, once put together, solve the puzzle characterizing Mill's supposedly conflicting views.

Before presenting this assessment, brief mention should be made of his

11. This passage exactly matches the arguments put forward in the last pages of the essay "Of the Influence of Consumption upon Production" (1844, 70–74), whose conclusion reads: "The essentials of the doctrine [rejecting general overproduction] are preserved when it is allowed that there cannot be permanent excess of production, or of accumulation; though it be at the same time admitted, that as there may be a temporary excess of any one article considered separately, so may there of commodities generally, not in consequence of over-production, but of a want of commercial confidence" (1844, 74).

methodology, which is not one of the pieces of the puzzle but rather constitutes its frame. Mill, together with Nassau Senior and John Cairnes, is a major figure of classical apriorism (Blaug [1980] 1992, chap. 3), which appraises theories only from the perspective of internal consistency, independently of their predictive power.[12] Thus, he either refuses to consider the empirical evidence or regards it as misunderstood by other authors.[13]

The interpretation of Mill's viewpoint on the efficacy of monetary impulses mainly involves questions of pure theory. In his equilibrium model of the economy, which is embedded in Say's law, the nature and availability of information are essential and condition the final outcome. Different assumptions about the availability of information and their impact on expectations within the equilibrium model explain the apparent puzzle of Mill's analysis.

In the essay "Of the Influence of Consumption upon Production" (1844), information about the causes of price changes is assumed to be so scant as to lead agents to confuse changes in the price level with the variations in relative prices and to hamper the revision of inflationary expectations. Hence, output expansion, though only temporary, can well occur and is followed by recession. In the article "The Currency Juggle" ([1833] 1967), this analysis is maintained, but in the *Principles*, the discussion takes a different turn. The effects of an issue of inconvertible paper money on prices are perceived at once so that individuals do not make any mistake with regard to the real variables governing their choices. As a result, aside from redistributive effects, output is unaffected. Even con-

12. Mark Blaug clearly describes the classical view: "Over and over again, in Senior, in Mill, in Cairnes, and even in Jevons, we have found the notion that 'verification' is not a testing of economic theories to see whether they are true or false, but only a method of establishing the boundaries of application of theories deemed to be obviously true: one verifies in order to discover whether 'disturbing causes' can account for the discrepancies between stubborn facts and theoretically valid reasons; if they do, the theory has been wrongly applied, but the theory itself is still true. The question of whether there is any way of showing a logically consistent theory to be false is never even contemplated" ([1980] 1992, 71–72).

13. Dealing with the topic of overproduction, Mill observes: "What then is it by which men who have reflected much on economical phenomena, and have even contributed to throw new light upon them by original speculations, have been led to embrace so irrational a doctrine? I conceive them to have been deceived by a mistaken interpretation of certain mercantile facts. They imagined that the possibility of a general over-supply of commodities was proved by experience. They believed that they saw this phenomenon in certain conditions of the markets, the true explanation of which is totally different" (Mill [1848] 1909, 560). Hollander (1985, chap. 2, especially pp. 125–31), however, has cautioned about the standard interpretation of Mill's methodology and has called attention to his interest for verification, which would make his approach more balanced.

sidering Hume's hypothesis of varying adjustment speed of commodity prices, Mill defends the assumption of full information and, hence, of inefficacy of monetary expansion. Only in the case where the producer of some goods does not perceive the change in money does he suffer a loss, but this is balanced by the gain of those who increased prices earlier. Therefore, in the *Principles*, Mill follows the same analytical framework of the essays but assumes a larger dimension to the information set. Indirect evidence is provided when another source of price increase sets off the business cycle. In the earliest paper, it is either growth in the money stock or speculation (1844, 67). In "The Currency Juggle," the former "accompanied rather than caused" ([1833] 1967, 191) the latter. Finally, in the *Principles*, the origin of price variations at the beginning of the cycle are entirely nonmonetary—for example, "an extra demand, a short crop, obstruction to importation" and "the opening of a new foreign market, or simultaneous indications of a short supply of several great articles of commerce" ([1848] 1909, 526, 527)—because, in order to consistently obtain a change in output, Mill can no longer adduce changes in money, having excluded their effectiveness.

The implicit assumption of the *Principles'* larger information set may be related, as both Neil Skaggs and an anonymous referee have suggested, to a different type of monetary system, fiat money, instead of convertible paper currency. This is an important consideration, but its congruence with the problem at stake needs to be qualified. In fact, the crucial section 4 of chapter 13, "Of an Inconvertible Paper Currency," criticizes "the notion that an increase of the currency quickens the industry" ([1848] 1909, 550) independently of the type of monetary system, since it opens with a reference to Hume's essay ([1752] 1970), which unquestionably posits a metallic money world. Mill then charges Attwood with confusing the price rise due to an increase in fiat money with that caused by speculation in a convertible currency regime. Only in the latter case do speculators gain in real terms following the price recoil in the final stage of economic fluctuations. In the former, instead, producers fully anticipate the effects on prices, hence output remains constant. The same conclusion also applies, with some qualifications, to Hume's analysis of an increase in metallic money. All in all, there is an apparent link between the type of monetary system and the agents' information set, the dimension of which gets larger as we move from convertible currency to fiat money. But the real basis of the link lies in the fact that while an inconvertible paper money leaves the issuer broad scope to vary the monetary stock, a convertible currency does not. In fact, Mill contrasts the definitive price increase due to a change in money supply with the temporary price increase generated by a speculative wave and assumes more information to be available and hence agents' responsiveness to be prompter in the former instance.

In Mill's work, the analytical distinction between barter, money, and credit seems more relevant than the distinction between commodity currency and fiat money. In fact, at the beginning of chapter 13, he clearly states for theoretical purposes the equivalence between commodity and fiat money.[14] From a policy viewpoint, however, Mill attaches great importance to the latter distinction and again anticipates some concepts of contemporary monetary economics. In his purely classical "vision," the economy is a self-adjusting system. His staunch defense of the gold standard, which to modern readers may appear at odds with his emphasis on the role of credit and his Banking School approach, can be explained by his adherence to the equilibrium model of the economy, which squares with a monetary system that provides a firm monetary anchor and disposes of any meddling with the real sector. Furthermore, his call for convertibility ([1848] 1909, 545–46), in place of a rule fixing the price of gold in an inconvertible paper currency system, is founded upon the key role of information. Convertibility can be enforced more effectively because it is simpler and therefore intelligible to the public at large; hence, it is less likely to be broken by the issuer who may instead attempt to tamper with a complicated rule.[15] Mill certainly allows for

14. "In the case supposed [of an inconvertible paper money], the functions of money are performed by a thing which derives its power for performing them solely from convention; but convention is quite sufficient to confer the power; since nothing more is needful to make a person accept anything as money, and even at any arbitrary value, than the persuasion that it will be taken from him on the same terms by others" (Mill [1848] 1909, 542).

15. "But a still stronger consideration is the importance of adhering to a simple principle, intelligible to the most untaught capacity. Everybody can understand convertibility; every one sees that what can be at any moment exchanged for five pounds is worth five pounds. Regulation by the price of bullion is a more complex idea, and does not recommend itself through the same familiar associations. There would be nothing like the same confidence, by the public generally, in an inconvertible currency so regulated, as in a convertible one: and the most instructed person might reasonably doubt whether such a rule would be as likely to be inflexibly adhered to. The grounds of the rule not being so well understood by the public, opinion would probably not enforce it with as much rigidity, and, in any circumstances of difficulty, would be likely to turn against it; while to the government itself a suspension of convertibility would appear a much stronger and more extreme measure, than a relaxation of what might possibly be considered a somewhat artificial rule. There is therefore a great preponderance of reasons in favour of a convertible, in preference to even the best regulated inconvertible currency. The temptation to

monetary policy (see Hicks's quotation in footnote 2), but only to protect the credit system and correct the agents' mistakes, which drive the economy off its equilibrium path. Therefore, in the middle of a speculative wave, tightening credit conditions would curb speculation while, in the final stage of the cycle, an issue of paper currency can attenuate the effects of the "price recoil," namely bankruptcies and a fall in output (Hollander 1985, 573–80). Anyway, the scope for policy is limited to compensating for an information failure that impairs the stability of the economy. Mill's conception, in fact, does not permit active monetary management to stimulate output. This would clash with his overall approach, which is centered on the notion of equilibrium and, thus, confines economic policy to a supplementary role arising from the agents' misinterpretation of market signals.

III

The history of economic analysis, though seldom appreciated by fellow economists, can at times shed light on current questions by calling attention to original but forgotten ideas (Cesarano 1983; Negishi 1989, 5). Mill's versatile treatment of information suggests a theory of monetary policy that can allow both for effectiveness and for ineffectiveness of money stock variations. Going beyond the two polar cases of complete information and no information at all, it can be assumed that information is obtained at a cost because it is scarce. Resources, therefore, are optimally allocated to seek information for expected benefit (Stigler 1961). According to this hypothesis, agents expect a net benefit from collecting and processing the necessary information. If the benefit is a positive function of the size of policy measures and the cost a negative function—because the "true" model of the economy used by rational agents has a greater predictive power in case of large changes in the instrument variables—then the smaller the policy action, the greater its effectiveness, since agents would not revise their expectations if this involved a net expected loss. In this approach, policy effectiveness does not follow from the ad hoc nature of the policy maker's superior information or from the presence of long-run nominal contracts, but from postulating that information is neither a free good nor completely inaccessible. A

over-issue, in certain financial emergencies, is so strong, that nothing is admissible which can tend, in however slight a degree, to weaken the barriers that restrain it" (Mill [1848] 1909, 546).

critical value of the policy measure dimension, then, will discriminate between the resulting effectiveness and ineffectiveness, depending on whether policies actually implemented are below or above that critical value.

In conclusion, Mill's seemingly inconsistent and puzzling view of the effectiveness of monetary impulses is related to the different role of information in his early writings and in the *Principles*. Nevertheless, he follows a coherent theoretical framework, founded on an equilibrium model of the economy. From the perspective of contemporary monetary theory, Mill's position can be looked at with more sympathy than Schumpeter showed.[16] Mill's advance on money and credit does not bring about support for active monetary management because he never abandons the equilibrium hypothesis. Thus, his favorable attitude toward monetary activism is strictly limited to protecting the liquidity and solvency of the credit system and supplementing market forces when incomplete information may temporarily drive the economy away from equilibrium.

References

Blaug, Mark. [1980] 1992. *The Methodology of Economics*. Cambridge: Cambridge University Press.

Cesarano, Filippo. 1983. On the Role of the History of Economic Analysis. *HOPE* 15.1:63–82.

Corry, B. A. 1962. *Money, Saving and Investment in English Economics 1800–1850*. London: Macmillan.

Fetter, Frank W. 1965. *Development of British Monetary Orthodoxy 1797–1875*. Cambridge: Harvard University Press.

Forget, Evelyn L. 1989. J. S. Mill and J. E. Cairnes on Natural Value: The Role of Expectations in Late-Classical Thought. *HOPE* 21.1:103–21.

Hicks, John R. 1967. *Critical Essays in Monetary Theory*. Oxford: Oxford University Press.

16. While acknowledging Mill's outstanding contributions, Schumpeter makes this rather harsh judgment: "There are but two qualifications to be added to this appraisal of a considerable achievement that, had it been better understood, might have been instrumental in bringing about a new epoch of monetary analysis. First, though his retention of the theorem that an increase in money will, *ceteris paribus*, raise prices *in the same proportion* (the property peculiar to money) is all right when hedged in as he hedged it in, he also retained the erroneous Ricardian doctrine that variations in quantity of money and variations in physical volume of output have nothing to do with one another and will never coincide except by chance. Second, this denial of the possibility of 'monetary stimulation' is but the most important instance of the narrow views on the ideas of monetary management that emerged in the twenties and thirties of the nineteenth century" (Schumpeter 1954, 710–11).

Hollander, Samuel. 1985. *The Economics of John Stuart Mill*. Toronto: University of Toronto Press.

Hume, David. [1752] 1970. Of Money. In *Writings on Economics*. Edited by Eugene Rotwein. Madison: University of Wisconsin Press.

Laidler, David. 1991. *The Golden Age of the Quantity Theory*. New York: Philip Allan.

Mill, John Stuart. [1833] 1967. The Currency Juggle. In vol. 4 of *Collected Works of John Stuart Mill*. Edited by John M. Robson. Toronto: University of Toronto Press.

———. 1844. Of the Influence of Consumption upon Production. In *Essays on Some Unsettled Questions of Political Economy*. London: Parker.

———. [1848] 1909. *Principles of Political Economy*. Edited by William Ashley. London: Longmans, Green & Co.

Mints, Lloyd W. 1945. *A History of Banking Theory in Great Britain and the United States*. Chicago: University of Chicago Press.

Negishi, Takashi. 1989. *History of Economy Theory*. Amsterdam: North-Holland.

O'Brien, D. P. 1975. *The Classical Economists*. Oxford: Oxford University Press.

Schumpeter, Joseph A. 1954. *History of Economic Analysis*. Oxford: Oxford University Press.

Schwartz, Pedro. 1972. *The New Political Economy of J. S. Mill*. London: Weidenfeld & Nicolson.

Skaggs, Neil T. 1994. The Place of J. S. Mill in the Development of British Monetary Orthodoxy. *HOPE* 26.4:539–67.

Smith, Adam. [1776] 1976. *An Inquiry into the Nature and Causes of the Wealth of Nations*. Edited by Edwin Cannan. Chicago: University of Chicago Press.

Stigler, George J. 1961. The Economics of Information. *Journal of Political Economy* 69.3:213–25.

Viner, Jacob. 1937. *Studies in the Theory of International Trade*. New York: Harper.

Wicksell, Knut. [1906] 1935. *Lectures on Political Economy*. Vol. 2. London: Routledge.

Journal of International Economics 45 (1998) 173–186

[5]

Hume's specie-flow mechanism and classical monetary theory: An alternative interpretation

Filippo Cesarano*

Banca d'Italia, Ufficio Ricerche Storiche, Via Milano, 64, 00184 Rome, Italy

Received 29 April 1997; received in revised form 10 July 1997; accepted 29 July 1997

Abstract

Hume's celebrated essay on the international distribution of money has always been criticized for ignoring the law of one price. Contrary to the traditional interpretation, however, Hume actually maintains that law and argues for the stability of long-run equilibrium. Putting money market equilibrium in the foreground, his analysis is essentially founded on the same hypothesis as the modern monetary approach, albeit focusing on the supply rather than on the demand side of the money market. © 1998 Elsevier Science B.V.

Keywords: Balance of payments; Classical monetary theory; Specie-flow mechanism

JEL classification: F40; B12; B31

1. Introduction

Hume's essay "Of the Balance of Trade" (Hume, 1752a) is the *locus classicus* of international monetary adjustment. Despite its time-honored fame, however, this contribution has always been controversial. Even before its appearance in the *Political Discourses*, Hume's close friend James Oswald of Dunnikier set forth a penetrating critique, initiating a debate that has continued down to our own days. As Samuelson (1980, p. 141) bluntly puts it, "Hume's account is both wrong and incomplete". This widespread thesis rests on Hume's purported neglect of the law of one price. In fact, the traditional description of Hume's analysis, which is

*Tel.: + 39 6 4792 3254; fax: + 39 6 4792 5444.

PII S0022-1996(97)00036-6

common throughout the literature on international monetary economics, hinges on a variation in domestic prices vis-à-vis the rest of the world. An increase in money supply following a trade surplus pushes up the country's price level, which by discouraging exports and stimulating imports redresses the balance and siphons off the extra money. In order to mend the supposed violation of the law of one price, a price effect in the adjustment process was resurrected through changes in the terms of trade and the introduction of non-traded goods. But these reconstructions entail "sophisticated fallacies" (Samuelson, 1980) and, above all, are beside the point because, as the present paper argues, they originate from an erroneous interpretation of Hume. On a more attentive reading a consistent theoretical framework emerges, showing these recurrent criticisms to be entirely misplaced. Despite the unavoidable abundance of quotations in Sections 2 and 3, necessary to overturn the received view, this alternative appraisal is no mere exegetical exercise of antiquarian interest. Besides vindicating Hume it shows, in contrast with the prevailing opinion, that the modern monetary approach is closely related to his contribution (Section 4).

2. The Hume–Oswald exchange

The centuries-old controversy surrounding "Of the Balance of Trade" is indeed a peculiar story in that the arguments fuelling it had already been illustrated to the author more than a year before publication. In a letter dated 10 October 1750,[1] Oswald raised some crucial objections, which gave Hume the opportunity to ponder them in his rejoinder (Hume, 1750) and strengthen his analysis. However, several economists have since faulted Hume for the same reasons. The importance of this correspondence, therefore, goes beyond the history of economics because it shows how Hume would have answered his modern critics.

In his critique, Oswald points out the disregard for the law of one price and for the output effect of variations in the money stock. For both reasons, domestic prices do not change in proportion to money supply.

> "The increased quantity of money would not necessarily increase the price of all labour and commodities; because the increased quantity, not being confined to the home labour and commodities, might, and certainly would, be sent to purchase both from foreign countries, which importation, unless obstructed by arbitrary and absurd laws, would keep down the price of commodities to the level of foreign countries; and if the price of labour still continued for a short time at a higher rate than that level, it would only serve, by attracting foreigners, to increase the number of useful inhabitants

[1] Due to a misprint in Rotwein's edition, Oswald's letter is often referred to as being dated 10 October 1749 instead of 1750 (Greig, 1932, p. 132).

in proportion to the increased quantity of money...it does not therefore follow that the quantity of money either is the same, or naturally will become the same, in all such countries; because the cultivation and population of the one may increase, and naturally will increase, while the cultivation and population of the other may diminish." (Oswald of Dunnikier, 1750, pp. 191–192)

Furthermore, the capital experiences a permanent trade surplus vis-à-vis distant provinces, and thus a monetary expansion that raises prices and enhances growth. Contrary to Hume's equilibrium hypothesis, therefore, this state of affairs is not reversed by self-correcting forces (Oswald of Dunnikier, 1750, pp. 193–195).

Hume replies by spelling out his analysis in two respects. In the first place, the money stock is not equally distributed in all countries, but in proportion to output and population.[2] This proposition disposes of Oswald's charge of neglecting the law of one price, since, abstracting from velocity, the ratio between money and output is equal to the price level, which must be the same everywhere. This equilibrium condition is central to Hume's theoretical framework. Secondly, Hume agrees with Oswald that, due to the law of one price, domestic prices do not vary with the money supply and, during transition from one equilibrium to another, an output effect may result. Hence, the money stock does not necessarily return to the former equilibrium level.

"You allow, that if all the money in England were increased four-fold in one night, there would be a sudden rise of prices; but then, say you, the importation of foreign commodities would soon lower the prices. Here, then, is the flowing out of the money already begun. But, say you, a small part of this stock of money would suffice to buy foreign commodities, and lower the prices. I grant it would for one year, till the imported commodities be consumed. But must not the same thing be renewed next year? No, say you; the additional stock of money may, in this interval, so increase the people and industry, as to enable them to retain their money. Here I am extremely pleased with your reasoning. I agree with you, that the increase of money, if not too sudden, naturally increases people and industry, and by that means

[2] "I never meant to say that money, in all countries which communicate, must necessarily be on a level, but only on a level proportioned to their people, industry, and commodities. That is, where there is double people, &c. there will be double money, and so on; and that the only way of keeping or increasing money is, by keeping and increasing the people and industry; not by prohibitions of exporting money, or by taxes on commodities, the methods commonly thought of. I believe we differ little on this head" (Hume, 1750, p. 197). Hume made this point more than a year before in a letter to Montesquieu: "It does not seem that money, any more than water, can be raised or lowered anywhere much beyond the level it has in places where communication is open, but that it must rise and fall in proportion to the goods and labour contained in each state" (Hume, 1749, p. 189).

> may retain itself; but if it do not produce such an increase, nothing will retain it except hoarding. Suppose twenty million brought into Scotland; suppose that, by some fatality, we take no advantage of this to augment our industry or people, how much would remain in the quarter of a century? Not a shilling more than we have at present. My expression in the Essay needs correction, which has occasioned you to mistake it." (Hume, 1750, pp. 197–198)

This passage clarifies Hume's view of international adjustment in detail and suggests several comments. First, it is the operation of the law of one price that triggers the equilibrating money flows. Second, if it is to stimulate output the increase in money must be unexpected ("not too sudden").[3] Third, inasmuch as the rise in output during transition helps to annul the disequilibrium, the country ends up with a higher money stock in the final equilibrium position.[4] Fourth, Hume's attention ultimately centers on long-run equilibrium. Besides the reference to "the quarter of a century" needed for adjustment, he rejects Oswald's argument that a rich country, or London vis-à-vis outlying provinces, can grow more than poor ones forever. And, in the final paragraph, Hume gives his own interpretation of the essay, emphasizing the equilibrium conception and the abandonment of mercantilist policies.[5] As this correspondence shows, the main criticisms raised against "Of the Balance of Trade", i.e. the presumed neglect of the law of one price and of the output effect of a money increase, had been correctly discussed by the author before publication. It is somewhat surprising, therefore, that the same criticisms, in particular the former, should be raised time and again in the ensuing centuries. Either Hume failed to incorporate his rejoinder to Oswald in the published version or his readers have misinterpreted the analytical content of his writing.

---

[3]In the essay "Of Money" (Hume, 1752b, p. 39, f. 1), Hume relates the output effectiveness of money variations to their slow and unannounced implementation (Cesarano, 1983, 1998). It may further be noted that Oswald's objection does not concern the effect on the terms of trade of spending excess cash balances, a point at the center of the transfer problem debate, but the effect on output and the price level of excess money supply. The issue at stake, therefore, regards absolute, not relative, prices. In other words, it belongs to the realm of monetary theory, not price theory.

[4]In this quotation, "hoarding" does not refer to a shift in the demand for money, as a modern economist might be tempted to think, but to the accumulation of a treasure by the sovereign. See Hume (1752a, pp. 73–75).

[5]"On the whole, my intention in the Essay was both to remove people's errors, who are apt, from chimerical calculations, to imagine they are losing their specie, though they can show in no instance that either their people or industry diminish; and also to expose the absurdity of guarding money otherwise than by watching over the people and their industry, and preserving or increasing them. To prohibit the exportation of money, or the importation of commodities, is mistaken policy; and I have the pleasure of seeing you agree with me" (Hume, 1750, p. 199).

3. An alternative interpretation

There is no direct evidence to answer this question, since the draft on which Oswald commented is not known. Besides the possible addition of a footnote (see footnote 6), the published essay has been assumed not to differ substantially from the manuscript (Greig, 1932, p. 143; Low, 1952, pp. 315–316; Berdell, 1995, p. 1206). This conjecture does not necessarily give rise to a conundrum, since Hume may have deemed the final version to be solid enough to stand up to Oswald's criticism. The present section, I believe, shows that this is indeed the case.

"Of the Balance of Trade" opens with a plea for free trade to increase the country's output and avoid outflows of money. Hume's chief objective is to put an end to the mercantilist fear of losing money and "prove the impossibility of this event, as long as we preserve our people and our industry" (Hume, 1752a, p. 62). The ratio of money to output, like water in communicating vessels, cannot diverge from a given "level". But this ratio is simply the price level, which must be everywhere the same. The core of Hume's analysis, therefore, is an equilibrium condition founded on the law of one price.

> "[A]ny man who travels over Europe at this day, may see, by the prices of commodities, that money, in spite of the absurd jealousy of princes and states, has brought itself nearly to a level; and that the difference between one kingdom and another is not greater in this respect, than it is often between different provinces of the same kingdom. Men naturally flock to capital cities, sea-ports, and navigable rivers. There we find more men, more industry, more commodities, and consequently more money; but still the latter difference holds proportion with the former, and the level is preserved." (Hume, 1752a, p. 66)[6]

This equilibrium condition is grounded on an unsophisticated version of the quantity theory that abstracts from and "does not [even] mention the velocity of circulation" (Holtrop, 1929, p. 513). However, though it is based on simplifying

[6]In a footnote appended to this passage, Hume strengthens and further clarifies his standpoint. "It must carefully be remarked, that throughout this discourse, wherever I speak of the level of money, I mean always its proportional level to the commodities, labour, industry, and skill, which is in the several states. And I assert, that where these advantages are double, triple, quadruple, to what they are in the neighbouring states, the money infallibly will also be double, triple, quadruple. The only circumstance that can obstruct the exactness of these proportions, is the expense of transporting the commodities from one place to another; and this expense is sometimes unequal. Thus the corn, cattle, cheese, butter, of Derbyshire, cannot draw the money of London, so much as the manufactures of London draw the money of Derbyshire. But this objection is only a seeming one: For so far as the transport of commodities is expensive, so far is the communication between the places obstructed and imperfect" (Hume, 1752a, p. 66, f. 1).

assumptions, Hume's approach is eminently correct. Dwelling upon the postulate of self-interest underlying money market equilibrium,[7] it maintains rather than ignores the law of one price. In the remaining pages (Hume, 1752a, pp. 67–77), he examines two instances – the establishment of banks and the accumulation of a public treasure – that, though seemingly contradicting his analysis by decreasing and increasing "money beyond its natural level", actually corroborate the equilibrium hypothesis.

The published article thus does reflect Hume's rejoinder to Oswald, but the first part only, dealing with equilibrium; the second part, relating to adjustment (see pp. 3–4 above), is not discussed at all. Such neglect should not be seen as a rearguard defense or an escape from Oswald's criticisms, since the latter had been efficaciously answered. The explanation should rather be sought in the nature of the issue addressed, namely the critique of mercantilism, as Hume himself argued (see footnote 5). The main message of his writing concerns the stability of equilibrium founded on the operation of forces that prevent money from falling or growing continuously. As stressed in the water analogy (Hume, 1749, p. 189; Hume, 1752a, pp. 63, 64, 72, 73 (lines 1 and 30), 77), the money stock, as long as communication is unobstructed, cannot deviate from the "natural level" determined by the law of one price. Hume's analysis, therefore, clashes head-on with the traditional account pointing at the discrepancy between domestic and foreign prices on the basis of two paragraphs[8] quoted ad nauseam in virtually all articles

[7]Aside from hindrances to communication like huge transport costs, equilibrium is maintained by "a moral attraction, arising from the interests and passions of men, which is full as potent and infallible [as physical attraction]. How is the balance kept in the provinces of every kingdom among themselves, but by the force of this principle, which makes it impossible for money to lose its level, and either to rise or sink beyond the proportion of the labour and commodities which are in each province?" (Hume, 1752a, p. 65). Waterman (1988) has drawn attention to the influence of Newton's contributions to physics on Hume.

[8]"Suppose four-fifths of all the money in Great Britain to be annihilated in one night, and the nation reduced to the same condition, with regard to specie, as in the reigns of the Harrys and Edwards, what would be the consequence? Must not the price of all labour and commodities sink in proportion, and everything be sold as cheap as they were in those ages? What nation could then dispute with us in any foreign market, or pretend to navigate or to sell manufactures at the same price, which to us would afford sufficient profit? In how little time, therefore, must this bring back the money which we had lost, and raise us to the level of all the neighbouring nations? Where, after we have arrived, we immediately lose the advantage of the cheapness of labour and commodities; and the farther flowing in of money is stopped by our fullness and repletion. Again, suppose, that all the money of Great Britain were multiplied fivefold in a night, must not the contrary effect follow? Must not all labour and commodities rise to such an exorbitant height, that no neighbouring nations could afford to buy from us; while their commodities, on the other hand, became comparatively so cheap, that, in spite of all the laws which could be formed, they would be run in upon us, and our money flow out; till we fall to a level with foreigners, and lose that great superiority of riches, which had laid us under such disadvantages?" (Hume 1752a, pp. 62–63).

and textbooks (a recent example is Krugman and Obstfeld, 1997, pp. 541–542). However, taken out of context, this passage is quite misleading. Hume is not analyzing the actual adjustment mechanism but simply a thought experiment describing the forces underlying a stable equilibrium. This appears patently in the paragraph, almost never quoted, that immediately follows the familiar ones.

> "Now, it is evident, that the same causes, which would correct these exorbitant inequalities, *were they to happen miraculously, must prevent their happening in the common course of nature*, and must for ever, in all neighbouring nations, preserve money nearly proportionable to the art and industry of each nation. All water, wherever it communicates, remains always at a level. Ask naturalists the reason; they tell you, that, were it to be raised in any one place, the superior gravity of that part not being balanced, must depress it, till it meet a counterpoise; and that the same cause, which redresses the inequality when it happens, must for ever prevent it, without some violent external operation." (Hume, 1752a, pp. 63–64, italics added)

Hume is evidently explaining the hypothetical character of those money stock variations that, just because the law of one price holds, cannot occur in reality as the italicized passage makes clear. This interpretation is confirmed by Hume himself when dealing with the impossibility of accumulating money, unless it is withdrawn from circulation in order to heap up a public treasure.[9] The change in money is just a "supposition", i.e. a thought experiment, to prove the stability result. Indeed, equilibrium is re-established "immediately" (Hume, 1752a, pp. 63, 69, 73) or "suddenly" like water in communicating vessels as emphasized in the letter to Montesquieu, the first statement of his theory (Hume, 1749, pp. 188–189). Yet this does not refer to the speed of the actual adjustment process but to the power of equilibrium forces deemed so strong as to make adjustment virtually instantaneous.

The question posed at the end of Section 2 can now be answered. "Of the Balance of Trade" reflects Hume's reply to Oswald and answers the same criticisms subsequently raised by others. The received view mistakenly takes Hume to task for ignoring the law of one price and misunderstands the essay entirely. The concentration on two single paragraphs (see footnote 8) has produced a caricatured interpretation centering on the adjustment mechanism. However, nowhere in this essay does Hume discuss transition; rather, positing the equality

[9] "To prove this, we need only return to our first *supposition*, of annihilating the half or any part of our cash; where we found, that the immediate consequence of such an event would be the attraction of an equal sum from all the neighbouring kingdoms" (Hume, 1752a, p. 72, italics added).

between domestic and foreign prices, he focuses on the stability property of long-run equilibrium.

4. Hume and classical monetary theory

Jacob Viner (1937) and Jürg Niehans (1990) are among the few who have not been caught in the trap laid by the mesmerizing passage quoted in footnote 8. In particular, Niehans (1990, p. 56) regards it as a *reductio ad absurdum* of the persistence of price differentials, thus hinting at the interpretation put forward in the present paper. Both recognize that Hume maintained, rather than ignored, the law of one price.[10] But Viner, deeming it "anachronistic" to ascribe to Hume the notion of price level because price indexes were not yet available, follows a relative price approach via the terms-of-trade channel (see the excellent treatment given by Negishi, 1989, pp. 40–48). If Viner falls short of a correct appraisal, Niehans goes beyond it by crediting Hume with a more sophisticated analysis involving the demand for real cash balances.[11] However, Hume has no such notion and, concentrating on the ratio between money and output, abstracts entirely from velocity. In fact, with the possible exception of Locke (Holtrop, 1929; Cesarano,

[10]In this respect, Viner is quite outspoken though his warning has remained unheeded. "The classical school and its important followers all held the same views on this point: after allowance for transportation costs, the market prices of identical transportable commodities must everywhere be equal or tend to be equal when expressed in or converted to a common currency. When, therefore, critics of the classical theory have taken it to task on the ground that it explained the adjustment of international balances by the influence on the course of trade of divergent market prices in different markets of identical transportable commodities, or when followers of the classical theory have attempted to defend it although themselves giving it such an interpretation, they have misinterpreted the classical doctrine" (Viner, 1937, pp. 316–317). That even authorities have been led astray on this essential point is shown by the following remark by Samuelson. "Gold's finding its proper geographical distribution by analogy with the way water finds its own level is merely a persuasive metaphor. If Hume had bothered to think the matter through, he'd have recognized that the analogy would have fit better if he likened the common price of wheat in two places to the common level of water in two places – a P rather than a Q or M analogy. No later writers have been harmed by Hume's level-of-water analogy" (Samuelson, 1980, pp. 146–47). But Hume did recognize the P analogy as extensively documented in the present paper (see especially the quotation on p. 5 and footnote 6).

[11]"Hume's expression of money everywhere maintaining its proper level clearly means that the ratio between the stock of money and the demand for real cash balances must everywhere be the same; but that ratio is simply the price level (if prices are expressed in coins with the same gold content). The economic substance of Hume's argument, therefore, though not innovative, was more solid than was often supposed. His exposition, however, though effective, was more misleading than Cantillon's or Smith's" (Niehans, 1990, p. 56). In a letter he sent me, Niehans agreed that Hume did not explicitly deal with the concept of real cash balances, although his water analogy might imply it (see footnotes 2 and 6).

1983), economists at the time had a rather mechanical conception of velocity assuming that its variations were tantamount to variations in the stock of money. Velocity was thus viewed as a factor impinging upon money supply rather than demand.[12] In the monetary transmission mechanism, an increase in money shifts the demand for goods, which raises output and eventually the price level (Cantillon, 1755, pp. 159–167). The real balance effect sets the mechanism in motion, but the discrepancy between desired and actual real cash balances is not even suggested. Indeed, the classics, albeit grasping the real balance effect, did not develop a fully-fledged conception of the demand for real cash balances and, particularly, of the adjustment of real balances to their equilibrium level. According to Patinkin (1965, p. 164 and Notes E and F), such adjustment was described only a century and a half later by Wicksell and Fisher. This point is important to arrive at a deeper assessment of Hume's contribution and to settle the much disputed question of the Humean character of the monetary approach to the balance of payment.

Hume is commonly criticized for neglecting the direct effect of the excess supply of money on the demand for foreign commodities and focusing, instead, on price differentials (Samuelson, 1980, p. 142). Of course, these are two sides of the same coin in that the violation of the law of one price results from the failure of arbitrage. As is shown in the previous section, however, equality between domestic and foreign prices is a central tenet of Hume's theory. Hence, the customary distinction between Hume's "price"-specie-flow mechanism and the modern approach based on arbitrage is unfounded. The point is not whether Hume

[12]Cantillon notes: "I have already remarked that an acceleration or greater rapidity in circulation of money in exchange, is equivalent to an increase of actual money up to a point" (Cantillon, 1755, p. 161). Holtrop (1929, pp. 508–509) aptly distinguishes the *motion theory* of velocity from the *cash-balance theory* and shows their theoretical implications. "These two theories diverge in the first place in their conception of the notions of supply and demand of money. The partisans of the motion theory are more or less inclined to regard the velocity of circulation as a property of money, as a kind of energy which is inherent to it. To be sure they do not say this in so many words, but all comparisons that are made, as e.g. with the carrying-capacity of a ship, go in this mechanical direction. If, however, the velocity is a property of money, then the supply of money is not a singular but a compound magnitude, being constituted of the product of quantity and velocity. Opposite to this supply they then put a demand for money, which is identified with the total supply of goods, thus coming to a formulation of the quantity theory, according to which the value of money is determined by supply and demand in the just mentioned sense. Otherwise the supporters of the cash-balance theory, who perceive that the size of the cash-balances is not dependent on the properties of the coins, but on the will of the owner, which is governed by economic motives. To them the demand for money is the sum-total of the individual demands for a cash-balance, and the supply of money is simply constituted by its quantity. It is self-evident that, according to this view, the velocity of circulation, being nothing but the expression of the relative size of the cash-balances, is not a factor of supply, but of demand" (Holtrop, 1929, pp. 522–23).

upheld a direct effect on the demand for foreign goods, which he certainly did, as it follows from the law of one price, but whether his analysis is consistent with that law. Bearing in mind Oswald's criticisms, Hume avoids tackling the dynamics of transition to the new steady state and instead aims to demonstrate the stability of equilibrium. To this purpose, he can rely on *notional* changes in the price level, which do not refer to the actual adjustment process but to a thought experiment. This analytical apparatus, while quite consistent, does not spell out a theory of transition from one equilibrium to another in the presence of the law of one price. This was eventually accomplished by the modern monetary approach (Niehans, 1984, chapters 2 and 3). Hume restricts himself to an analysis of the adjustment process in the closed economy set-up of his essay "Of Money", where the problem of the law of one price does not arise. In fact, if a distinction can be drawn in Hume's work, the relevant one is between the analysis of equilibrium and that of transition, dealt with respectively in "Of the Balance of Trade" and "Of Money". The latter essay shows how employment and output are affected, while prices respond after a lag, during adjustment in consequence of the agents' incomplete information (Cesarano, 1998).[13] But there is no conflict between the two essays, because they address different topics on the basis of the same analytical framework grounded on the equilibrium hypothesis.

The problem Hume dealt with, namely the stability of long-run equilibrium, was entirely neglected by neo-classical economists (Patinkin, 1965, pp. 168, 186). This should be emphasized because his work has always been considered devoid of originality, its main tenets having been anticipated by Gervaise, Cantillon and Vanderlint (Vickers, 1959, p. 218; Allen, 1987, p. 431; Niehans, 1990, p. 55). His simple yet powerful box of tools explains the international distribution of money as well as the endogeneity of money supply inside a country, dwelling upon the equilibrium hypothesis and the forces underlying the stability of equilibrium. A fast-growing country, for instance, attracts money from the rest of the world. Moreover, the argument for free trade that opens and closes the essay is instrumental to growth, the only viable source of money accumulation.

This appraisal bears on the relationship between Hume and the monetary approach, whose exponents claim a Humean heritage (Johnson, 1972; Frenkel, 1976; Frenkel and Johnson, 1976) but maintain the traditional interpretation of

[13] In an often quoted passage, Keynes considers Hume the beginner of the classical equilibrium tradition, even though he argued partly in a mercantilist vein. "Hume... had a foot and a half in the classical world. For Hume began the practice amongst economists of stressing the importance of the equilibrium position as compared with the ever-shifting transition towards it, though he was still enough of a mercantilist not to overlook the fact that it is in the transition that we actually have our being" (Keynes, 1936, p. 343, f. 3). The quotation then refers to "Of Money" (Hume, 1752b) whereas, with regard to "Of the Balance of Trade", Hume certainly had both feet in the classical world.

Hume, thus failing to make a convincing case[14]. Indeed, the standard view in the literature points out the contrast between the "price"-specie-flow mechanism and the law of one price upon which the modern theory is built (Fausten, 1979; Samuelson, 1980; Berdell, 1995). Although this distinction has been shown to be baseless, it would be overhasty to suggest that a close link exists. On the one hand, Hume undoubtedly upholds the law of one price in a simple quantity theory set-up. On the other, he does not refer to the notion of demand for real cash balances, let alone of the equilibrating mechanism annulling the discrepancy between actual and desired real money balances, which is the core of the monetary approach. If the latter aspect, developed only a century and a half later, is deemed essential to the monetary approach, then we must agree with the standard view. Otherwise, we must affirm with Harry Johnson that "the mainstream of the classical tradition [is] epitomized in David Hume's 'price-specie flow mechanism'" (Johnson, 1976, p. 9). This, in fact, appears to be the case because the starting point of both Hume's theoretical framework and modern theory is money market equilibrium. The main difference is that while Hume's equilibrating mechanism is centered on the hydraulic process focusing on the money to output ratio and looks at the supply side of the market, contemporary economists emphasize the behavioral hypothesis underlying the notion of desired real cash balances and points at the demand side. Nevertheless, the two strains of thought originate from a common source, since both approach the balance of payments from a money market perspective and view it as a monetary phenomenon. Certainly, the modern theory displays greater sophistication and generality, which leads to a fully-fledged analysis of the dynamics of transition. But Hume's contribution, two centuries in advance, demonstrates considerable explanatory power within a simplified theoretical framework. In fact, it reaches the main results of the monetary approach (Fausten,

[14]See the following remark by Harry Johnson. "[I]n the detailed analysis of the mechanism there is a rather awkward compromise between the assumption of a closed and of an open economy, in which it is assumed that domestic prices can vary from purchasing-power parity under the influence of imbalances between money demand and money supply, but that such variations give rise to changes in trade flows which alter the balance of payments and hence the domestic stock of money in the longer run. As we shall see, the new approach to balance-of-payments theory, while basically Humean in spirit, places the emphasis not on relative price changes but on the direct influence of excess demand for or supply of money on the balance between income and expenditure, or more generally between total acquisition and disposal of funds whether through production and consumption or through borrowing and lending, and therefore on the overall balance of payments" (Johnson, 1972, p. 230). Frenkel (1976, p. 41), besides quoting a passage from Hume's "Of the Jealousy of Trade", refers to Gervaise and Cantillon in order to provide evidence for the direct effect on the demand for foreign goods. And, with regard to the "famous paragraph" (see footnote 8 above), he notes: "Hume's statements concerning the changes in prices raise some questions whether his price adjustment assumes failure of arbitrage" (Frenkel, 1976, p. 42).

1979, p. 661) – the endogeneity of money supply, the transitory and self-correcting character of payments disequilibria, and the concentration on the longer-run consequences of balance-of-payments policies – thus showing a common analytical foundation.

5. Conclusion

As economists are well aware, the classics are more often quoted than read. Theories mistakenly named after a classical author survive in the economic jargon with the wrong label. An example is the Ricardian Equivalence Theorem, which was in fact refuted by Ricardo (O'Driscoll, 1977). Likewise, textbooks will continue to dispense a popularized version of Hume's writing as the classic statement of international adjustment based on the divergence between domestic and foreign prices. Had readers not focused only on the passage cited in footnote 8, they would have recognized that the changes in money that Hume refers to represent a thought experiment relating to the stability of equilibrium and not to the actual adjustment mechanism. Admittedly, Hume's exposition can be confusing, but an attentive reading of the essay together with the correspondence with Oswald leads to a straightforward interpretation. Hume was perfectly aware of the objection concerning the violation of the law of one price long before publication. Not surprisingly, then, the definitive version of his work is immune to that critique. Hence, the received view of the "price"-specie-flow mechanism clashes with Hume's overall analysis. His theoretical framework hinges on money market equilibrium and, albeit concentrating on the supply rather than the demand side, can be seen as the epitome of the modern monetary approach to the balance of payments.

Acknowledgements

Thanks are due to William Allen, John Berdell, Mark Blaug, Robert Clower, Dietrich Fausten, Milton Friedman, David Laidler, Robert Mundell, Jürg Niehans, Eugene Rotwein, A.M.C. Waterman and two referees for their perceptive comments. The paper was presented at the History of Economics Society conference in Charleston, S.C., in June 1997. I am grateful to the discussant, Allin Cottrell, and to other participants for their helpful suggestions. The usual caveat applies.

References

Allen, W.R., 1987. Specie-flow mechanism. In: Eatwell, J., Milgate, M., Newman, P. (Eds.), The New Palgrave. A Dictionary of Economics, Vol. 4. Macmillan, London.

Berdell, J.F., 1995. The present relevance of Hume open-economy monetary dynamics. Economic Journal 105, 1205–1217.

Cantillon, R., 1755. Essai sur la Nature du Commerce en Général. Cass, London, 1959.

Cesarano, F., 1983. The rational expectations hypothesis in retrospect. American Economic Review 73, 198–203.

Cesarano, F., 1998. Expectations and monetary policy: A historical perspective. Manchester School of Economic and Social Studies, forthcoming.

Fausten, D.K., 1979. The Humean origin of the contemporary monetary approach to the balance of payments. Quarterly Journal of Economics 93, 655–673.

Frenkel, J.A., 1976. Adjustment mechanisms and the monetary approach to the balance of payments: A doctrinal perspective. In: Claassen, E., Salin, P. (Eds.), Recent Issues in International Monetary Economics. North-Holland, Amsterdam.

Frenkel, J.A., Johnson, H.G., 1976. The monetary approach to the balance of payments: Essential concepts and historical origins. In: Frenkel, J.A., Johnson, H.G. (Eds.), The Monetary Approach to the Balance of Payments. Allen & Unwin, London.

Greig, J.Y.T. (Ed.), 1932. The Letters of David Hume, Vol. I. Oxford University Press, Oxford.

Holtrop, M.W., 1929. Theories of the velocity of circulation of money in earlier economic literature. Economic Journal (Supplement), Economic History Series 4, 503–524.

Hume, D., 1749. Letter to Montesquieu, 10 April 1749. In: Rotwein, E. (Ed.), David Hume. Writings on Economics. The University of Wisconsin Press, Madison, 1970.

Hume, D., 1750. Letter to Oswald, 1 November 1750. In: Rotwein, E. (Ed.), David Hume. Writings on Economics. The University of Wisconsin Press, Madison, 1970.

Hume, D., 1752a. Of the balance of trade. In: Rotwein, E. (Ed.), David Hume. Writings on Economics. The University of Wisconsin Press, Madison, 1970.

Hume, D., 1752b. Of money. In: Rotwein, E. (Ed.), David Hume. Writings on Economics. The University of Wisconsin Press, Madison, 1970.

Johnson, H.G., 1972. The monetary approach to balance-of-payments theory. In: Johnson, H.G. (Ed.), Further Essays in Monetary Economics. Allen & Unwin, London.

Johnson, H.G., 1976. Money and the balance of payments. Banca Nazionale del Lavoro, Quarterly Review 29, 3–18.

Keynes, J.M., 1936. The General Theory of Employment, Interest and Money. Macmillan, London.

Krugman, P.R., Obstfeld, M., 1997. International Economics, 4th ed. Addison-Wesley, Reading, Mass.

Low, J.M., 1952. An Eighteenth Century Controversy in the Theory of Economic Progress. Manchester School of Economic and Social Studies, 20, pp. 311–330, reprinted in Blaug (1991).

Negishi, T., 1989. History of Economic Theory. North-Holland, Amsterdam.

Niehans, J., 1984. International Monetary Economics. The Johns Hopkins University Press, Baltimore.

Niehans, J., 1990. A History of Economic Theory. The Johns Hopkins University Press, Baltimore.

O'Driscoll, G.P., 1977. The Ricardian nonequivalence theorem. Journal of Political Economy 85, 207–210.

Oswald of Dunnikier, J., 1750. Letter to Hume, 10 October 1750. In: Rotwein, E. (Ed.), David Hume. Writings on Economics. The University of Wisconsin Press, Madison, 1970.

Patinkin, D., 1965. Money, Interest, and Prices. Harper & Row, New York.

Samuelson, P.A., 1980. A corrected version of Hume's equilibrating mechanisms for international trade. In: Chipman, J.S., Kindleberger, C.P. (Eds.), Flexible Exchange Rates and the Balance of Payments. North-Holland, Amsterdam.

Vickers, D., 1959. Studies in the Theory of International Trade. Owen, London.
Viner, J., 1937. Studies in the Theory of International Trade. Harper, New York.
Waterman, A.M.C., 1988. Hume, Malthus, and the stability of equilibrium. History of Political Economy 20, 85–94.

[6]

Keynes's Revindication of Classical Monetary Theory

Filippo Cesarano

John Maynard Keynes's insightful critique of the classical economists in his *General Theory of Employment, Interest, and Money* (1936) aimed at rebuilding economic analysis from its very foundations. Most, if not all, historians of economics agree that he succeeded, as they ascribe the discipline's only scientific revolution, in Thomas Kuhn's sense (1970), to the *General Theory*.[1] Keynes's pathbreaking contribution held the stage for most of the twentieth century. It prompted the response of the monetarist counterrevolution (Johnson 1971), giving rise to a heated debate that is still going on, fueled by novel arguments, between new classicals and new Keynesians.

The propensity for radical innovation is not confined to Keynes's magnum opus but characterizes many of his writings and especially those regarding the international monetary system, a topic of foremost interest to him throughout his life. Keynes's unflagging quest for monetary reform is grounded in his theoretical work on money. Until the early thirties, it was based upon an elaboration of the classical model. Afterward, the *General Theory* provided an alternative model, leading to an

Correspondence may be addressed to Filippo Cesarano, Banca d'Italia, Ufficio Ricerche Storiche, Via Nazionale 191, Rome 00184, Italy; e-mail: cesarano.filippo@insedia.interbusiness.it. Thanks are due to Robert Clower, David Laidler, Allan Meltzer, Scott Sumner, John Williamson, and an anonymous referee for their useful comments. Any errors or omissions are mine.

1. The marginalist literature is a much more controversial candidate. Recently, David Laidler's important book (1999) has cast serious doubts on the revolutionary character of Keynes's work.

History of Political Economy 35:3 © 2003 by Duke University Press.

overall rethinking of international monetary arrangements. As one of the architects of the postwar monetary order, Keynes began to deal with this topic as early as the fall of 1940, producing the final draft of the plan that bears his name in April 1943.

The plan, which was the culmination of three decades of reflection on the international monetary system, was motivated by Keynes's rejection of the gold standard and eventually of classical monetary theory altogether. It is striking, therefore, that in his last published article, in 1946, Keynes revives classical monetary economics and, albeit not recanting the message of the *General Theory*, points out the mistake of neglecting the international adjustment mechanism based on the equilibrium hypothesis of classical economics. Written shortly before his death, this little-known paper on the issue of dollar scarcity can be viewed as his intellectual testament. Since the followers of Keynesian economics departed from the economics of Keynes in many respects (Leijonhufvud 1968), a reconsideration of his last essay is important in order to dispel further misinterpretations and give a more accurate assessment of his thought. After a reconstruction of his main contributions to monetary reform (section 1), the 1946 article is examined, showing Keynes's revindication of classical monetary theory (section 2).

1. Keynes on the International Monetary System

Keynes's concern for international monetary problems goes back to the very beginnings of his career. His first book, *Indian Currency and Finance* (1913), written in the heyday of the gold standard, supports the gold exchange standard. Although lacking originality from both a theoretical and an institutional viewpoint (Laidler 1991, 169–70), this work shows his unyielding effort to reform the monetary system. This is indeed a constant feature of Keynes's writings on the subject and is founded on a critique of the model of commodity money. Instead of having rigid rules shackling the economy's performance, monetary institutions should be molded with sufficient flexibility to allow the pursuit of domestic targets.[2]

2. The present section concentrates on the analytical aspects of Keynes's various reform proposals and skips institutional details. For more on the analytical aspects, see the excellent essays by John Williamson (1983), Donald Moggridge (1986), and Allan Meltzer (1988, 1989). Emphasizing Keynes's prolificness in suggesting new projects, Moggridge (1986, 66–67) notes, "By the time Keynes came to draft his proposals for the post-World War II monetary system, he

After the First World War, the main objective of policymakers was to reestablish the gold standard. The Cunliffe Committee report ([1918] 1985, 175) contended that the return to gold would bring monetary stability, the prerequisite for economic stability, both to Britain and to the rest of the world. However, noted economists, among others Gustav Cassel and Irving Fisher, criticized the deflationary and redistributive impact of the restoration rule, which required going back to the original parity after a temporary suspension. This opened a crack in the edifice of the gold standard, since the rule was the keystone of the system's credibility.[3] Besides providing the basis for economic policy discipline, the rule enhanced the adjustment mechanism insofar as, by virtually eliminating exchange rate risk, it fostered capital movements (Eichengreen 1996, 30–32). The search for an alternative monetary setup was also prompted by a further, crucial shortcoming of the gold standard, namely, its leaving the determination of the money stock to the vagaries of the gold market, thus jeopardizing price level stability. Several scholars had already pointed out this problem in the decades preceding the war and put forward proposals to reform the monetary system accordingly. Alfred Marshall's symmetallism, Léon Walras's *billon régulateur*, and Fisher's compensated dollar are the best-known examples. Knut Wicksell (see footnote 6 below) went so for as to suggest a paper money totally divorced from commodity money. Yet, these contributions had little impact on central bankers, even after the war. Among economists, the prevailing

had at one time or another recommended almost every exchange rate regime known to modern analysts except completely freely floating exchange rates." In fact, Keynes consistently rejects flexible exchange rates throughout his writings. In an early draft of his 1943 plan, he considers as a false approach "the idea that a freely fluctuating exchange would discover for itself a position of equilibrium" (1980a, 22).

3. Stephen Clarke (1973, 11–12) underscores the central place of the restoration rule in the approach followed by the Cunliffe Committee: "In an interim report published in August of the same year, the committee presented a classical description of what its authors took to be the working of the pre-1914 gold standard. The report is relevant for this study because its international monetary model was in many respects the one that was accepted by virtually everyone at Genoa and even eleven years later by the Continental European countries that participated in the London conference. It was, of course, a system in which the parities of currencies were assumed to be permanently fixed in terms of gold and in which gold movements associated with payment imbalances brought equilibrating adjustments in domestic interest rates, wages, prices, and spending. The conception was of a unified world in which the component national economies adjusted in order to maintain international monetary stability. Not only was this view accepted without dissent by the committee, but its members conducted their discussions *on the assumption* that sterling would eventually be stabilized at its prewar parity equivalent to $4.86."

idea put forward in response to the shortcomings of the gold standard was to introduce a managed money like the gold exchange standard, "the favourite of currency theorists" in Ralph Hawtrey's words (1919, 437), although dissenting views were not lacking. On the one hand, conservative scholars like Ludwig von Mises and Friedrich Hayek upheld the gold standard because its demise would pave the way to inflation and economic instability. On the other hand, Keynes, in the *Tract on Monetary Reform*, took a diametrically opposite position and, in order to stabilize "trade, prices, and employment, . . . [made] the proposal—which may seem, but should not be, shocking—of separating entirely the gold reserve from the note issue" (Keynes 1923, 196).

This is an anti-classical prescription and yet is grounded on classical foundations. Far from being inconsistent, in chapters 1 and 2 of the *Tract* Keynes thoroughly analyzes the distributive effects of price level changes, inflation as a tax on real cash balances, the burden of public debt, and the like, arriving at a clear-cut statement of classical monetary economics. Dwelling on Marshall's and Fisher's[4] ideas about the role of expectations in the monetary transmission mechanism and on the Cambridge approach to the quantity theory, Keynes relates the amplitude of business cycles to both actual and expected purchasing power variations, which affect the entrepreneur's investment and production decisions. Since changes in price expectations tend to be cumulative, the policymaker should defy the rules of a commodity standard and intervene readily to neutralize them from the very beginning, instead of "sitting quietly by, whilst a standard of value, governed by chance causes and deliberately removed from central control, produces expectations which paralyse or intoxicate the government of production" (Keynes 1923, 39). Hence, an activist policy, preventing shifts in the demand for money and for bank reserves, is necessary to avoid price level fluctuations, which ultimately have significant repercussions on output and employment.

Keynes's break with the past concerns policy rather than theory. Using the works of A. C. Pigou, Marshall, and Fisher to buttress the hypothesis

4. Keynes's first publication (1911) is a review of Irving Fisher's classic *The Purchasing Power of Money*, in which (see especially chapter 13) expectations play a key role in explaining the effectiveness of monetary impulses in different monetary systems. In a letter sent to Fisher on 7 July 1944 during the Bretton Woods conference, Keynes ([1944] 1997, 218) recognizes his intellectual debt. "You were one of my earliest teachers on these matters and nothing is more satisfactory to any of us than to satisfy one of those from whom we have learned." For an exhaustive treatment of the development of the quantity theory in the 1870–1914 period, see Laidler 1991.

that money is nonneutral in the short run, he makes output variability depend on the operation of the gold standard and consequently calls for the latter's removal. Given the conspicuous postwar depreciations, it is impossible to comply with the restoration rule. And a partial revaluation would not do insofar as only the return to the prewar parity would leave the credibility of the standard untainted.[5] Even in ordinary circumstances, the adjustment process embodied in David Hume's specie-flow mechanism is too slow so that, in the presence of major disequilibria, it is changes in output, not changes in prices, that bear the brunt of adjustment:

> The fault of the pre-war régime, under which the rates of exchange between a country and the outside world were fixed, and the internal price level had to adjust itself thereto (*i.e.* was chiefly governed by external influences), was that it was too slow and insensitive in its mode of operation. . . . Thus when there are violent shocks to the pre-existing equilibrium between the internal and external price-levels, the pre-war method is likely to break down in practice, simply because it cannot bring about the re-adjustment of internal prices *quick enough*. Theoretically, of course, the pre-war method must be able to make itself effective sooner or later, provided the movement of gold is allowed to continue without restriction, until the inflation or deflation of prices has taken place to the necessary extent. But in practice there is usually a limit to the rate and to the amount by which the actual currency or the metallic backing for it can be allowed to flow abroad. If the supply of money or credit is reduced faster than social and business arrangements allow prices to fall, intolerable inconveniences result. (Keynes 1923, 159–62)

All in all, the shocks caused by World War I inevitably brought about a certain degree of flexibility in the monetary system so that "gold itself has become a 'managed' currency" (1923, 167). The diffusion of managed money is a fait accompli. Following the message of the *Tract* emphasizing the destabilizing effects of price level variability, the

5. "It is of the essence of the argument that the *exact* pre-war parity should be recovered" (Keynes 1923, 150). Stressing the consequences of a severe deflationary policy, Keynes (1923, 153–54) recalls that David Ricardo was against restoration if the currency had depreciated more than 5 percent. Furthermore, he rejects the argument that the restoration rule repairs the "injustice" suffered by bond holders, since the main part of government debt had been issued after, not before, the war began (147–49).

determination of the money stock should not be left to the market in the money commodity but assigned to the monetary authority.[6] This goes beyond a mere institutional modification and paves the way for modern monetary policy. The bank rate, as an instrument, then plays quite a different role: instead of triggering capital movements to enhance the adjustment process as under the gold standard, it is directed at stabilizing the price level and other policy targets.

Unquestionably, the analysis of the *Tract* is based on the Cambridge approach to the quantity theory—"This Theory is fundamental. Its correspondence with fact is not open to question" (Keynes 1923, 74)—and takes for granted the equilibrium hypothesis, that is, the self-adjusting property of the economy, the central tenet of classical economics. Yet Keynes, emphasizing the effectiveness of monetary impulses and the slowness of the gold standard adjustment mechanism, makes the case for an active monetary policy with a view to dampening price variability and ultimately reducing unemployment.[7] Hence, the link between note

6. In his classic *Interest and Prices*, Wicksell ([1898] 1965, 193–94) anticipates this view, arguing for the demise of the gold standard in order to stabilize the price level: "It would be possible to avoid such a rise of prices only by the *suspension of the free coinage of gold*. This would mark the first step towards the introduction of an ideal standard of value. Monetary discussions of recent years have made us more and more familiar with such an international paper standard. . . . The introduction of such a scheme offers no difficulty, at any rate on the theoretical side. Neither a central bureau nor international notes would be necessary. Each country would have its own system of notes (and small change). These would have to be redeemable at par by every central bank, but would be allowed to circulate only inside the one country. It would then be the simple duty of each credit institution to regulate its rate of interest, both relatively to, and in unison with, other countries, so as both to maintain in equilibrium the international balance of payments and to stabilise the general level of world prices."

7. Keynes makes this point very clearly in the opening paragraph of the *Tract*'s preface. "We leave Saving to the private investor, and we encourage him to place his savings mainly in titles to money. We leave the responsibility for setting Production in motion to the business man, who is mainly influenced by the profits which he expects to accrue to himself in terms of money. Those who are not in favour of drastic changes in the existing organisation of society believe that these arrangements, being in accord with human nature, have great advantages. But they cannot work properly if the money, which they assume as a stable measuring-rod, is undependable. Unemployment, the precarious life of the worker, the disappointment of expectation, the sudden loss of savings, the excessive windfalls to individuals, the speculator, the profiteer—all proceed, in large measure, from the instability of the standard of value." Several other references to the task of decreasing income and employment variability can be found in chapters 4 and 5 (172, 176, 196, 197). The policymaker, however, should not rely on "a precise, arithmetical formula" like Fisher's compensated dollar but should consider all available information on "actual price-movements . . . the state of employment, the volume of production, the effective demand for credit as felt by the banks, the rate of interest on investments of various types, the volume of new issues, the flow of cash into circulation, the statistics of foreign trade and the level of the exchanges" (186–89).

issue and gold is severed and the basic rule governing the monetary system is turned upside down: instead of maintaining parity, the monetary authority must stabilize purchasing power.

Despite its originality, the *Tract*, obscured by the *General Theory* and even by the much criticized *Treatise on Money*, has been decidedly underrated,[8] particularly as regards its influence on the evolution of monetary arrangements. Starting from the heterodox position of cutting the connection with gold,[9] Keynes predicts several future developments. International cooperation will be a "pious hope" (1923, 174) because the dynamics of credit, prices, and economic activity will actually be determined by the policy of the most powerful country, the United States. The gold exchange standard, therefore, will retain the defects of the gold standard but not its qualities. This is a key issue: if central bank policy replaces the impersonal workings of commodity money, a political element arises, since a country's own welfare targets, broadly conceived, are necessarily brought into play, thus making cooperation difficult. Not

8. In this regard, Milton Friedman's appraisal should be recalled. "In listing 'the' classic of each of these great economists, historians will cite the *General Theory* as Keynes's pathbreaking contribution. Yet, in my opinion, Keynes would belong in this line even if the *General Theory* had never been published. Indeed, I am one of a small minority of professional economists who regard his *Tract on Monetary Reform* (1923), not the *General Theory*, as his best book in economics. Even after sixty-five years, it is not only well worth reading but continues to have a major influence on economic policy" (Friedman 1997, 2).

9. The contrast between Keynes's analysis and the mainstream is vividly illustrated by Ralph Hawtrey's entry on money in the 1929 edition of the *Encyclopaedia Britannica*. "The Genoa plan is based on the continued general use of the gold standard. Proposals have been put forward (particularly by Mr. J.M. Keynes) for applying the policy of stabilization of purchasing power to a paper currency entirely dissociated from gold. The practicability of such a plan is a matter of controversy, and the general return to the gold standard throughout the greater part of the world has made the question an academic one. Apart from schemes of the type favoured by Mr. Keynes, paper money dissociated from gold is a monetary disease. The abuse of paper money became so prevalent during and after the World War, that it has been given an almost disproportionately important place in latter-day monetary theory" (Hawtrey 1929, 698). Hawtrey's judgment of the debate about Keynes's proposals as an "academic one" sounds unintentionally ironic on the eve of the downfall of the gold standard. In the cultural climate of the time, however, the danger of inflationary abuses was emphasized not only by conservative economists but also by those, such as Pigou, who were not against a managed money: "The main argument in favour of a gold standard, as against a paper standard, is that, whereas Governments and banks can create paper money at will, they can only obtain gold money by buying it. To leave the Bank of the Government a free hand in currency manufacture, without any obligation to convert notes into gold and without any legal limit to the quantity of notes that may be created, is to open the door to grave abuse. Moreover, even if grave abuse does not in fact take place, the fear that it may take place and the suspicion that it will are likely to weaken the general sense of security, which is an important factor in industrial progress" (Pigou 1927, 297).

casually, in the *Tract* (1923, 203–4) the establishment of a single authority in charge of international money is deemed unfeasible, although Keynes's future reform plans provide for such an authority, a weak point of those plans for the very reason that cooperation is implausible.

The analytical apparatus of the *Tract* is the basis of the pamphlet *The Economic Consequences of Mr Churchill* (1925), a forceful critique of England's return to the gold standard, showing the effects of the deflationary policies necessary to make prices and wages coherent with the prewar parity.

> Our problem is to reduce money wages and, through them, the cost of living, with the idea that, when the circle is complete, real wages will be as high, or nearly as high, as before. By what *modus operandi* does credit restriction attain this result?
>
> *In no other way than by the deliberate intensification of unemployment.* The object of credit restriction, in such a case, is to withdraw from employers the financial means to employ labour at the existing level of prices and wages. The policy can only attain its end by intensifying unemployment without limit, until the workers are ready to accept the necessary reduction of money wages under the pressure of hard facts. (Keynes [1925] 1972, 218)

Keynes emphasizes the presence of frictions in the adjustment mechanism, the lack of labor mobility between sectors of the economy, and the risk of major disequilibria due to the increasing rigidity of the economic system.[10] All these factors work against the smooth and costless operation of the gold standard and instead suggest the design of alternative, more pliable, monetary institutions that would widen the scope of economic policy.

This research program is carried further in the more ambitious *Treatise on Money* (1930), which, in the author's intentions, was to provide an exhaustive account of the subject but was in fact widely criticized.

10. In the following passage, he envisages the possibility of a crisis of great proportions. "The gold standard, with its dependence on pure chance, its faith in 'automatic adjustments,' and its general regardlessness of social detail, is an essential emblem and idol of those who sit in the top tier of the machine. I think that they are immensely rash in their regardlessness, in their vague optimism and comfortable belief that nothing really serious ever happens. Nine times out of ten, nothing really serious does happen—merely a little distress to individuals or to groups. But we run a risk of the tenth time (and are stupid into the bargain), if we continue to apply the principles of an economics, which was worked out on the hypotheses of *laissez-faire* and free competition, to a society which is rapidly abandoning these hypotheses" (224).

The "fundamental equations" have been regarded as extremely formalistic and mechanical, if not downright tautological, and the analysis of monetary dynamics as an incomplete revisitation of Wicksell's cumulative process (Patinkin 1976, 47–53). Despite these weaknesses,[11] the discussion of international monetary arrangements is of some interest. Adherence to the gold standard constrains bank rate policy, the basic instrument for maintaining equality between saving and investment that is the core of Keynes's model. The resulting dilemma must be solved through a compromise giving the policymaker sufficient room for maneuver (Keynes 1930, 2:304). As in the *Tract*, Keynes stresses the slowness of the adjustment mechanism due to market rigidities, making the operation of an automatic monetary system unreliable. An "international standard," introducing highly mobile capital flows in an otherwise rigid economic structure, may give rise to serious disturbances.

> This leads us to the heart of our argument. If we deliberately desire that there should be a high degree of mobility for international lending, both for long and for short periods, then this is, admittedly, a strong argument for a fixed rate of exchange and a rigid international standard. What, then, is the reason for hesitating before we commit ourselves to such a system? Primarily a doubt whether it is wise to have a Currency System with a much wider ambit than our Banking System, our Tariff System and our Wage System. Can we afford to allow a disproportionate degree of mobility to a single element in an economic system which we leave extremely rigid in several other respects? If there was the same mobility internationally in all other respects as there is nationally, it might be a different matter. But to introduce a mobile element, highly sensitive to outside influences, as a connected part of a machine of which the other parts are much more rigid, may invite breakages. (2:334–35)

Nevertheless Keynes (1930, 2:338), considering flexible exchange rates an unfeasible solution, pragmatically suggests sticking to the Genoa conference resolutions and assigning the management of the value of

11. This is recognized by the author himself in the preface. "As I read through the page proofs of this book I am acutely conscious of its defects. It has occupied me for several years, not free from other occupations, during which my ideas have been developing and changing, with the result that its parts are not all entirely harmonious with one another. . . . it represents a collection of material rather than a finished work" (1930, v–vi). In his masterly study on the Keynesian revolution, David Laidler (1999, 131 n. 1) remarks, "Keynes himself was unhappy with the *Treatise*, describing it as 'an artistic failure' in a letter to his mother."

gold to a supernational authority. This is indicative of the then overwhelming support for the gold standard, especially among policymakers. The formulation of two reform plans, the "minimum" and the "maximum," was anything but a breakthrough. The former follows the outlines of the Genoa conference and, besides excluding gold from circulation, introduces a 2 percent difference between the selling and buying price for gold (in the *Tract* [1923, 190] the proposed margin was 0.5 to 1 percent) to hamper capital mobility. The latter gives the supernational bank the same policy instruments as any central bank in order to stabilize the value of gold in the long run and dampen short-run business fluctuations. These suggestions are scarcely innovative, with the possible exception of that of establishing a supernational monetary authority, an "ideal arrangement" whose successful implementation, however, depends on "the exercise of daily wisdom by the monetary authorities of the world" (1930, 2:402). Yet such a suggestion poses more questions than it answers, raising again the issue of achieving successful cooperation, which, previously doubted by Keynes himself, is not supported by compelling arguments (2:374–77). More attention should instead be given to the explanation of the persistence of the Great Depression as due to the retention of mistaken monetary policies, that is, the return to the gold standard in 1925 and the settlement of war reparations, both of which helped to drive the market rate of interest above the natural rate. The crisis could have been avoided, but only if the policymakers' mentality had been quite different.[12]

12. "If, then, these [misguided monetary policies] are the causes, was the slump avoidable? And is it remediable? The causes to which we have assigned it were the outcome of policy; and in a sense, therefore, it was avoidable. Yet it is evident that the policy could not have been radically different, unless the mentality and ideas of our rulers had also been greatly changed. That is to say, what has occurred is not exactly an accident; it has been deeply rooted in our general way of doing things" (Keynes 1930, 2:385). In the paragraph immediately following this quotation Keynes warns of the danger of letting the adjustment process run its course and argues instead for an expansionary monetary policy *à outrance* by both the Bank of England and the Fed. It should be recalled that the *Treatise* was published in October 1930 when the Great Depression was in its initial stage. "But, granted that the past belongs to the past, need we be fatalistic about the future also? If we leave matters to cure themselves, the results may be disastrous. Prices may continue below the cost of production for a sufficiently long time for entrepreneurs to feel that they have no recourse except an assault on the money-incomes of the factors of production. This is a dangerous enterprise in a society which is both capitalist and democratic. It would be foolish of us to come to grief at a time when the pace of technical improvements is so great that we might, if we choose, be raising our standard of life by a measurable percentage every year. It has been my rôle for the last eleven years to play the part

The Great Depression was a watershed in the reflection on the monetary system. Apart from Keynes, other scholars, anticipating some results of modern research, focused on the defective operation of the gold standard to account for the sharp fall in prices and economic activity, thus making the case for managed money much stronger. In his Rhodes Memorial Lectures, Cassel (1932, 41–49) associated the distinctive nature of the Great Depression with the decline in purchasing power, which is a monetary phenomenon and thus admits only a monetary explanation. This view was shared by many. Putting forward his 100 percent money proposal, Fisher ([1935] 1945, 6–7) referred to the huge decline in bank deposits between 1929 and 1933 as "the chief sinister fact in the depression from which followed the two chief tragedies, unemployment and bankruptcies." And Hawtrey ([1932] 1970, 219) emphasized the breaking of the rules of the game related to gold accumulation by the United States and France and, given wage rigidity, the inevitable decrease in income. Moreover, John Williams (1937, 24) pointed out the multiplier effects of international gold flows. All in all, the Great Depression taught economists that the money stock should be stabilized in order to prevent major price and output fluctuations, thus swinging the pendulum toward the position taken by Keynes beginning in 1923. Of course, the epochal transition toward managed money, subverting two and a half millennia of monetary history, could not happen overnight. Besides conservative economists, central bankers were especially reluctant to abandon the gold standard model. Yet that model progressively lost support and, especially in the academic world, Keynes's once isolated, heterodox position became representative of the state of the art.[13]

By the middle of the 1930s, however, Keynes had gone much further, having almost completed the *General Theory*. His writings on the

of Cassandra, first on the Economic Consequences of the Peace and next on those of the Return to Gold;—I hope that it may not be so on this occasion" (Keynes 1930, 2:385).

13. "The classical doctrine of the automatic standard was thus opposed by the conception of a managed currency. More and more economists were accepting the principles of the new school. Today Keynes appears to have the greatest number of adherents; according to him the gold parity should be changed from time to time. Foreign-exchange quotations should fluctuate within limits broader than those of the gold point, for instance within 5 per cent of a given parity. The issue of bank notes should be severed from gold movements and controlled only from the point of view of stabilizing the purchasing power of money as the most important consideration. Without going into technical details, and without discussing the shortcomings or advantages of the new doctrine, it can be stated that it is a complete reversal of the Ricardian theory and hence quite revolutionary with regard to the classical doctrine" (Mlynarsky 1937, 272).

monetary system, therefore, take a new turn. In the pamphlet *The Means to Prosperity* the recipe for emerging from the depression entails "raising world prices . . . by increasing loan-expenditure" ([1933] 1972, 352). Besides providing credit at low interest rates, the government should increase public expenditures to improve the profit prospects of entrepreneurs and thus stimulate investment.[14] To implement such a design, central banks must be relieved of the task of maintaining sufficient international reserves, in keeping with a reform plan that was part of the British position at the World Economic Conference (Howson and Winch 1977, 114–21). The plan, whose main tenets go back to Keynes's highly influential "Notes on the Currency Question" (1931), anticipates many features of the Bretton Woods proposal. In fact, gold maintains a central place in the system,[15] but an element of flexibility is introduced in that the stock of reserves other than gold is increased or decreased to contrast a downward or an upward price trend respectively. A 5 percent margin between the gold points deters short-term capital movements, creating maneuvering room for monetary policy; in particular circumstances, the parity can be changed. The adoption of the plan should allow the dismantlement of all kinds of controls fettering world trade (Keynes [1933] 1972, 361). Some of these ideas are again illustrated in a subsequent

14. "It is unlikely that private enterprise will, on its own initiative, undertake new loan-expenditure on a sufficient scale. Business enterprise will not seek to expand until *after* profits have begun to recover. Increased working capital will not be required until *after* output is increasing. Moreover, in modern communities a very large proportion of our *normal* programmes of loan-expenditure are undertaken by public and semi-public bodies. The new loan-expenditure which trade and industry require in a year is comparatively small even in good times. Building, transport, and public utilities are responsible at all times for a very large proportion of current loan-expenditure. Thus the first step has to be taken in the initiative of public authority; and it probably has to be on a large scale and organised with determination, if it is to be sufficient to break the vicious circle and to stem the progressive deterioration, as firm after firm throws up the sponge and ceases to produce at a loss in the seemingly vain hope that perseverance will be rewarded" ([1933] 1972, 354).

15. An international authority issues gold-notes against an equal value of gold-bonds of the participating countries up to a maximum quota for each country based on gold reserves. Members of the board have a voting power proportional to their quota. The governing board sets the quantity of notes or the interest rate to achieve the target of price level stabilization ([1933] 1972, 358–60). The key role assigned to gold was interpreted by many commentators as a sudden shift in Keynes's position. He rejects this interpretation in a letter to the editor of the *Economist* on 20 March 1933 vindicating the substantial continuity of his thought ([1933] 1982, 186). It should be added in passing that Keynes's great fertility in proposing new monetary schemes (see footnote 2) is accompanied by a high degree of analytical eclecticism. In a different context, Gottfried Haberler (1948, 434 n. 10) once remarked: "Whatever one's view there is always a Keynes to whom one can look for support!"

article on the future of the foreign exchanges emphasizing the rejection of the gold standard and the use of policy instruments "with exclusive regard to internal conditions and, in particular, the state of employment" ([1935] 1982, 366). However, should a structural disequilibrium arise, a change in parity would be the right course of action. Those, like the Bank for International Settlements Council, who still favor "a return to a régime of fixed gold parities . . . are living in an unreal world, a fool's world" (367).

These two essays ([1933] 1972, [1935] 1982), especially the first one, are but further stages of Keynes's research program aimed at overcoming the limitations of a commodity standard through international monetary arrangements that, while retaining a role for gold, had sufficient elasticity to prevent money supply gyrations and thus price and output instability. The model is now that of the *General Theory*, whose essential message is anticipated in a radio broadcast eloquently titled "Poverty in Plenty: Is the Economic System Self-Adjusting?" Dividing economists into two groups according to whether they answer the question positively or negatively, Keynes puts himself in the second, among the "heretics," and, challenging the followers of orthodoxy on their own ground, announces to have spotted a basic weakness in classical economics:

> Now *I* range myself with the heretics. I believe their flair and their instinct move them towards the right conclusion. But I was brought up in the citadel and I recognise its power and might. A large part of the established body of economic doctrine I cannot but accept as broadly correct. I do not doubt it. For me, therefore, it is impossible to rest satisfied until I can put my finger on the flaw in that part of the orthodox reasoning which leads to the conclusions which for various reasons seem to me to be inacceptable. I believe that I am on my way to do so. There is, I am convinced, a fatal flaw in that part of the orthodox reasoning which deals with the theory of what determines the level of effective demand and the volume of aggregate employment; the flaw being largely due to the failure of the classical doctrine to develop a satisfactory theory of the rate of interest. (Keynes [1934] 1973, 489)[16]

16. Epitomizing Lionel Robbins as the representative of orthodoxy, Keynes ([1934] 1973, 487) efficaciously summarizes the received view. "Professor Robbins . . . stresses the effect of business mistakes under the influence of the uncertainty and the false expectations due to the faults of post-war monetary systems. These authorities do not, of course, believe that the system is automatically or immediately self-adjusting. But they do believe that it has an inherent

The *General Theory* deals with a closed economy, although, in the penultimate chapter, it touches upon international monetary problems, revisiting the much disparaged mercantilist doctrine. Under a metallic standard in which authorities have no direct control over the money stock and domestic investment, a trade surplus is a correct policy target, since it is the only means to lower the interest rate and increase foreign investment ([1936] 1964, 335–38). More generally, Keynes's revaluation of mercantilism builds on that doctrine's disbelief in the self-adjusting property of the economy and its concern with increasing the money supply to lower the interest rate and foster economic growth. Hence, he takes the classical economists to task for failing to consider the employment effects of the gold standard adjustment mechanism in the presence of fixed money contracts:

> The part played by orthodox economists, whose common sense has been insufficient to check their faulty logic, has been disastrous to the latest act. For when in their blind struggle for an escape, some countries have thrown off the obligations which had previously rendered impossible an autonomous rate of interest, these economists have taught that a restoration of the former shackles is a necessary first step to a general recovery. In truth the opposite holds good. It is the policy of an autonomous rate of interest, unimpeded by international preoccupations, and of a national investment programme directed to an optimum level of domestic employment which is twice blessed in the sense that it helps ourselves and our neighbours at the same time. And it is the simultaneous pursuit of these policies by all countries together which is capable of restoring economic health and strength internationally, whether we measure it by the level of domestic employment or by the volume of international trade. (349)

While in the classical doctrine balance-of-payments difficulties were dealt with by an increase in interest rates, with repercussions for economic activity, Keynes calls for the opposite policy course, whose implementation, however, requires the abandonment of a rigid commodity standard.[17] In the *General Theory*, the interest rate is not controlled for

tendency towards self-adjustment, if it is not interfered with and if the action of change and chance is not too rapid."

17. Scott Sumner (1999) has recently argued that the analysis of monetary policy ineffectiveness developed in the *General Theory* is consistent with the assumption of a gold standard model, albeit a modified or flexible gold standard more like the Bretton Woods system than the

monetary policy purposes, but to favor investment. His work on monetary reform, which until the early thirties expanded on the classical approach, takes an entirely new turn afterward following his rejection of the equilibrium hypothesis. Whereas in the classical model departures from equilibrium are only temporary, in the 1936 model equilibrium is not necessarily attained and it is policy action that is assigned the task of bringing the economy back to full employment. Indeed, the *General Theory* seeks to create a discontinuity in the evolution of economics, since it aims to upset the received view constructed over two centuries. Whether it accomplished that objective remains a much debated issue. Recently, David Laidler (1999, chap. 11) has cast serious doubts on the existence of a Keynesian revolution, showing, in particular, that contemporary reviewers, albeit recognizing his contribution in clarifying some intricate questions, denied the originality of his work. With regard to the design of the monetary system, however, the introduction of novel proposals is a constant feature of Keynes's writings. In the interwar period, the state of the art lagged steadily behind his contributions, catching up years later. When in the 1920s economists called for the gold exchange standard, which he supported as early as in 1913, Keynes was already arguing for severing the link with gold. In the midst of the Great Depression, this position gained wider acceptability, but he was far ahead of the mainstream in building an entirely different paradigm. Armed with this innovative analytical framework, he reinforced the case for a managed money, eventually arriving at a full-fledged reform of the international monetary system, the Keynes Plan.

2. The Keynes Plan, the Dollar Shortage, and Monetary Equilibrium

Keynes's trilogy (the *Tract* [1923], the *Treatise* [1930], and the *General Theory* [1936]) has been viewed as "The Saga of Man's Struggle for Freedom from the Quantity Theory" (Patinkin 1976, 18 n. 13). The starting point is Keynes's critique of the gold standard, under which there was no control of the money stock; without control of the money stock, price and output instability occur in the presence of changing expectations and of frictions in the adjustment mechanism. In a sense, Keynes

classical gold standard. The latter would indeed be at odds with Keynes's thought both in that book and in his overall writings on the subject.

first rejects classical monetary arrangements but maintains the classical model, and only at a subsequent stage does he construct an alternative model, escaping from classical monetary economics. In fact, the *Tract* rejects the gold standard altogether, yet it is grounded in the quantity theory. The central idea is that welfare targets can be more successfully reached by an active monetary policy, so monetary institutions must be designed to serve that objective instead of fettering the policymaker as in a commodity standard. Throughout his writings Keynes's continuous effort is to lay the theoretical foundations for this idea and devise a coherent institutional setup. The so-called Keynes Plan—"Proposals for an International Clearing Union," 21 April 1943 (Horsefield 1969, 19–36)—is the crowning achievement of this effort.

The *General Theory* opened a wide-ranging debate, and Keynes wished to answer criticisms and apply his new model to specific fields of inquiry, namely, international trade and business cycles. But starting in 1937 serious heart problems slowed down his research work (Patinkin 1976, 142–43). At the outbreak of the war, then, he became deeply involved in government. International economic issues, in particular the reconstruction of the international monetary system, absorbed most of his time and energy. After the recurrent crises of the interwar period, the design of new monetary institutions represented an intellectual challenge. Essentially, the new system envisaged by Keynes is grounded on the principle of clearing to overcome the shortcomings of the gold exchange standard. Keynes's plan went through several drafts and was discussed with officials at the Treasury, the Board of Trade, and the Bank of England, and with fellow economists—Hawtrey, Richard Kahn, James Meade, Lionel Robbins, and Dennis Robertson—before it was published; the main features of the final version, however, were the same as in the earliest version circulated in September 1941 (Keynes 1980a, 21–40). The plan shares the radical character of Keynes's previous proposals, but it was given much closer attention, not only because of the rising fame of the author of the *General Theory* but also because it was the official British proposal in the negotiations with the United States leading up to Bretton Woods.

The emphasis of the Keynes Plan is on the independence of domestic economic policy, with a view to maintaining full employment. The reestablishment of a stable monetary framework is based on the introduction of an international currency defined in terms of gold; Keynes calls this proposed currency the "bancor," and it is intended to mend the defects of the post–World War I gold exchange standard—bilateral trade, competitive devaluations, a volume of international reserves dependent upon the gold industry and on the policies of individual countries, asymmetry in the adjustment process. More generally, the essence of the plan is to avoid an adjustment mechanism that gives rise to sharp changes in liquidity and thus in output and employment. The Clearing Union, by extending the "principle of banking" to the international scene, brings monetary arrangements to a more advanced stage. It parallels the "ideal case," in which all payments are made by check, envisaged by John Stuart Mill ([1848] 1987, 524) and developed later by Wicksell ([1906] 1946, 87–126) in his analysis of the "ideal banking system."

Although the link of the bancor to gold solves the Wicksellian problem of price level indeterminacy, the Keynes Plan has serious limitations. Controls on capital movements, which are also included in the White Plan, would make the implementation of domestic policies consistent with fixed exchange rates, but the efficacy of such controls is questionable. Moreover, the reestablishment of symmetry in the system, a main objective of the plan, seems doubtful. Under the gold standard, symmetry held, since gold was the "*n*th currency" which solved the Mundellian redundancy problem (McKinnon 1993, 17). In the plan, however, gold is simply the unit of account, and the sanctioning power of the Clearing Union may not be sufficient to effectively constrain the economic policy of member countries, making it coherent with a symmetric, fixed exchange rate regime. In fact, an international agency's ability to enforce rules differs in kind, not just in degree, from the inescapable operation of commodity money.[18] Hence, the pursuit of autonomous domestic policies, in the absence of the gold standard's credibility, may make a fixed exchange rate system unsustainable.

At the time of its publication, however, the most common criticism of the Keynes Plan was that it might cause inflation. When preliminary drafts were circulated, this point was often raised and was thus carefully considered. Not surprisingly, in the final version, debtor countries are subject to strict limitations and the quotas of members are reduced "if it seems necessary to correct . . . an excess of world purchasing power" (Horsefield 1969, 25). Yet, in the absence of credible rules governing

18. In the concluding section of the Keynes Plan, the problem of the surrender of sovereignty by members is considered but, far from its relevance to the viability of the Clearing Union being truly weighed, it is played down with the claim that "no greater surrender [of sovereign rights] is required than in a commercial treaty" (Horsefield 1969, 36).

the Clearing Union, countries hit by an adverse shock might eventually resort to inflation, thus disrupting the system. All in all, most of the criticisms that can be raised against the plan are specific instances of the general, latent inconsistency between a fixed exchange rate regime and the significant role assigned to domestic economic policy, in keeping with the message of the *General Theory*.

The Keynes Plan provoked a variety of reactions, critical (De Vegh 1943; Graham 1943; Lutz 1943) as well as favorable (Robertson 1943; Robinson 1943; Schumacher 1943), with Jacob Viner ([1943] 1951) taking a more balanced view. An article of Hayek's (1943), however, must be singled out because, although lacking originality, it prompts a rebuttal in which Keynes (1943) gives his own interpretation of his plan. Hayek revives the commodity reserve currency, which would purportedly maintain the advantages of the gold standard—creation of an international currency without submitting national monetary policy to an international authority, an automatic and thus predictable monetary policy, the stabilizing character of money stock changes—and mend its main defect, which was the slow adjustment of the gold supply to changes in demand. In his rejoinder, Keynes first points out the novelty of the Clearing Union remedy for the gold standard shortcoming, that is, working through changes in the velocity rather than in the volume of money. He then emphasizes its solution to the most serious problem with the gold standard, namely, the increase in unemployment deriving from the limit to wage increases set by the quantity of money, allowing each country to pursue independent wage and price policies. When the latter diverge substantially from those of other countries, either the policy design must be corrected or, if efficiency wage rates move at different speeds, the exchange rate must be altered (1943, 186). The ultimate basis of the plan, therefore, is to provide the policymaker with sufficient scope for maneuver to attain full employment. Under the gold standard, an opposite mechanism was at work that bent economic policies to the maintenance of parity. It is to avoid just such a mechanism that the Keynes Plan admits exchange rate changes:

> The fundamental reason for thus limiting the objectives of an international currency scheme is the impossibility, or at any rate the undesirability, of imposing stable price-levels from without. The error of the gold-standard lay in submitting national wage-policies to outside dictation. It is wiser to regard stability (or otherwise) of internal prices as

a matter of internal policy and politics. Commodity standards which try to impose this from without will break down just as surely as the rigid gold-standard. (187)[19]

The International Clearing Union carries out the basic idea of designing monetary arrangements that allow the implementation of an active economic policy, thus turning the rules governing the commodity standard upside down. It is well known that after the Bretton Woods negotiations little was left of Keynes's proposal. Nevertheless, he sternly defended the project[20] right up until the inaugural meeting of the IMF and the World Bank in Savannah in March 1946. It is rather surprising, therefore, that in his last published paper Keynes (1946) revindicates some fundamental hypotheses of the classical theory, which he mostly helped to explode. The article was sent to the *Economic Journal* in January 1946 but did not appear until after Keynes's death because he had asked the editor, Roy Harrod, to wait until the American loan to Britain had passed Congress (Keynes 1980c, 427; Moggridge 1986, 56; Moggridge 1992, 822).[21] Despite a dry aspect due to a detailed analysis of several statistical tables, the paper, as is shown by its original title ("Will the Dollar Be Scarce?") addresses an important issue at the center of the postwar debate.

The body of statistics is deployed to disprove some commonplaces about the U.S. balance of payments, namely, a substantial surplus on

19. The same point is made in a short note (Keynes 1944) commenting on an article by Frank Graham.

20. In the House of Lords debate on the document to be discussed at Bretton Woods—the *Joint Statement by Experts on the Establishment of an International Monetary Fund* (21 April 1944)—Keynes (1980b, 18–19) restates in simple words the essence of his thought: "The plan not merely confirms the de-thronement [of gold] but approves it by expressly providing that it is the duty of the Fund to alter the gold value of any currency if it is shown that this will be serviceable to equilibrium.

"In fact, the plan introduces in this respect an epoch-making innovation in an international instrument, the object of which is to lay down sound and orthodox principles. For instead of maintaining the principle that the internal value of a national currency should conform to a prescribed *de jure* external value, it provides that its external value should be altered if necessary so as to conform to whatever *de facto* internal value results from domestic policies, which themselves shall be immune from criticism by the Fund. Indeed, it is made the duty of the Fund to approve changes which will have this effect. That is why I say that these proposals are the exact opposite of the gold standard. They lay down by international agreement the essence of the new doctrine, far removed from the old orthodoxy."

21. After the present essay had been accepted for publication, Donald Moggridge (2001) made an interesting reconstruction of the vicissitudes of the publishing history of Keynes's last article.

current account, a fall of imports relative to exports during depressions, and, particularly, the net creditor position of the United States at the end of the war. The first two points, Keynes argues, reflect the evidence of 1938 only, and the third depends on the large U.S. gold reserves. In fact, abstracting from gold holdings, the United States was a debtor country at the end of 1945 (Keynes 1946, 174–78). With regard to future prospects, a trade surplus of 2–3 billion dollars may be offset by an increasing deficit on invisibles due to tourist expenditures not fully compensated by interest on loans. Summing up the huge mass of statistical information, Keynes seriously questions the hypothesis that the dollar will be scarce in five to ten years' time, a view "widely held . . . on the basis . . . of mere impression" (185). His doubts about the emergence of dollar scarcity had already been raised in a letter commenting on Jacob Viner's 1943 article on the British and American reform plans (Keynes 1980a, 324–25) and were shared by Viner himself (Keynes 1980a, 329), who reaffirms this position in a subsequent paper (Viner [1944] 1951, 240 n. 6). The importance of Keynes's correspondence with Viner, however, goes far beyond this specific point in that Viner poses the key question of distinguishing the short-run problems of the postwar period from those of the long-run more stable future (Keynes 1980a, 330–31), a distinction that looms large in Keynes's last writings.

The consensus view that a dollar shortage would arise after the war was an instance of the general skepticism about the efficacy of market forces in solving disequilibrium problems.[22] A large, persistent, U.S. balance-of-payments surplus was deemed impervious to adjustment. On the one hand, the classical model was rejected especially because the central bank sterilizes gold flows in order to avoid major output and price variations. On the other hand, the Keynesian model certainly does not lead to a complete balancing of a current account surplus if the increase in income is not accompanied by an increase in investment (Metzler 1948, sec. 2). Against the mainstream, however, Keynes (1946, 185) discards the possibility of a dollar shortage not simply on the basis of

22. Asking whether there was a unifying principle linking the new theories of international trade, Metzler (1948, 253) remarks: "The connecting idea, however, is essentially negative. Historically, the interwar period will probably be remembered as a period of retreat from the price system, when all sorts of temporary or provisional measures were adopted to regulate economic activity. The market mechanism had broken down and no one seemed to know quite why or just what to do about it. This was perhaps even more true of the international mechanism than of domestic markets, and to a very great extent the theoretical developments reflected the empirical."

statistical evidence but on theoretical grounds emphasizing the equilibrium hypothesis, the foundation of classical economics:

> In the long run more fundamental forces may be at work, if all goes well, tending towards equilibrium, the significance of which may ultimately transcend ephemeral statistics. I find myself moved, not for the first time, to remind contemporary economists that the classical teaching embodied some permanent truths of great significance, which we are liable to-day to overlook because we associate them with other doctrines which we cannot now accept without much qualification. There are in these matters deep undercurrents at work, natural forces, one can call them, or even the invisible hand, which are operating towards equilibrium. If it were not so, we could not have got on even so well as we have for many decades past.

The solution of the dollar shortage, therefore, is given by the classical adjustment mechanism operating through a change in the price level. The United States was, in fact, "becoming a high-living, high-cost country beyond any previous experience" (1946, 185), and this phenomenon, unless offset by import tariffs and export subsidies, would lead to external equilibrium. In fact, for the classical adjustment mechanism to be effective, there must be no obstacles to trade. The free-trade objective, which can be traced back to the Atlantic Charter of 1941, figured prominently in postwar commercial policy and was especially pursued by the United States. However, since the effects of the classical recipe are felt only in the long run, other measures must be implemented for immediate relief. Yet such measures do not provide a true solution, which only the classical adjustment process can deliver.

> I must not be misunderstood. I do not suppose that the classical medicine will work by itself or that we can depend on it. We need quicker and less painful aids of which exchange variation and overall import control are the most important. But in the long run these expedients will work better and we shall need them less, if the classical medicine is also at work. And if we reject the medicine from our systems altogether, we may just drift on from expedient to expedient and never get really fit again. (Keynes 1946, 186)

The explicit reference to Adam Smith's invisible hand and the stern defense of the classical equilibrium model by the economist who most contributed to its demise may well be surprising. Yet a comprehensive assessment of Keynes's thought clears this seeming contrast up. In the *General Theory* classical economics, far from being rejected altogether, retains its validity in accounting for optimal resource allocation for a given level of output.[23] It is the determination of the latter that belongs to the realm of a "monetary economy," in which money enters in an essential way through changes in expectations that in turn affect employment (Keynes [1936] 1964, vii). In the discussion of the quantity theory (chapter 21), this two-tier conception is in the forefront. With highly simplified assumptions, increases in the money stock increase employment proportionally as long as the economy is below full employment, while beyond this point the price level rises. However, since this L-shaped aggregate supply curve is unlikely to obtain when those simplifying assumptions are removed,[24] prices will begin to rise before full employment is attained. Leaving aside a detailed examination of the many channels leading to this result, the important point is that Keynes's analysis accords with and extends a basic proposition of classical monetary theory, namely, the short-run nonneutrality of changes in the money stock. Of course Keynes's analysis, besides being more sophisticated given his study of the interactions between the many complicating factors (see footnote 24 of the present essay), stems from the model of the *General Theory*. Hence, some of the channels of the monetary transmission mechanism are peculiar to this theoretical framework; the mechanism works through the interest rate, whose influence on effective demand is determined by liquidity preference, or through the marginal efficiency of capital and the investment multiplier ([1936] 1964, 298). But other

23. "Our criticism of the accepted classical theory of economics has consisted not so much in finding logical flaws in its analysis as in pointing out that its tacit assumptions are seldom or never satisfied, with the result that it cannot solve the economic problems of the actual world. But if our central controls succeed in establishing an aggregate volume of output corresponding to full employment as nearly as is practicable, the classical theory comes into its own again from this point onwards. If we suppose the volume of output to be given, *i.e.* to be determined by forces outside the classical scheme of thought, then there is no objection to be raised against the classical analysis of the manner in which private self-interest will determine what in particular is produced, in what proportions the factors of production will be combined to produce it, and how the value of the final product will be distributed between them" ([1936] 1964, 378–79).

24. The complications considered by Keynes ([1936] 1964, 296) include the following: (1) effective demand does not change in proportion to the quantity of money; (2) diminishing returns occur because resources are not homogeneous; (3) conditions of inelastic supply are reached even in the presence of unemployed resources since the latter are not interchangeable; (4) the wage-unit tends to rise before full employment is attained; and (5) factor remunerations do not all change in the same proportion.

channels relating to the availability of unemployed resources and to wage changes (items 3 and 4 in footnote 24) had been developed along the same lines by the classicals, particularly by Hume in his celebrated essay "On Money" ([1752] 1970, 37–40).[25] Although some of Keynes's arguments are cast in terms of Marshallian microeconomics, the essential emphasis on the different timing of the effectiveness of money stock variations—that is, the immediate impact of those variations on employment and output in contrast with the sluggish response of wages and prices—is a basic feature common to Keynesian and classical theory:

> It is probable that the general level of prices will not rise very much as output increases, so long as there are available efficient unemployed resources of every type. But as soon as output has increased sufficiently to begin to reach the "bottle-necks," there is likely to be a sharp rise in the prices of certain commodities. . . . However, . . . the elasticity of supply partly depends on the elapse of time. If we assume a sufficient interval for the quantity of equipment itself to change, the elasticities of supply will be decidedly greater eventually. Thus a moderate change in effective demand, coming on a situation where there is widespread unemployment, may spend itself very little in raising prices and mainly in increasing employment; whilst a larger change, which, being unforeseen, causes some temporary "bottle-necks" to be reached, will spend itself in raising prices, as distinct from employment, to a greater extent at first than subsequently. . . . In addition to the final critical point of full employment at which money-wages have to rise, in response to an increasing effective demand in terms of money, fully in proportion to the rise in the prices of wage-goods, we have a succession of earlier semi-critical points at which an increasing effective demand tends to raise money-wages though not fully in

25. In the chapter on mercantilism, Keynes quotes a passage from that essay but considerably plays down Hume's contribution. After crediting Locke with having been "the parent of twin quantity theories," identifying the influence of money on both the interest rate and the price level and thus "standing with one foot in the mercantilist world and with one foot in the classical world" ([1936] 1964, 343), Keynes goes on: "Hume a little later had a foot and a half in the classical world. For Hume began the practice amongst economists of stressing the importance of the equilibrium position as compared with the ever-shifting transition towards it, though he was still enough of a mercantilist not to overlook the fact that it is in the transition that we actually have our being" (343 n. 3). The failure to duly recognize Hume's contribution is related to the fact that, in the *General Theory*, Keynes characterizes classical economics as a full employment model, almost creating a straw man in order to enhance the contrast with his own model.

> proportion to the rise in the price of wage-goods; and similarly in the case of a decreasing effective demand. ([1936] 1964, 300–301)

Hence, Keynes reaches, although partly through different channels, results quite similar to those of classical monetary theory with regard to the short-run effectiveness of monetary impulses. And like the classical economists, he maintains the hypothesis of a long-run relationship between money and prices. Although grounding it in liquidity preference, he argues for a stable equilibrium level of the Cambridge *k*, which provides the foundation of the money-price relationship. The latter, however, is asymmetric in that, due to frictions in the transmission mechanism, a prolonged decrease in the quantity of money affects not only prices but also output and employment. Hence, in the course of history, lengthy deflationary trends gave rise to changes in the monetary standard, which explains the secular rise in the price level ([1936] 1964, 306–7).

Going back to Keynes's last article, then, its message concerns the distinction between short- and long-run equilibrium and the implications of the distinction for economic policy effectiveness. While measures such as import controls have immediate effects and may be appropriate in the short term, it is illusory to use them to redress long-run disequilibrium. The currency and commercial policy proposals suitably combine both types of policy:

> The great virtue of the Bretton Woods and Washington proposals, taken in conjunction, is that they marry the use of the necessary expedients to the wholesome long-run doctrine. It is for this reason that, speaking in the House of Lords, I claimed that "Here is an attempt to use what we have learnt from modern experience and modern analysis, not to defeat, but to implement the wisdom of Adam Smith." (1946, 186)

In the article's conclusion, however, Keynes is cautious about the success of the new monetary order, given the uncertainties and glaring inconsistencies of the modern economy.[26] And in his speech at the inaugural meeting in Savannah of the Fund, he hinted at possible obstacles

26. "No one can be certain of anything in this age of flux and change. Decaying standards of life at a time when our command over the production of material satisfactions is the greatest ever, and a diminishing scope for individual decision and choice at a time when more than before we should be able to afford these satisfactions, are sufficient to indicate an underlying contradiction in every department of our economy. No plans will work for certain in such an epoch. But if they palpably fail, then, of course, we and everyone else will try something different" (1946, 186).

stemming from the influence of political factors in managing the newborn institutions (1980b, 216). More generally, Keynes is aware of the highly innovative and yet difficult task of the Bretton Woods system—"attempting a great step forward towards the goal of international economic order amidst national diversities of policies" (1979, 621)—and is keen to make clear the conditions for its viability. From this standpoint, the firm revindication of classical monetary theory in his last article is readily accounted for. While providing the solution to the dollar shortage, the essay defines the limits of policy effectiveness and brings Keynes's unremitting quest for an active economic policy, the guiding principle of his research program, into clearer focus.[27] The *General Theory*, in fact, uses a short-run model ([1936] 1964, 306). As such it cannot be resorted to in approaching long-term equilibrium problems that are amenable to classical economics. The international adjustment mechanism is a prime example. Having always supported fixed exchange rates (see footnote 2), he finds the solution in Hume's price-specie-flow mechanism, the *locus classicus* of international adjustment. Keynes's last published paper, therefore, reestablishes the relevance and the validity of classical monetary theory grounded on the equilibrium hypothesis, showing his wide-ranging view of economic theory. His followers, however, have dwelled above all on the *General Theory*, thus considering only part of his thought, narrowing the scope of his contributions and distorting his analytical message.

3. Conclusion

It is a commonplace to portray Keynes's work as a break in the evolution of economic analysis, the claim being that it introduced an original paradigm that was an alternative to classical economics. Even taking due

27. In the House of Lords debate on the joint statement (see footnote 20), Keynes (1980b, 16) summarizes his viewpoint on monetary reform: "Three [conclusions], in particular, are highly relevant to this discussion. We are determined that, in future, the external value of sterling shall conform to its internal value as set by our own domestic policies, and not the other way round. Secondly, we intend to retain control of our domestic rate of interest, so that we can keep it as low as suits our own purposes, without interference from the ebb and flow of international capital movements or flights of hot money. Thirdly, whilst we intend to prevent inflation at home, we will not accept deflation at the dictate of influences from outside. In other words, we abjure the instruments of Bank rate and credit contraction operating through the increase of unemployment as a means of forcing our domestic economy into line with external factors. . . . To establish those three principles which I have just stated has been my main task for the last twenty years."

account of Laidler's important qualifications (1999), the *General Theory*, underscoring fluctuations in investment and the role of uncertainty in defining the essential properties of a monetary economy, provides a model of effective demand in which the economy does not necessarily settle at a full-employment equilibrium. Making a compelling case for active economic policy, this model helps to fulfill the lifelong research program on monetary reform that would culminate in the Keynes Plan. The central idea is to design monetary arrangements that, instead of fettering the policymaker's action as under the gold standard, allow sufficient leeway to attain welfare targets. However, in his last article, on the dollar shortage, Keynes forcefully revindicates the classical theory of money, showing its relevance to long-run adjustment problems.

Far from being inconsistent with the *General Theory*, Keynes's final paper clarifies the limits of applicability of the economic model in the *General Theory* to the short run. The *General Theory*, in fact, does not reject classical economics outright. Rather it seeks to explain, for a given level of output, resource allocation and the long-run relationship between money and prices. So to dispose of the threatened dollar scarcity, Keynes emphasizes the soundness of the equilibrium hypothesis underlying the classical adjustment mechanism. His last article thus shows the comprehensive, balanced character of his overall contributions, in which the classical theory retains a not inconspicuous role. The economics of Keynes is removed from Keynesian economics as developed by his epigones, whose neglect of the long-run dimension of economic policy opened a crack in the Keynesian edifice, weakening its theoretical structure and eventually leading to its demise.

References

Cassel, Gustav. 1932. *The Crisis in the World's Monetary System*. Oxford: Clarendon Press.

Clarke, Stephen V. O. 1973. *The Reconstruction of the International Monetary System: The Attempts of 1922 and 1933*. Princeton Studies in International Finance, no. 33. Princeton, N.J.: Princeton University.

Cunliffe Committee on Currency and Foreign Exchanges after the War. [1918] 1985. *First Interim Report*. In *The Gold Standard in Theory and History*, edited by Barry Eichengreen. New York: Methuen.

De Vegh, I. 1943. The International Clearing Union. *American Economic Review* 33 (September): 534–56.

Eichengreen, Barry. 1996. *Globalizing Capital: A History of the International Monetary System*. Princeton, N.J.: Princeton University Press.

Fisher, Irving. 1913. A Compensated Dollar. *Quarterly Journal of Economics* 27 (February): 213–35.

———. [1935] 1945. *100% Money*. New Haven, Conn.: City Printing Company.

Friedman, Milton. 1997. John Maynard Keynes. Federal Reserve Bank of Richmond *Economic Quarterly* 83 (spring): 2–23.

Graham, Benjamin. 1943. The Critique of Commodity-Reserve Currency: A Point-by-Point Reply. *Journal of Political Economy* 51 (February): 66–69.

Haberler, Gottfried. 1948. Dollar Shortage? In *Foreign Economic Policy for the United States*, edited by Seymour E. Harris. Cambridge: Harvard University Press.

Hawtrey, Ralph G. 1919. The Gold Standard. *Economic Journal* 29 (December): 428–42.

———. 1929. Money. In vol. 15 of *The Encyclopaedia Britannica*. 14th ed. New York: Encyclopaedia Britannica.

———. [1932] 1970. *The Art of Central Banking*. London: Frank Cass.

Hayek, Friedrich A. 1943. A Commodity Reserve Currency. *Economic Journal* 53 (June–September): 176–84.

———. [1932] 1984. The Fate of the Gold Standard. In *Money, Capital, and Fluctuations: Early Essays*, edited by Roy McCloughry. London: Routledge & Kegan Paul.

Horsefield, J. Keith. 1969. *The International Monetary Fund 1945–1965: Twenty Years of International Monetary Cooperation*. Vol. 3, *Documents*. Washington, D.C.: International Monetary Fund.

Howson, Susan, and Donald Winch. 1977. *The Economic Advisory Council: 1930–1939*. Cambridge: Cambridge University Press.

Hume, David. [1752] 1970. Of Money. In *David Hume: Writings on Economics*, edited by Eugene Rotwein. Madison: University of Wisconsin Press.

Johnson, Harry G. 1971. The Keynesian Revolution and the Monetarist Counter-Revolution. *American Economic Review* 61 (May): 1–14.

Keynes, John M. 1911. Review of Irving Fisher, *The Purchasing Power of Money*. *Economic Journal* 21 (September): 393–98.

———. 1923. *A Tract on Monetary Reform*. London: Macmillan.

———. 1930. *A Treatise on Money*. 2 vols. London: Macmillan.

———. 1943. The Objective of International Price Stability. *Economic Journal* 53 (June–September): 185–87.

———. 1944 . Keynes vs. Hayek on a Commodity Reserve Currency: Note. *Economic Journal* 54 (December): 429–30.

———. 1946. The Balance of Payments of the United States. *Economic Journal* 56 (June): 172–87.

———. [1936] 1964. *The General Theory of Employment, Interest, and Money*. London: Macmillan.

———. [1913] 1971. *Indian Currency and Finance*. Vol. 1 of *The Collected Writings of John Maynard Keynes*. London: Macmillan.

———. [1925] 1972. *The Economic Consequences of Mr Churchill.* In vol. 9 of *The Collected Writings of John Maynard Keynes*. London: Macmillan.

———. [1933] 1972. *The Means to Prosperity*. In vol. 9 of *The Collected Writings of John Maynard Keynes*. London: Macmillan.

———. [1934] 1973. Poverty in Plenty: Is the Economic System Self-Adjusting? In vol. 13 of *The Collected Writings of John Maynard Keynes*, edited by Donald Moggridge. London: Macmillan.

———. 1979. *Activities 1944–1946: The Transition to Peace*. Vol 24 of *The Collected Writings of John Maynard Keynes*, edited by Donald Moggridge. London: Macmillan.

———. 1980a. *Activities 1940–1944. Shaping the Post-War World: The Clearing Union*. Vol. 25 of *The Collected Writings of John Maynard Keynes*, edited by Donald Moggridge. London: Macmillan.

———. 1980b. *Activities 1941–1946. Shaping the Post-War World: Bretton Woods and Reparations*. Vol. 26 of *The Collected Writings of John Maynard Keynes*, edited by Donald Moggridge. London: Macmillan.

———. 1980c. *Activities 1940–1946. Shaping the Post-War World: Employment and Commodities*. Vol. 27 of *The Collected Writings of John Maynard Keynes*, edited by Donald Moggridge. London: Macmillan.

———. [1931] 1982. Notes on the Currency Question. In vol. 21 of *The Collected Writings of John Maynard Keynes*, edited by Donald Moggridge. London: Macmillan.

———. [1933] 1982. Letter to *The Economist*, 20 March. In vol. 21 of *The Collected Writings of John Maynard Keynes*, edited by Donald Moggridge. London: Macmillan.

———. [1935] 1982. The Future of the Foreign Exchanges. In vol. 21 of *The Collected Writings of John Maynard Keynes*, edited by Donald Moggridge. London: Macmillan.

———. [1944] 1997. Letter to Irving Fisher, 7 July 1944. In vol. 14 of *The Works of Irving Fisher*. Edited by William J. Barber. London: Pickering & Chatto.

Kuhn, Thomas S. 1970. *The Structure of Scientific Revolutions*. 2d ed. Chicago: University of Chicago Press.

Laidler, David. 1991. *The Golden Age of the Quantity Theory*. New York: Allan.

———. 1999. *Fabricating the Keynesian Revolution*. Cambridge: Cambridge University Press.

Leijonhufvud, Axel. 1968. *On Keynesian Economics and the Economics of Keynes*. London: Oxford University Press.

Lüke, Rolf E. 1985. The Schacht and the Keynes Plans. *Banca Nazionale del Lavoro Quarterly Review*, no. 152, March, 65–76.

Lutz, Friedrich A. 1943. *The Keynes and White Proposals*. In *Essays in International Finance*, no. 1. Princeton, N.J.: Princeton University Press.

McKinnon, Ronald I. 1993. The Rules of the Game: International Money in Historical Perspective. *Journal of Economic Literature* 31 (March): 1–44.

Meltzer, Allan H. 1988. *Keynes's Monetary Theory: A Different Interpretation*. Cambridge: Cambridge University Press.

———. 1989. Keynes on Monetary Reform and International Economic Order. In *Monetary Economics in the 1980s*, edited by Forrest Capie and Geoffrey E. Wood. London: Macmillan.

Metzler, Lloyd A. 1948. The Theory of International Trade. In *A Survey of Contemporary Economics*, edited by Howard S. Ellis. Philadelphia: Blakiston.

Mill, John S. [1848] 1987. *Principles of Political Economy*. Edited by William Ashley. New York: Kelley.

Mlynarsky, Feliks. 1937. Proportionalism and Stabilization Policy. In *The Lessons of Monetary Experience*, edited by Arthur D. Gayer. London: George Allen and Unwin.

Moggridge, Donald E. 1986. Keynes and the International Monetary System 1909–46. In *International Monetary Problems and Supply-Side Economics: Essays in Honour of Lorie Tarshis*, edited by Jon S. Cohen and G. C. Harcourt. London: Macmillan.

———. 1992. *Maynard Keynes: An Economist's Biography*. London: Routledge.

———. 2001. "Maynard would not have wished"? Second-Guessing the Author of "The Balance of Payments of the United States." *HOPE* 33.4:815–24.

Patinkin, Don. 1976. *Keynes's Monetary Thought: A Study of Its Development*. Durham, N.C.: Duke University Press.

Pigou, Arthur C. 1927. *Industrial Fluctuations*. London: Macmillan.

Robertson, Dennis H. 1943. The Post-War Monetary Plans. *Economic Journal* 53 (December): 352–60.

Robinson, Joan. 1943. The International Currency Proposals. *Economic Journal* 53 (June–September): 161–75.

Schumacher, E. F. 1943. The New Currency Plans. *Bulletin of the Oxford Institute of Statistics*, vol. 5, supplement no. 5, pp. 8–29.

Sumner, Scott. 1999. The Role of the Gold Standard in Keynesian Monetary Theory. *Economic Inquiry* 37 (July): 527–40.

Viner, Jacob. [1943] 1951. Two Plans for International Monetary Stabilization. In *International Economics*. Glencoe, Ill.: Free Press.

———. [1944] 1951. The Bretton Woods Agreements. In *International Economics*. Glencoe, Ill.: Free Press.

Wicksell, Knut. [1906] 1946. *Lectures on Political Economy*. London: Routledge.

———. [1898] 1965. *Interest and Prices*. New York: Kelley.

Williams, John H. 1937. International Monetary Organization and Policy. In *The Lessons of Monetary Experience*, edited by Arthur D. Gayer. London: George Allen and Unwin.

Williamson, John. 1983. Keynes and the International Economic Order. In *Keynes and the Modern World*, edited by David Worswick and James Trevithick. Cambridge: Cambridge University Press.

Part 2

Expectations and Monetary Policy

[7]

The Rational Expectations Hypothesis in Retrospect

By FILIPPO CESARANO*

The rational expectations hypothesis is at the center of current debates in economic theory. The importance of this theoretical innovation has stimulated a number of studies, including analyses in the unfashionable field of the history of thought, the 1979 article by Brian Kantor being a first example. Historical investigations on the subject of rational expectations are of interest since it is held that this theory has revived the teachings of the classics, inasmuch as it provides the cornerstone of the recently developed approach known as "new classical macroeconomics." The present note examines some specific aspects, as yet not emphasized in the literature, concerning the relationship between rational expectations and classical monetary theory. In particular, the following results will be shown: the fundamental implication of the rational expectations hypothesis, that is, that only unexpected changes in the money stock influence the real sector of the economy, is a basic tenet of classical monetary theory as well and is founded upon the very argument according to which agents efficiently use the available information in order to take account of the consequences of policy measures (Section I). This common analytical framework notwithstanding, classical analysis of the role to be assigned to the monetary authority reflects a different appraisal of the dimension of the information set (Section II).

I

Classical economists have discussed at length the effects of both unexpected and expected changes in the money stock, but have paid far greater attention to the former. In the monetary system of the time, that is, a metallic standard, variations in money supply essentially originated from the balance of trade and from the discovery of new mines. Thus, given the lack of regularly collected statistics, the classics normally assumed such variations to be unexpected.[1] Debasement of the currency by the prince, the other possible source of variation in the nominal money stock, represented, under certain conditions, the case of expected change in money, but was regarded more as an exceptional measure than an ordinary course of action.

Classical economists viewed the transmission mechanism of unexpected monetary impulses as a sequential process determined by the gradual propagation of the increase in money in the economy. It takes time for this sequential process to be completed and, in the transition, real income and employment are affected before the price level adjusts. The *locus classicus* of this mechanism is a

*Banca d'Italia. A first draft of this paper was written while I was a visiting scholar at Harvard University. Helpful comments from Benjamin Friedman, David Laidler, and the referee are gratefully acknowledged. The usual disclaimer applies.

[1] In his thorough examination of the subject, Richard Cantillon notes: "It is also usually the case that the increase or decrease of actual money in a State is not perceived because it flows abroad, or is brought into the State, by such imperceptible means and proportions that it is impossible to know exactly the quantity which enters or leaves the State" (1755, p. 163). The assumption was also discussed in hypothetical terms. This clearly appears in the following passage in which John Locke describes the effects of a reduction in the quantity of money, focusing on the notion of an equilibrium amount of cash balances:

> "If one-third of the money employed in trade were locked up, or gone out of England, must not the landholders necessarily receive one-third less for their goods, and consequently rents fall; a less quantity of money by one-third being to be distributed amongst an equal number of receivers? Indeed, *people not perceiving the money to be gone*, are apt to be jealous one of another; and each suspecting another's inequality of gain to rob him of his share, every one will be employing his skill and power the best he can to retrieve it again, and to bring money into his pocket in the same plenty as formerly." [1691, pp. 70–71, emphasis added]

The distinction should be made between *unexpected* and *unperceived* changes in the money stock, Such a distinction, however, does not significantly bear upon the main arguments of the present paper.

celebrated passage by David Hume,[2] who clearly identifies the basic argument accounting for the short-run effectiveness of monetary impulses. Through the several stages of the transmission mechanism, agents have no information about the change in the money stock and, thus, do not modify their behavior accordingly. Hume states:

> When any quantity of money is imported into a nation, it is not at first dispersed into many hands, but is confined to the coffers of a few persons, who immediately seek to employ it to advantage.... They are thereby enabled to employ more workmen than formerly, *who never dream of demanding higher wages*, but are glad of employment from such good paymasters.... It is easy to trace the money in its progress through the whole commonwealth; where we shall find, that it must first quicken the diligence of every individual, before it encrease the price of labour.
> [1752, p. 38, emphasis added]

It should be stressed that, in analyzing the efficacy of changes in money, classic authors did not refer to peculiar assumptions relating to institutional features, such as rigid prices or long-term contracts. They focused, instead, upon the lack of information during the time necessary for the mechanics of the increase in money to work its effects through the economy.[3] Indeed, the world of the classics is one of flexible wages and prices where long-term contracts do play a role but account only for the redistributive effects of inflation (for example, see Cantillon, 1755, pp. 163–65). Thus, it is not price or wage rigidity that distinguishes classic writers from rational expectations theorists on this specific point, but the particular element which is missing in the information set: the former consider the unavailability of information on the change in the money stock, which does not allow individuals to shift their behavior functions; the latter look at the lack of data on the current price level, which does not enable private agents to assess the relative prices of their outputs.[4]

A rudimentary version of the second hypothesis can nevertheless be found in Ferdinando Galiani's analysis of the effects of an "augmentation," that is, a once-and-for-all increase in the nominal quantity of money implemented through currency debasement. He puts forward a theory of the agents' "connection of ideas about the prices of commodities and money," according to which individuals conceive their "ideas" about prices from "truth," that is, from the

[2] "...[W]e must consider, that though the high price of commodities be a necessary consequence of the encrease of gold and silver, yet it follows not immediately upon that encrease; but some time is required before the money circulates through the whole state, and makes its effect be felt on all ranks of people. At first, no alteration is perceived; by degrees the price rises, first of one commodity, then of another; till the whole at last reaches a just proportion with the new quantity of specie which is in the kingdom. In my opinion, it is only in this interval or intermediate situation, between the acquisition of money and rise of prices, that the encreasing quantity of gold and silver is favourable to industry." [1752, pp. 37–38]

[3] Cantillon notes: "I have already remarked that an acceleration or greater rapidity in circulation of money in exchange, is equivalent to an increase of actual money up to a point.... On the other hand money flows in detail through so many channels that it seems impossible not to lose sight of it seeing that having been amassed to make large sums it is distributed in the little rills of exchange, and then gradually accumulated again to make large payments." [1755, pp. 161–63]

The discussion of the transmission mechanism by Cantillon (pp. 159–99) is far more detailed and, it should be stressed, predates Hume's *Discourses* since the *Essai* was actually written sometime in the 1720's or early 1730's. In particular, Cantillon attempts to show that: (*i*) the effectiveness of variations in money supply depends on the channel through which money is injected (this has been called the "Cantillon Effect" by Mark Blaug, 1978, p. 22); (*ii*) the price level does not necessarily change in proportion to the variation in the money stock; (*iii*) the structure of relative prices is also affected.

[4] Therefore, it does not seem entirely correct to contrast the rational expectations theorists' "information lag hypothesis," which assumes flexible wages and prices, with the classics' "adjustment lag hypothesis" related "at least partially to the existence of long-term contracts" (Charles Nelson, 1981, pp. 1–2). A not-inconspicuous consequence of these interpretation failures is to attribute a Keynesian character to the work of Milton Friedman and of the St. Louis economists on the grounds that both postulate a slowly adjusting price level in the transmission mechanism (see Nelson, pp. 3–4).

true state of things; and, to those "ideas," they pair the "sound of names," that is, actual or called prices. (See Galiani, 1751, pp. 68–72.) Augmentation does not affect the true state of things but only actual prices. The latter, however, do not change immediately since agents take some time to get accustomed to higher prices. It is this delayed response which allows the monetary authority to gain from an inflationary measure. Galiani states:

> Augmentation of money is a profit that the prince and the state make from the slowness with which the multitude changes the connection of ideas about the prices of goods and money.... It [augmentation] does not produce any change in things, but in names; thus in order for the prices of things to remain the same, they have also to change with regard to their names. If this happened on the same day in which the augmentation was carried out and happened entirely, and entirely in proportion, then the augmentation would have no consequences; just as a law which established that money, instead of being called by Italian names, should be called by Latin or Greek or Hebrew names would have no consequences.
> [pp. 68–70]

It could be pointed out that, essential to the theory of rational expectations, is the inclusion in the agents' information set of the "true" model of the economy. This is, without doubt, a novel assumption in the modelling of individual behavior that has not been set forth in earlier writings. In the historical reconstruction of economics, however, what is to be investigated are not precise and formal descriptions of a theory—since this would be a preposterous task—but rather the essential concepts underlying them. It can be shown that the classics commonly adopted the assumption, albeit failing to state it explicitly, according to which agents correctly anticipate the implications of announced decisions by the monetary authority with the help of the relevant theoretical framework. In fact, this is a necessary condition for those correct implications to be derived: this obtains only if agents do make use of a theory which links together the available data. The remainder of this section provides evidence for the latter proposition.

As explained earlier, the classics gave less weight to discussions of expected variations in the quantity of money. Nevertheless, in those cases in which a change in money supply was deliberately engineered by the prince,[5] and publicly announced, classic authors emphasize the consequent shift in the agents' behavior, thereby accounting for the inefficacy of such policies. Cantillon (1755, p. 289 ff.) refers to the deflationary measure implemented by the king of France in 1714 when, by decree, the nominal value of the *écu* was decreased from 5 to 4 *livres*, 1 percent per month for a twenty-month period. He describes in detail the implications of this measure and, notwithstanding the inconsistency of some of the arguments, shows that the agents responded to an announced policy as if they understood the correct model. Hence, their behavior is not policy invariant.[6]

Hume was also aware of the inefficacy of expected monetary impulses. Therefore, while proposing an inflationary measure, he pur-

[5]An increase in the money stock could be implemented in three ways: by decree, giving a new face value to the coins without altering their metallic content; by melting and coining again the money stock, but lowering the titer of each coin; by cutting a hole in the middle of the coins.

[6]Cantillon states:

> "Enlightened people in France hoard their money in these times. The King finds means to borrow much money on which he willingly loses the diminution, proposing to compensate himself by an augmentation at the end of the diminution. With this object after several diminutions they begin to hoard money in the King's Treasury, to postpone the payments, pensions, and army pay. In these circumstances money becomes extremely rare at the end of the diminutions both by reason of the sums hoarded by the King and various individuals and by reason of the nominal value of the coin, which value is diminished." [1755, pp. 289–91].

While explaining the failure of the king of France to gain from the augmentation of 1726, Cantillon again establishes that individuals react differently to unexpected policies: "The diminutions which had preceded this augmentation were made suddenly without warning, which prevented the ordinary operations of diminutions" (p. 295).

posely wished it to be a "surprise."[7] Finally, Galiani's analysis stems from his theory of the "connection of ideas about the prices of commodities and money." Once the information on the monetary shock is available, individuals promptly revise their "ideas" on prices and the latter increase without lags: the inflationary policy becomes ineffective.[8]

II

In Section I, it was shown that the proposition concerning the efficacy of unexpected monetary impulses, advanced by the classics, is founded upon the very principle of rational behavior on the part of agents, characteristic of modern monetary theory. It may be natural, then, to ask which implications for the conduct of the monetary authority were derived from this common analytical groundwork.

In a commodity standard, the scope for the authority's action is constrained by the very rules of the monetary system. Hence, with regard to the works of the classics, it is not appropriate to refer to "monetary policy" as in relation to modern writings, since the role of the authority in the respective institutional frameworks, a commodity standard on the one side and a fiat-money system on the other, can hardly be compared. Indeed, the classics could not have arrived at a full-fledged conception of policy design, linking instruments to targets, since the prerequisites for such a conception were missing. This impossibility of comparison notwithstanding, it is of interest to inquire about the classics' analyses of the authority's role inasmuch as this can be suggestive of a better understanding of the relationship between classical and contemporary monetary theory.

Currency debasement was within the prince's range of power, but was commonly regarded as an interference with the smooth working of a commodity standard. Even those few authors who spoke favorably of debasement were careful to qualify their position. Galiani, for example, does not regard "augmentation" of money as an ordinary measure to be resorted to in normal times, but as an exceptional one to be taken only in emergencies. The monetary authority should evaluate the benefits and costs of such a measure and implement it whenever the net effect is positive (1751, p. 68). This is likely to be the case when the prince faces a critical situation and cannot raise taxes or issue securities or sell his own property. In these circumstances, augmentation is the right course of action since its effects will be slow and will be spread over the entire population (see Galiani, pp. 87–117).

The negative attitude of the classics towards debasement was related not only to the view of debasement as a disruption of the monetary arrangements, but also to its characteristic of being often a once-and-for-all change as well as an expected change in the money stock. On the contrary, variations in the quantity of money inherent in the functioning of a metallic standard (for example, those originating from the balance of trade and from the discovery of new mines) were both continuous and unexpected and, thus, were thought to influence real variables for a not ephemeral period. Cantillon, aware of the effects on output stemming from balance of trade adjustment, does advocate a norm of conduct designed to control the quantity of money in order to prevent economic fluctuations:

> When a State has arrived at the highest point of wealth (I assume always that the comparative wealth of States consists principally in the respective quantities of money which they possess) it will inevitably fall into poverty by the ordinary course of things. The too great abundance of money, which so long as it lasts forms the power of States, throws them back imperceptibly but

[7] "In executing such a project [taking from every shilling a penny's worth of silver], it would be better to make the new shilling pass for 24 halfpence, *in order to preserve the illusion, and make it be taken for the same*" (1752, p. 39, emphasis added).

[8] Galiani states:

> "If he [the prince] abused it [augmentation], the connection collapses, names change their significance, things remain the same and the unsurpassable force of nature wins.... Finally, a prince who, abusing augmentation, practised it every month, destroying every connection of ideas between prices and commodities, would render it quite useless and inefficacious; and only with other policies would obtain what today is obtained with augmentation." [1751, pp. 70–71]

> naturally into poverty. Thus it would seem that *when a State expands by trade and the abundance of money raises the price of Land and Labour, the Prince or the Legislator ought to withdraw money from circulation, keep it for emergencies, and try to retard its circulation by every means except compulsion and bad faith, so as to forestall the too great dearness of its articles and prevent the drawbacks of luxury.*
> [1755, p. 185, emphasis added]

In the subsequent statement, however, Cantillon recognizes the difficulties of implementing such a stabilizing action: "...it is not easy to discover the time opportune for this, nor to know when money has become more abundant than it ought to be for the good and preservation of the advantages of the State" (p. 185).

In an earlier passage, he also points out the scanty knowledge about the properties of the transmission mechanism:

> The proportion of the dearness which the increased quantity of money brings about in the State will depend on the turn which this money will impart to consumption and circulation. Through whatever hands the money which is introduced may pass it will naturally increase the consumption; but this consumption will be more or less great according to circumstances. It will be directed more or less to certain kinds of products or merchandise according to the idea of those who acquire the money....I conceive that when a large surplus of money is brought into a State the new money gives a new turn to consumption and even a new speed to circulation. But it is not possible to say exactly to what extent.[pp. 179–81]

Cantillon's recommendation for controlling the time path of the money stock parallels, keeping in mind the caveat stated at the beginning of this section, the policy rule called for by both Friedman and rational expectations theorists. This very rule of conduct, however, is founded upon quite distinct arguments. According to Milton Friedman, a discretionary monetary policy is likely to increase rather than decrease instability, because of the insufficient knowledge of the transmission mechanism, together with the presence of long and variable lags. According to rational expectations theorists, instead, private agents, and a fortiori the monetary authority, have complete knowledge of the "true" model of the economy; a discretionary policy will increase the variance of output because, by conveying wrong signals to agents, it blurs the assessment of relative prices. Hence, there seems to be a clear-cut divergence between the rational expectations theorists' and Friedman's standpoint concerning the dimension of the information set. All in all, it is Friedman's work which appears to be closer to the classical tradition.[9]

Following the message of this short note, much care should be taken in representing the rational expectations literature as a punctilious continuation of the teachings of classical monetary theory. There are, in fact, some conspicuous asymmetries and their study may well provide stimulating ideas for the further advancement of monetary economics.[10]

[9] See especially where Friedman states: "As I see it, we have advanced beyond Hume in two respects only: first, we now have a more secure grasp on the quantitative magnitudes involved; second, we have gone one derivative beyond Hume" (p. 177).

[10] The role the history of economic analysis can play in furthering current research is thoroughly investigated in my 1983 article.

REFERENCES

Blaug, Mark, *Economic Theory in Retrospect*, New York: Cambridge University Press, 1978.

Cantillon, Richard, *Essai sur la Nature du Commerce en Général*, London, 1755 (Henry Higgs, ed., London: Macmillan, 1931).

Cesarano, Filippo, "On the Role of the History of Economic Analysis," *History of Political Economy*, Spring 1983, *15*.

Friedman, Milton, "25 Years After the Rediscovery of Money: What Have We Learned? Discussion," *American Economic Review*

Proceedings, May 1975, *65*, 176–79.

Galiani, Ferdinando, *Della Moneta*, Naples, 1751; reprinted in Pietro Custodi, ed., *Scrittori Classici Italiani di Economia Politica*, Vol. IV, Milan: Destefanis, 1803.

Hume, David, "Of Money," in *Political Discourses*, Edinburgh, 1752; reprinted in Eugene Rotwein, ed., *Writings on Economics*, Toronto: Nelson, 1955.

Kantor, Brian, "Rational Expectations and Economic Thought," *Journal of Economic Literature*, December 1979, *17*, 1422–41.

Locke, John, *Some Considerations of the Consequences of Lowering the Interest and Raising the Value of Money*, 1691; reprinted in *Works*, Vol. V, London, 1823.

Nelson, Charles R., "Adjustment Lags Versus Information Lags," *Journal of Money, Credit, and Banking*, February 1981, *13*, 1–11.

The Manchester School Vol 66 No. 4 September 1998
0025–2034 439–452

[8]

EXPECTATIONS AND MONETARY POLICY: A HISTORICAL PERSPECTIVE*

by

FILIPPO CESARANO†

Banca d'Italia

Classical economists developed a surprisingly sophisticated analysis of money supply variations that, anticipating the main features of contemporary theory, emphasizes the role of information in the transmission mechanism. Drawing on the classical contributions, this paper outlines a general approach to monetary policy, treating information as a scarce commodity allocated optimally by rational agents.

1 Introduction

The subject of monetary policy remains controversial. At least since the currency–banking school debate throughout the monetarist–Keynesian strife, opposite views of the effectiveness of money supply changes have contested the field.[1] At the root of these disputes, there are distinct conceptions of a monetary economy and of the model that links money to output and the price level. In the last decades, the introduction of the rational expectations hypothesis and the application of game theory have made the pendulum swing further towards the classical approach, eventually leading to a regrouping of rival currents of thought. The New Keynesians, through the search for the theoretical underpinnings of price and wage rigidity and the related short-run effectiveness of monetary impulses, are now much closer to the monetarist position of the 1960s (Tobin, 1980, pp. 21–22; Mankiw, 1992), so that both together contrast with the New Classicals.

* Manuscript received 19.2.96; final version received 21.2.97.

† Thanks are due to Robert Clower, Milton Friedman, David Laidler, Bennett McCallum and two referees for their helpful comments. The usual caveat applies.

[1] In the preface of his *Critical Essays*, Hicks notes: 'It is useful to recognize that pre-Keynesian economics was not monolithic, in order to understand how it is that in our day monetary economics is not monolithic either. Some of our present differences echo much older differences. There is one in particular, that came to the surface in the Currency School–Banking School controversy of the eighteen-forties (but is older than that), and which persists to this day. We still have a Currency School, seeking in vain—but one sees why—for a monetary system that shall be automatic. It is represented, over its long history, not only by Lord Overstone and his friends, but by Ricardo himself; not only by Mises and Hayek and Friedman, but also by Pigou. The Banking School (or Credit School, as I wish they had called it) has a history of almost equal antiquity. It has greater names upon its roll than that of Tooke: Mill and Bagehot among the Victorians; Hawtrey and Robertson, as well as Keynes, in the twentieth century' (1967, pp. VII–VIII).

Published by Blackwell Publishers Ltd, 108 Cowley Road, Oxford OX4 1JF, UK, and 350 Main Street, Malden, MA 02148, USA.

These developments draw attention to the monetary economics of the past. In this respect, leading authors went much further than a mere intuitive grasp of the subject: they pointed out the essential factors in the explanation of the effects of changes in the money stock that distinguish the two strands of the contemporary literature. In particular, the classics identified the key role of information showing that the effectiveness of money changes is inversely related to the information available to economic agents. While eighteenth-century authors assumed a small information set, thus regarding variations in the money stock as highly effective (Section 2), John Stuart Mill made the opposite assumption, ruling out any effect on real variables (Section 3). The analysis of classical economic thought then suggests a more general approach that goes beyond these extreme assumptions and considers information as a scarce commodity allocated optimally by rational agents. Following this approach, a different view of monetary policy effectiveness is outlined (Section 4).

2 The Effectiveness of Changes in Money Supply

Classical economists distinguished the money stock variations that were perceived by individuals from those that were not, thus paralleling the modern distinction between anticipated and unanticipated changes in money. In a metallic standard, variations in the money stock were endogenous, originating from mine discoveries and the trade balance. Nevertheless, a second type of variation could be engineered by the monetary authority whose room for manoeuvre was not entirely abolished. Major public finance crises, in the aftermath of wars or other shocks, were often tackled by an 'augmentation' or 'raising' of money. Both classes of money supply changes were usually considered as once-and-for-all and unanticipated. Since the classics took it for granted that the only effect of anticipated variations was on the price level, they were mainly interested in unanticipated money changes, the only ones affecting the real economy.

The transmission of monetary impulses is viewed as a sequential, multi-stage process whose dynamics rest on agents' reactions to such impulses which, in turn, impinge on the adjustment speed of wages and prices. The *locus classicus* of this analysis is Hume's (1752a, pp. 37–38) discussion of gold flows from America, where he contrasts the ineffectiveness of a money supply change in the final equilibrium position with its effectiveness during the transition from one equilibrium to another. The rise in employment and output that follows an increase in money stems from the slow response of wages and prices to the shift in demand for labour and commodities.

> They [merchants] are thereby enabled to employ more workmen than formerly, *who never dream of demanding higher wages*, but are glad of employment from such good paymasters. If workmen become scarce, the manufacturer gives higher wages, but at first requires an encrease of labour; and this is willingly submitted to by the artisan, who can now eat and drink better, to compensate his additional toil and fatigue. He carries his money to market, where he finds every thing at the same price as formerly, but returns with greater quantity and of better kinds, for the use of his family. ... It is easy to trace the money in its progress through the whole commonwealth; where we shall find, that it must first quicken the diligence of every individual, before it encrease the price of labour. (Hume, 1752a, p. 38, italics added)

Cantillon and Galiani also relate the effectiveness of monetary expansion to the slowness of the adjustment mechanism and note the impact of information availability on agents' behaviour. Cantillon points out incomplete information with respect to both money data and the model of the transmission mechanism.[2] After a mine discovery, the increase in both consumption and lending reduces unemployment but, in the presence of long-term rent and wage contracts, the eventual price rise causes income redistribution at the expense of landowners and workers. When contracts expire, individuals adjust their behaviour to the higher price level and thus rents and wages go up, bringing about a trade deficit and a fall in output. In contrast, an increase in money due to a trade surplus stimulates growth because of the inhabitants' higher propensity to save (1755, pp. 163–171). Therefore, the effect of money variations depends on the channel through which money is injected. Blaug (1985, p. 21) has called this proposition the 'Cantillon effect'.

While Cantillon focuses on long-term nominal labour contracts, which, together with incomplete information, are the key factors of modern explanations of monetary policy effectiveness (Blackburn and Christensen, 1989, p. 11), Galiani points to agents' sluggish responsiveness and sets forth a rudimentary hypothesis that explains the low adjustment

[2]See the following two quotations respectively. '[A]n acceleration or greater rapidity of circulation of money in exchange, is equivalent to an increase of actual money up to a point. . . . On the other hand money flows in detail through so many channels that it seems impossible not to lose sight of it seeing that having been amassed to make large sums it is distributed in the little rills of exchange, and then gradually accumulated again to make large payments. . . . It is also usually the case that the increase or decrease of actual money in a State is not perceived because it flows abroad, or is brought into the State, by such imperceptible means and proportions that it is impossible to know exactly the quantity which enters or leaves the State' (1755, pp. 161–163).

'M. Locke . . . has clearly seen that the abundance of money makes every thing dear, but he has not considered how it does so. The great difficulty of this question consists in knowing in what way and in what proportion the increase of money raises prices' (1755, p. 161).

speed of the equilibrium process and the efficacy of monetary expansion (1751b, pp. 166–167). Individuals conceive their ideas about prices from 'truth', i.e. from the true state of things; and, to those ideas, they match the 'sound of words', i.e. actual or called prices. Augmentation of money does not affect the true state of things but only called prices. The latter, however, do not change immediately since agents revise their ideas about prices slowly and the prince can thus gain from inflating the currency.[3]

As Friedman and Schwartz (1986, p. 43) note with reference to the earliest commodity money systems, it is the lag in price adjustment that allows the issuing authority to profit from debasement. And this lag is closely related to agents' slow response to money changes. The result of the long-run neutrality and short-run non-neutrality of money, therefore, is based on the hypothesis that links the dimension of the information set, including both the data and the model of the economy, to individual behaviour. Since the information available to agents is not sufficient to enable them to revise their behaviour promptly, money variations first affect output and employment and, only after a substantial lag, prices and wages. This is the core of the classical analysis of the effectiveness of money changes, a main tool in the economists' kit, which has survived to our day (Keynes, 1923, Ch. II; Friedman, 1968, pp. 103–104). To illustrate just one application, it is the basis of Hume's refutation of a monetary theory of interest. Different levels of the money stock do not impinge, in equilibrium, on the rate of interest.[4] Only a *continual* increase in the money supply can lower it, such as occurred in Spain after the persistent money flow from America (Hume, 1752b, p. 58), but this episode was indeed an exceptional one in terms of both size and duration.

To corroborate this theory, the classics often refer to the policies implemented in France in the early eighteenth century. Besides Hume's cursory mention (1752a, p. 39), both Cantillon (1755, pp. 287–299) and

[3]'*Augmentation of money is a profit that the prince and the state make because of the slowness with which the multitude changes the connection of ideas about the prices of commodities and money*. . . . It does not produce any change in things but in words: thus, in order for the prices of commodities to remain the same (with respect to things), they have also to change with regard to words. If this followed on the same day in which the augmentation takes place, and if it followed entirely and entirely in proportion, then the augmentation would have no consequences whatever, just as a law which established that money, instead of being called by Italian names, should be called by Latin or Greek or Hebrew names' (1751a, p. 188, italics in the original). Whenever Galiani's translation (1751b) diverges somewhat from the original (1751a), reference is to the latter in order to provide the most literal rendering.

[4]The essay 'Of interest' opens: 'Nothing is esteemed a more certain sign of the flourishing condition of any nation than the lowness of interest: And with reason; though I believe the cause is somewhat different from what is commonly apprehended. Lowness of interest is generally ascribed to plenty of money. But money, however plentiful, has no other effect, *if fixed*, than to raise the price of labour' (Hume, 1752b, p. 47, italics in the original).

Galiani (1751b, pp. 191–198) dedicate a whole chapter to French monetary history. Following Cantillon, in 1714 a deflationary measure was first carried out—a decree lowered the écu 1 per cent per month for 20 months to reduce its nominal value from 5 to 4 livres—simply to prepare the ground for a sudden, unanticipated augmentation of the écu back to 5 livres, thus bringing about an increase in public revenues.[5] Cantillon contrasts this episode with another one in 1726 which did not produce the desired effect because the lowering of the currency did not allow sufficient time for the demand for money to go up and generate a trade surplus (1755, pp. 293–295). In all these discussions, individual behaviour is closely related to available information and reacts to new data accordingly. Hence, the success of policies designed to raise seignorage depends on an element of surprise. Hume thus stresses the need to surprise the public in his proposal to increase money supply by recoining it and taking a penny's worth of silver from every shilling. 'In executing such a project, it would be better to make the new shilling pass for 24 halfpence, *in order to preserve the illusion*, and make it be taken for the same' (1752a, p. 39, italics added). Furthermore Galiani notes that, if changes in the money stock are carried out too frequently, the assumption of policy invariance of individual behaviour falls apart and agents do not stick to the once-prevailing prices. Augmenting money becomes wholly ineffective.[6]

The policy recipe the classics derive from their analysis is to avoid sharp fluctuations in the money stock. Given a small information set, these fluctuations are highly effective and thus a stable money supply path prevents output and employment variability. In support of this design, Cantillon again stresses the lack of knowledge on the part of the monetary authority, especially with regard to the timing of policy actions (1755, p. 185). Likewise, Galiani rejects increasing the money supply and calls for

[5]'Enlightened people in France hoard their money in these times. The King finds means to borrow much money on which he willingly loses the diminution, proposing to compensate himself by an augmentation at the end of the diminution. With this object after several diminutions they begin to hoard money in the King's Treasury, to postpone the payments, pensions, and army pay. In these circumstances money becomes extremely rare at the end of the diminutions both by reason of the sums hoarded by the King and various individuals and by reason of the nominal value of the coin, which value is diminished. . . . Then the King augments anew the coinage, settles the new écu or ounce of silver of the new issue at 5 livres, begins with this new coinage to pay the troops and the pensions. The old coinage is demonetised and received at the Mint at a lower nominal value. The King profits by the difference' (Cantillon, 1755, pp. 289–291).

[6]Dwelling upon his theory of the 'connection of ideas between the prices of commodities and of money', Galiani remarks: 'If he [the prince] abused it [augmentation], the connection would be severed, words change their significance, things remain the same and the unsurpassable force of nature wins. . . . Finally, a prince who, abusing augmentation, practised it every month, destroying every connection of ideas between prices and commodities, would render it quite useless and inefficacious, and only with other policies would obtain what today is obtained with augmentation' (1751a, pp. 188–189).

measures to avoid a fall in both velocity and money (1751b, pp. 204ff.). Finally, Hume argues 'for a gradual and universal encrease of the denomination of money' (1752a, p. 39) to eschew the contractionary effects of deflation.

3 Mill and the Role of Expectations

In contrast with the authors just examined, an inflationist school of thought, active in Britain in the early decades of the nineteenth century, drew the opposite policy conclusion from the theory of money effectiveness. Thomas Attwood, in several pamphlets and parliamentary speeches, made the case for the active management of an inconvertible paper money aimed at the goal of full employment. Although Attwood and his followers did not leave a mark on the history of economics, they prompted a pervasive critique by John Stuart Mill. Mill's analysis has received attention more for the alleged contrast between his early essay 'Of the Influence of Consumption upon Production' (1844, but written around 1830) and the *Principles* (1848) than for his contribution, which was much ahead of its time and foreshadowed the modern theory of business cycles and of monetary policy.

Mill's starting point is the equilibrium hypothesis. A monetary expansion increases the employment of both capital and labour, but this is *not* an equilibrium position since it is the result of an information failure on the part of entrepreneurs who mistake a variation in the general price level for a change in relative prices. In an equilibrium model of the economy, the adjustment process eventually brings about a recession.[7]

As in contemporary business cycle theory, the economy departs from equilibrium because individuals do not correctly perceive market signals. The confused interpretation of price changes distorts agents' choices and

[7]'[P]eriods of "brisk demand", are also the periods of greatest production: the national capital is never called into full employment but at those periods. This, however, is no reason for desiring such times; it is not desirable that the whole capital of the country should be in full employment. For, the calculations of producers and traders being of necessity imperfect, there are always some commodities which are more or less in excess, as there are always some which are in deficiency. If, therefore, the whole truth were known, there would always be some classes of producers contracting, not extending, their operations. If *all* are endeavouring to extend them, it is a certain proof that some general delusion is afloat. The commonest cause of such delusion is some general, or very extensive, rise of prices (whether caused by speculation or by the currency) which persuades all dealers that they are growing rich. And hence, an increase of production really takes place during the progress of depreciation, as long as the existence of depreciation is not suspected; and it is this which gives to the fallacies of the currency school, principally represented by Mr. Attwood, all the little plausibility they possess. But when the delusion vanishes and the truth is disclosed, those whose commodities are relatively in excess must diminish their production or be ruined: and if during the high prices they have built mills and erected machinery, they will be likely to repent at leisure' (1844, pp. 67–68, italics in the original).

thus leads to instability. In Mill's thinking, monetary expansion cannot permanently increase real income, but is viewed as a source of disequilibrium that sets off economic fluctuations.

Mill criticizes Attwood's inflationary doctrine in other less known articles (1833), but his main contribution is in the *Principles* (1848) where he buttresses his earlier argument, explicitly introducing expectations. The failure of a monetary injection to increase output is due to the prompt revision of expectations. For output to grow, people must anticipate an increase in their real income, but this argument ultimately rests on agents' failure to revise expectations as prices go up, which must be excluded.

> I presume, however, that the inducement which, according to Mr. Attwood, excited this unusual ardour in all persons engaged in production, must have been the expectation of getting more commodities generally, more real wealth, in exchange for the produce of their labour, and not merely more pieces of paper. This expectation, however, must have been, by the very terms of the supposition, disappointed, since, all prices being supposed to rise equally, no one was really better paid for his goods than before. Those who agree with Mr. Attwood could only succeed in winning people on to these unwonted exertions by a prolongation of what would in fact be a delusion; contriving matters so, that by a progressive rise of money prices, every producer shall always seem to be in the very act of obtaining an increased remuneration which he never, in reality, does obtain. It is unnecessary to advert to any other of the objections to this plan than that of its total impracticability. It calculates on finding the whole world persisting for ever in the belief that more pieces of paper are more riches, and never discovering that, with all their paper, they cannot buy more of anything than they could before. (1848, p. 550)

Mill (1848, p. 551) then interprets Hume's argument for the effectiveness of money variations as based on a different price adjustment speed for different commodities which would allow the producers of the goods whose price rises first to gain. Mill objects that such gain must be balanced by the loss of those whose product is the last to increase in price. But, for this to occur, agents must not exploit the available information; otherwise the losers, perceiving the change in prices, will raise their prices too, thus stopping the expansionary process from its very beginning.

In Mill's theoretical framework, departures from equilibrium are due to incomplete information and can only be temporary. The role of information is central in his analysis of the effects of changes in money and of economic fluctuations. There is nothing inherent in the functioning of the economy that causes instability which, instead, arises from agents' misinterpretation of market signals. Mill, therefore, fiercely opposes fiat money on both theoretical and policy grounds.[8] His staunch defence of the gold standard, which to modern readers may appear at odds with his emphasis on banking school tenets, is consistent with the equilibrium model of the economy, which requires a firm monetary anchor to prevent any interference with the real sector (see footnote 8). In this connection, the importance of information in the expectation formation process emerges in his call for convertibility in place of a rule fixing the price of gold in an inconvertible paper currency system. In fact, convertibility is simpler and more intelligible to the public at large and thus is less likely to be broken by the issuer who, in financial emergencies, could instead try to tamper with a complicated rule. Simple rules, being easily monitored, enhance enforcement (Mill, 1848, pp. 545–546).[9]

The essential distinction between eighteenth-century classics and Mill centres on the size of agents' information set, assumed to be small or large respectively. This distinction mirrors the contemporary one between traditional monetarists and New Classicals (Cesarano, 1983a). In fact, while Friedman (1960, pp. 87–88; 1968, p. 107) repeatedly emphasized the lack of knowledge of the monetary transmission mechanism, knowledge of the 'true' model of the economy is an essential component of the rational expectations hypothesis. Hence, the common recipe of a constant rate of growth of money supply, supported by both past and contemporary Chicago school economists, rests on a very different basis. On the one hand, Friedman views monetary policy as an extremely powerful instrument whose discretionary use is a major source of output variability. On the other, rational expectations theorists regard changes in money as ineffective, even in the short run, in the presence of price flexibility.[10]

[8]'Such a power [of issuing inconvertible currency], in whomsoever vested, is an intolerable evil. All variations in the value of the circulating medium are mischievous: *they disturb existing contracts and expectations*, and the liability to such changes renders every pecuniary engagement of long date entirely precarious. . . . Not to add, that the issuers may have, and in the case of a government paper, always have, a direct interest in lowering the value of the currency, because it is the medium in which their own debts are computed' (1848, p. 544, italics added).

[9]Friedman also puts forward these arguments in supporting his *k* per cent rule. '[A] much simpler rule would also produce highly satisfactory results and would have two great advantages: first, its simplicity would facilitate the public understanding and backing that is necessary if the rule is to provide an effective barrier to opportunistic "tinkering"; second, it would largely separate the monetary problem from the fiscal and hence would require less far-reaching reform over a narrower area' (1960, p. 90).

[10]The following remark by Milton Friedman, referring to the unsettled empirical questions underlying the Keynesian–monetarist debate of the 1960s, shows how far he is from the contemporary rational expectations approach. 'The reason such differences have been able to persist is, I believe, that full adjustment to monetary disturbances takes a very long time and affects many economic magnitudes. If adjustment were swift, immediate, and mechanical, as some earlier quantity theorists may have believed, or, more likely, as was attributed to them by their critics, the role of money would be clearly and sharply etched even in the imperfect figures that have been available. But, if the adjustment is slow, delayed, and sophisticated, then crude evidence may be misleading, and a more

However, such changes meddle with the price system and, by introducing noisy signals into resource allocation, drive the economy away from equilibrium. In the *Principles*, Mill anticipates some crucial aspects of the latter approach, namely the equilibrium hypothesis and the role of expectations in the monetary transmission mechanism, while Cantillon, Galiani and Hume foreshadow the monetarist analysis of the 1960s. All in all, the classical theory of money supply variations is rather sophisticated in that it links the availability of information to agents' behaviour in order to explain the effectiveness of money changes in the transition from one equilibrium to another.

4 Information and Monetary Policy Effectiveness

The contributions of the classical economists suggest a more general approach to monetary policy effectiveness. The starting point is to go beyond the two polar cases of a large versus a small information set—posited by Mill and eighteenth-century authors respectively, or by New Classical macroeconomists and traditional monetarists nowadays—and consider information as a scarce commodity that individuals allocate optimally like any other good. This approach grafts Stigler's (1961) analysis onto the theory of monetary policy. To revise their expectations, agents must get a net benefit from the costly activity of gathering and processing information. This involves fitting data into the 'true' model of the economy, the two elements of agents' information set, to calculate expectations. The overwhelming evidence in favour of the short-run effectiveness of money variations (Friedman and Schwartz, 1963) has called forth explanations of incomplete information but these have focused on the data rather than the model. A well-known example is Lucas's (1972) conjecture concerning agents' confusion about changes in relative prices and in the general price level, which is found in Mill's work also (see pp. 444–446 above). With respect to Mill's times, however, the volume, accuracy and rapid availability of the data have enormously increased. Possible information failures are therefore likely to derive more from the explanatory power of the model, which has improved a mere trifle in comparison.[11]

The hypothesis set forth here is that the model's explanatory or predictive power varies with the value of exogenous or policy-determined variables, i.e. the variance of predictions is inversely related to the size of shocks or of policy measures. The cost and benefit of collecting and treating

subtle examination of the record may be needed to disentangle what is systematic from what is random and erratic' (1970, pp. 61–62).

[11]With regard to the scant progress of monetary theory, Friedman has observed: 'As I see it, we have advanced beyond Hume in two respects only: first, we now have a more secure grasp on the quantitative magnitudes involved; second, we have gone one derivative beyond Hume' (1975, p. 177).

information are then a negative and positive function respectively of the size of policy actions. To illustrate, the effect on the price level of, say, a doubling of the money stock can be predicted with much greater precision and less effort than that of a half per cent increase. Of course, the benefit from processing information, measured by the expected change in wealth, also differs in the two cases, making agents' responsiveness much greater in the former. According to this hypothesis, therefore, the smaller the policy action, the less agents are induced to revise their expectations since this involves a net loss. The point at which the cost and benefit functions intersect identifies the critical value of the policy measure dimension which triggers agents' revision of their expectations and thus divides the region of policy ineffectiveness from the region of policy effectiveness.

This approach does not make a case for or against discretion but only sketches a positive analysis of the effectiveness of money supply changes that considers information as a scarce commodity allocated optimally by rational agents. Policy effectiveness does not follow from assumptions relating to the institutional setting, such as the existence of long-run labour contracts, or from the policymaker's superior information or from the presence of fixed costs in expectation formation. Moreover, this analysis is removed from the hypotheses of bounded rationality (Simon, 1955) or near rationality (Akerlof and Yellen, 1985). Agents are, instead, fully rational but, since the information they elaborate is scarce, they may well fail to revise expectations if the optimizing calculus yields a net loss. From an empirical viewpoint, the relatively low inflation rates observed during the 1950s and 1960s, despite the activist approach of the authorities, can be related to the reduced scope of monetary policy allowed by the Bretton Woods rules, so that central bank actions seldom went farther than the critical dimension which sets off expectation revision. After the demise of Bretton Woods, the opposite scenario emerged.

The region of policy effectiveness changes as the cost and benefit curves of processing information shift, thereby modifying the critical value that triggers the agents' revision of expectations. An increase in the size of the information set, particularly in the form of an enhanced explanatory power of the model, shifts both curves leftward and reduces the policy effectiveness region. Muth's (1961) basic innovation obviously does not concern the rationality postulate, which is as old as economics, but the hypothesis of computing forecasts on the basis of the relevant economic theory. However, the efficiency of the model in producing forecasts can differ greatly with the complexity of the problem and, in extreme cases, can become so low as to make the usefulness of predictions, even in a simple non-strategic context, entirely negligible. To take an example outside economics, the rational forecast of the occurrence of an earthquake is hardly useful if, as happened in California in 1989, it is defined in an interval of zero to 30 years (*The Economist*, 1989, p. 99). Resort to the 'true' model of earthquakes may not furnish agents with an efficient enough prediction to avoid the undesired effects.[12] Hence, in the present state of advancement of geology, earthquake forecasts, even if unbiased, are so variable that it was rational for Californians not to leave their homes.

The analogy with monetary policy is appropriate. If the net benefit from processing information is negative, agents do not revise their expectations and can then be subject to money supply 'surprises' within the region of policy effectiveness. The size of the region depends on the dimension of the information set, so that an enlargement of the latter, especially through the improved efficiency of the model, makes it shrink. The extent of the region is an empirical question. And, in a futuristic scenario devoid of tangible exchange media (Black, 1970; Fama, 1980), the problem of effectiveness could even become irrelevant, though this proposition is disputable (Cesarano, 1995).

The foregoing analysis also has implications for the strategic aspects of monetary policy, which provide a further theoretical basis for rules rather than discretion. As long as the central bank's actions remain within the region of policy effectiveness, no trade-off between credibility and flexibility exists because the policy measures are not sufficiently large to trigger agents' revision of expected inflation. In the monetary policy game, a player must not incur a net loss in processing the information necessary to make a move; otherwise the game stops altogether. As long as central bank actions are confined within the region of policy effectiveness, credibility is untainted. Furthermore, if the central bank goes beyond that region in response to an exceptionally large shock—a war, a stock market crash, soaring oil prices and the like—credibility is not undermined because it is intentionally taking action to attenuate the consequences of such a shock (Lohmann, 1992).[13]

[12]*The Economist*'s conclusion stresses the negligible usefulness of such prediction: 'Earthquake scientists dare not make too much of their approximate prediction of last week's earthquake, or they will be accused of failing to warn. But what could they have done? Told San Franciscans to leave the area for 30 years or until the earthquake, whichever should prove the shorter period?' (1989, p. 100).

[13]The gold standard has also been interpreted as a credible contingent rule incorporating an escape clause to cope with major shocks (Bordo and Kydland, 1995). Going back for a moment to classical authors, Galiani made this point in his rejection of the critique that inflation 'mars the most precious treasure of the prince—the faith of the people' (1751b, p. 177). He notes: 'Finally, in augmenting the currency, faith in the ruler does not waiver except when this is not appropriate. Failure to fulfill one's promise, when it is necessary, does not diminish faith, it increases compassion. We saw this occur in the republic of Genoa not too many years ago. Misfortunes that proceed from natural causes do not make men fearful, but vices and bad faith do, when they cannot be checked by anxious fear and superior authority. The prince will be just and people will have faith in him. He will augment the currency when necessary and none shall complain. He will not pay when he cannot, and his not being able to do so is not his fault. He will not be pitied any more; he will be helped with great fervor' (1751b, pp. 178–179).

5 Concluding Remarks

Careful reading of the classics provides plenty of hints, intuitions and ideas for current research (Cesarano, 1983b; Negishi, 1989, Ch. 1). As Stigler notes in a paper that makes a case for studying the history of economics: '[I]f a great book such as Smith's *Wealth of Nations* is read repeatedly, on even a fifth or tenth reading one continues to learn new things' (1969, p. 218). With regard to the effectiveness of changes in the money supply, the classics show the crucial role of information in explaining the monetary adjustment mechanism. The dimension of the information set impinges on agents' behaviour and determines how far the system can be removed from equilibrium. The degree of policy effectiveness, therefore, is ultimately related to the availability of information. In this connection, the works of eighteenth-century authors and of traditional monetarists on the one hand, and of Mill and rational expectations theorists on the other, represent two polar cases. The former assume little or no information, which leaves much room for disequilibrium and makes monetary policy a powerful instrument, since both the size and duration of adjustment can be considerable. The latter assume an information set large enough to maintain the economy in equilibrium, thus denying, apart from specific information failures, any effects of money supply changes. The rules versus discretion debate has developed along these extreme lines. An approach that avoids either set of assumptions and treats information as a scarce commodity allocated optimally by rational agents could improve our knowledge of the transmission of monetary impulses.

References

Akerlof, G. A. and Yellen, J. L. (1985). 'A Near-rational Model of the Business Cycle, with Wage and Price Inertia', *Quarterly Journal of Economics*, Vol. 100, Supplement, pp. 823–838.

Black, F. (1970). 'Banking and Interest Rates in a World Without Money: the Effects of Uncontrolled Banking', *Journal of Bank Research*, Vol. 1, No. 3, pp. 9–20.

Blackburn, K. and Christensen, M. (1989). 'Monetary Policy and Policy Credibility: Theories and Evidence', *Journal of Economic Literature*, Vol. 27, No. 1, pp. 1–45.

Blaug, M. (1985). *Economic Theory in Retrospect* (4th edn), Cambridge, Cambridge University Press.

Bordo, M. D. and Kydland, F. (1995). 'The Gold Standard as a Rule', *Explorations in Economic History*, Vol. 32, No. 4, pp. 423–464.

Cantillon, R. (1931 [1755]). *Essai sur la Nature du Commerce en Général*, edited by Henry Higgs, London, Macmillan.

Cesarano, F. (1983a). 'The Rational Expectations Hypothesis in Retrospect', *American Economic Review*, Vol. 73, No. 1, pp. 198–203.

Cesarano, F. (1983b). 'On the Role of the History of Economic Analysis', *History of Political Economy*, Vol. 15, No. 1, pp. 63–82.

Cesarano, F. (1995). 'The New Monetary Economics and the Theory of Money', *Journal of Economic Behavior and Organization*, Vol. 26, No. 3, pp. 445–455.
The Economist (1989). 'The Shakiness of Predictions', Vol. 313, No. 7626, 28 October, pp. 99–100.
Fama, E. F. (1980). 'Banking in the Theory of Finance', *Journal of Monetary Economics*, Vol. 6, No. 1, pp. 39–57.
Friedman, M. (1960). *A Program for Monetary Stability*, New York, Fordham University Press.
Friedman, M. (1968). 'The Role of Monetary Policy', *American Economic Review*, Vol. 58, No. 1, pp. 1–17; reprinted in M. Friedman, *The Optimum Quantity of Money and Other Essays*, Chicago, IL, Aldine, 1969.
Friedman, M. (1970). 'A Theoretical Framework for Monetary Analysis', *Journal of Political Economy*, Vol. 78, No. 2, pp. 193–238; reprinted in R. J. Gordon (ed.), *Milton Friedman's Monetary Framework*, Chicago, IL, University of Chicago Press, 1974.
Friedman, M. (1975). '25 Years After the Rediscovery of Money: What Have We Learned?', *American Economic Review*, Vol. 65, No. 2, pp. 176–179.
Friedman, M. and Schwartz, A. J. (1963). *A Monetary History of the United States, 1867–1960*, Princeton, NJ, Princeton University Press.
Friedman, M. and Schwartz, A. J. (1986). 'Has Government Any Role in Money?', *Journal of Monetary Economics*, Vol. 17, No. 1, pp. 37–62.
Galiani, F. (1963 [1751a]). *Della Moneta*, Milan, Feltrinelli.
Galiani, F. (1977 [1751b]). *On Money*, translated by Peter R. Toscano, Ann Arbor, MI, University Microfilms International.
Hicks, J. R. (1967). *Critical Essays in Monetary Theory*, Oxford, Oxford University Press.
Hume, D. (1970 [1752a]). 'Of Money', in E. Rotwein (ed.), *Writings on Economics*, Madison, WI, University of Wisconsin Press.
Hume, D. (1970 [1752b]). 'Of Interest', in E. Rotwein (ed.), *Writings on Economics*, Madison, WI, University of Wisconsin Press.
Keynes, J. M. (1923). *A Tract on Monetary Reform*, London, Macmillan.
Lohmann, S. (1992). 'Optimal Commitment in Monetary Policy: Credibility versus Flexibility', *American Economic Review*, Vol. 82, No. 1, pp. 273–286.
Lucas, R. E. (1972). 'Expectations and the Neutrality of Money', *Journal of Economic Theory*, Vol. 4, No. 2, pp. 103–124.
Mankiw, N. G. (1992). 'The Reincarnation of Keynesian Economics', *European Economic Review*, Vol. 36, Nos. 2–3, pp. 559–565.
Mill, J. S. (1967 [1833]). 'The Currency Juggle', in *Collected Works of John Stuart Mill*, Vol. 4, edited by J. M. Robson, Toronto, University of Toronto Press.
Mill, J. S. (1844). 'Of the Influence of Consumption upon Production', in *Essays on Some Unsettled Questions of Political Economy*, London, Parker.
Mill, J. S. (1909 [1848]). *Principles of Political Economy* (1st edn), edited by William Ashley, London, Longmans, Green.
Muth, J. F. (1961). 'Rational Expectations and Theory of Price Movements', *Econometrica*, Vol. 29, No. 3, pp. 315–335.
Negishi, T. (1989). *History of Economy Theory*, Amsterdam, North-Holland.
Simon, H. A. (1955). 'A Behavioral Model of Rational Choice', *Quarterly Journal of Economics*, Vol. 69, No. 1, pp. 99–118.
Stigler, G. J. (1961). 'The Economics of Information', *Journal of Political Economy*, Vol. 69, No. 1, pp. 213–225.

Stigler, G. J. (1969). 'Does Economics Have a Useful Past?', *History of Political Economy*, Vol. 1, No. 2, pp. 217–230.

Tobin, J. (1980). *Asset Accumulation and Economic Activity*, Chicago, IL, University of Chicago Press.

Part 3

Monetary Theory and Monetary Systems

History of Political Economy 22:2
© 1990 by Duke University Press
CCC 0018–2702/90/$1.50

[9]

Law and Galiani on money and monetary systems

Filippo Cesarano

The introduction of a wholly fiduciary standard is a very late development in the history of monetary arrangements. As Milton Friedman has recently remarked (1986, 643), irredeemable paper money—a system in which no major currency has any link to a commodity—has emerged only in the 1970s, following a process begun after World War I. A key element explaining such delay can be found in the foremost place held, in the evolution of monetary analysis, by "theoretical metallism" as contrasted with "theoretical cartalism." These terms, both due to Knapp, are lucidly defined by Schumpeter along with their "practical" counterparts.

> By Theoretical Metallism we denote the *theory* that it is logically essential for money to consist of, or to be "covered" by, some commodity so that the logical source of the exchange value or purchasing power of money is the exchange value or purchasing power of that commodity, considered independently of its monetary role. . . . By Practical Metallism we shall denote sponsorship of a principle of monetary policy, namely, the principle that the monetary unit "should" be kept firmly linked to, and freely interchangeable with, a given quantity of some commodity. Theoretical and Practical Cartalism may best be defined by the corresponding negatives. (1954, 288, emphasis his)[1]

Although there is no necessary one-to-one correspondence between the theoretical and practical sides of either metallism or cartalism—inasmuch as the principles underlying the two aspects are quite distinct[2]—

Correspondence may be addressed to the author, Banca d'Italia, Servizio Studi, Via Nazionale 91, 00184 Roma, Italy.

1. Schumpeter emphasizes the overwhelming dominance of theoretical metallism: "Whatever may be its shortcomings, this theory [Aristotle's metallist theory of money], though never unchallenged, prevailed substantially to the end of the nineteenth century and even beyond. It is the basis of the bulk of all analytic work in the field of money" (1954, 63).

2. "An economist may, for instance, be fully convinced that theoretical metallism is untenable, and yet be a strong practical metallist. Lack of confidence in the authorities or politicians, whose freedom of action is greatly increased by currency systems that do not

the weakness of theoretical cartalism has helped to check the introduction of fiduciary standards by failing to provide their logical foundation.

Resort to this taxonomy may be troublesome because of the classic authors' ambiguity in distinguishing analytical from institutional arguments.[3] Nevertheless this classificatory device is a useful tool because, first, it brings about a synthetic description of the variegated viewpoints in the copious literature on money and, second, it sheds light on the relationship between monetary theory and monetary standards, a subject currently receiving increasing attention.[4] The work of two major economists, John Law and Ferdinando Galiani, offers a most interesting case for analyzing this topic, given the high level of their contribution but especially the controversial nature of the latter's. In section I a novel hypothesis is suggested according to which, contrary to common opinion, Law's and Galiani's theoretical approaches are respectively viewed as closer to metallism and cartalism. As regards the monetary standard instead (section II), their position is reversed, since they embrace practical cartalism and metallism. This contrast, characterizing both authors, is suggestive of sundry general propositions on the progress of monetary economics and its bearing upon the monetary arrangements that prompted Friedman's remark on irredeemable currency.

I

Before examining in turn the writings of these economists, their uneven character should be stressed. While Law appears as a hasty,[5] almost extemporaneous, writer mainly motivated by supplying proposals and

---

provide for prompt and unquestioning redemption in gold of all means of payment that do not consist of gold, is quite sufficient to motivate practical metallism in a theoretical cartalist; this does not involve any contradiction" (Schumpeter 1954, 289).

3. Despite making wide use of this terminology, Schumpeter cautions the reader about its clearness: "Finally, basic theories are malleable and writers are often inconsistent, still more often vague. When we find that a writer compares money to a ticket—a ticket that admits the bearer to the great social store of all goods—we feel inclined to register him as a cartalist. But the phrase need not mean much, and both J. S. Mill, who used it in the nineteenth century, and Berkeley, who used it in the eighteenth, are more properly called metallists. There is no denying that views on money are as difficult to describe as are shifting clouds" (1954, 289). And indeed they are, since Schumpeter, just five pages later (294), relabels Berkeley as a cartalist. In a footnote following the passage quoted above, he frankly admits his own interpretative doubts: "Such difficulties we have met already in the case of Aristotle. I am by no means absolutely sure that I was right to class him with the theoretical metallists. Galiani . . . interpreted him in the opposite sense" (290).

4. The whole January 1986 issue of the *Journal of Monetary Economics* is dedicated to this theme, which is closely related to the matter studied by the so-called new monetary economics (see note 33 below).

5. In the concluding paragraph of his book Law states: "I have not had time to put my Thoughts in that Order they ought to have been, and am forc't to leave out Answers I design'd to have given to some Objections I have heard made against this Proposal" (1705, 120).

framing policy, Galiani displays typical scholarly attitudes aimed at formulating explanatory hypotheses supported by well-pondered abstract analyses.

John Law's theoretical views on money, mostly contained in his 1705 volume, have been controversial, supposedly because of their wavering nature. Schumpeter's authoritative account (1954, 321–22) is revealing. After showing several arguments supporting Law's metallist stance, he classes him as a cartalist, primarily on the basis of Law's statement that "Money is not the value *for* which Goods are exchanged, but the Value *by* which they are exchanged" (1705, 100; Schumpeter 1954, 322, emphasis his). Along with Schumpeter, Law has been characterized as a theoretical cartalist by other authors, including Rist (1951, 43–44) and Vickers (1960, 31, 75, 103, 118, esp. 138). The efficacious and meaningful conciseness of the crucial quotation notwithstanding, any attempt at a conclusive assessment should rest on an analysis of Law's whole work.

The opening page of Law's *Money and trade* sets out a policy problem—the alleged scarcity of money in Scotland—and proposes to discuss the underlying issues, i.e., the nature of money, the relationship between money and trade, and the measures for solving the problem. He starts off with an exposition of value theory which, besides introducing a rudimentary demand-supply apparatus, emphasizes the different quality of commodities as the factor explaining price variability. This very feature plays a crucial role in Law's approach to the foundations of money.[6] While illustrating the inconveniences of barter, he goes beyond the problem of double coincidence of wants and lists two other points: uncertainty in the settlement of contracts due to the different quality of goods and lack of a unit of account. For this reason, he observes, silver was used as money, because "It could be brought to a Standard in Fineness, so was certain as to its Quality" (1705, 6) and because of other properties, i.e., its ease of delivery, transportability, durability, and homogeneity. These characteristics bestow four functions on the money commodity—unit of account, medium of exchange, standard of deferred payments, and store of value[7]—the identification of the latter two being one of Law's original contributions (Monroe 1923, 161–62).

6. The reconstruction of Law's arguments focuses on the elements that are relevant to identifying his position. However, other important topics, brilliantly analyzed—e.g. the welfare gains following the transition from a barter to a money economy (1705, 5–6)—are not considered in this context.

7. "Silver having these Qualities, 'its [*sic*] reasonable to think it was used as Money, before it was coin'd. What is mean't by being used as Money, is, that Silver in Bullion was the Measure by which Goods were valued: The Value by which Goods were Exchanged: And in which Contracts were made payable.

"He who had more Goods than he had use for, would choose to barter them for Silver,

In successive paragraphs, certainty in quality is again given particular prominence as the feature characterizing the commodity that performs monetary functions.[8]

> A.B. would choose to take the Bond payable in Silver, rather than in Horses: Because Silver was certain in Quality, and Horses differ'd much. So Silver was used as the value in which Contracts were made payable.
>
> Silver was likewise used as the Measure by which Goods were valued, because certain in Quality. . . . The Wine could not be valued by the Quantity of Oats it was worth at Glasgow, nor the Oats by the Quantity of Wine they were worth at Aberdeen. Wine or Oats might differ in Quality, or be more or less valuable at the one Place than at the other. The way to have known what Quantity of Oats was equal to the Wine, was by the Quantity of Silver each was worth at the places they were to be delivered. (1705, 8–9)

Therefore, the introduction of coinage accomplished the task of assuring a uniform quality of the money commodity.

> Silver being capable of a Stamp, Princes, for the greater Convenience of the People, set up Mints to bring it to a Standard, and Stamp it; Whereby its Weight and Fineness was known, without the Trouble of Weighing or Fyning; *But the Stamp added nothing to the Value*. (1705, 9, emphasis added)

These passages bring into focus Law's analysis of a monetary economy, whose main characterization is the emergence of a money commodity that does away with price uncertainties that arise from the variable qualities of different goods. The value of money is explained by the same demand-supply model that accounts for prices of goods, so that the additional demand for monetary use—stemming from the specific properties mentioned above—raises the value of silver. The latter can hardly be viewed as imaginary and exogeneously imposed; therefore Law is critical of Locke's approach to the origin of money as based on the "general Consent of Men." Silver, he argues, was employed as money because of its properties, whereas coinage was introduced subsequently, its role being simply to raise the efficacy of those properties

---

tho he had no use for it; Because, Silver was certain in its Quality: It was easie of delivery: It could be kept without Loss or Expense: And with it he could purchase other Goods as he had occasion, in Whole or in Part, at Home or Abroad, Silver being divisible without Loss, and of the same Value in different Places" (1705, 7).

8. Information about the quality of goods is a main element of some contemporary works on the fundamentals of money; see Brunner and Meltzer 1971, Alchian 1977, and King and Plosser 1986.

in order to improve the efficiency of the monetary system. Hence assigning an imaginary value to money is totally unfounded.[9]

Law's hypothesis on the origin of money dwells upon a centuries-old accepted opinion on this very topic, centered on the "conception of money as the most saleable commodity" (Schumpeter 1954, 99). The latter also underlies the now commonly accepted theory which acknowledges the market characteristics of certain goods which, because they overcome the inconveniences of barter, emerge as money through the unconcerted market behavior of individuals (Menger 1892; Jones 1976). This hypothesis fits into Law's general conception of money in a way that further supports his metallist stance. His reiterated argument negating any influence of coinage on the value of money is matched by his denial of attributing an imaginary value to money which could bypass a quid pro quo requirement (see note 9 above).

> Thus Silver having a Value, and Qualities fitting it for Money, which other Goods had not, was made Money, and for the greater convenience of the People was Coin'd.
>
> The Names of the different Pieces might have been Number 1. Number 2. and so on; Number 60 would have been the same as a Crown; *For the Name and Stamp was only to certify, that the Piece had such a Quantity of Silver in it, of such fineness*. (1705, 10–11, emphasis added)

The arguments illustrated in the preceding paragraphs all refer to the opening chapter of *Money and trade*. However, this topic is also discussed along the same metallist lines in other parts of the book, mostly concerned with policy proposals and reforming the standard. In particular, having excluded credit as an efficacious remedy for the scarcity of money, Law's feasible solution involves the selection of other goods having those specific properties which enable them to perform monetary functions.[10] Reference to commodities that have well-defined properties is indeed a firm and explicit point of his analysis.

9. "I cannot conceive how different Nations could agree to put an Imaginary Value upon any thing, especially upon Silver, by which all other Goods are valued; Or that any one Country would receive that as a Value, *which was not valuable equal to what it was given for;* Or how that Imaginary Value could have been kept up" (Law 1705, 9, emphasis added).

10. "It remains to be considered, whether any other Goods than Silver, can be made Money with the same safety and convenience.

"From what has been said about the nature of Money, Chap. I. it is evident, that any other Goods which have the Qualities necessary in Money, may be made Money equal to their Value, with Safety and Convenience. There was nothing of Humour or Fancy in making Silver to be Money; it was made Money, because it was thought best Qualified for that use" (1705, 60).

> *Money is not a pledge,* as some call it. It's a Value payed, or Contracted to be payed, with which 'tis supposed, the Receiver may, as his occasions require, Buy an equal Quantity of the same Goods he has Sold, or other Goods equal in Value to them: And that Money is the most secure Value, either to Receive, to Contract for, or to Value Goods by; which is least lyable to a change in its Value. Silver Money is more uncertain in its Value *than other Goods,* so less Qualified for the Use of Money. (1705, 61–62, emphasis added)

The clarity of this passage is impressive. Rejecting the fiduciary character of money, Law sets out to design a monetary system superior to a metallic standard inasmuch as it is founded on goods that have a lower price variability than silver. The details of his proposals are examined in the next section, but those aspects that carry theoretical relevance should be considered here.

Illustrating his choice of land as the standard, Law again refers to the essential properties of money and advances arguments which unambiguously derive from a metallist position.

> Any Goods that have the Qualities necessary in Money, may be made Money equal to their value. 5 Ounces of Gold is equal in value to 20 lib. and may be made Money to that Value. An Acre of Land rented at 2 Bolls of Victual, the Victual at 8 lib. and Land at 20 years purchase, is equal to 20 lib. and may be made Money equal to that Value, for it has all the Qualities necessary in Money. (1705, 83–84)

Considering the bulky and overwhelming evidence supporting the classification of Law as a theoretical metallist, one must account for the much-quoted sentence cited by Schumpeter (see above), which suggests an opposite interpretation. The explanation of this supposed contrast is straightforward when that sentence is considered in its context: the final part of Law's book, which deals with his proposals for reforming the monetary system. Describing a thought experiment in which the owner of an island introduces paper money with the purpose of raising income and employment (1705, 97–100), Law aims to show its several advantages. However, far from attaching to such a fiduciary instrument a self-contained monetary role, he explicitly assigns the latter to land. Hence the sentence in question belongs to a passage that, when quoted in full, hardly admits a cartalist standpoint:

> Money is not the value for which Goods are exchanged, but the Value by which they are Exchanged: The use of Money is to buy Goods, and Silver while Money is of no other use.
>
> Tho Silver were our product, yet it is not so proper to be made Money as Land. Land is what produces every thing, Silver is only

> the product. Land does not increase or decrease in Quantity, Silver or any other product may. So Land is more certain in its value than Silver, *or any other Goods*. (1705, 100, emphasis added)

The first paragraph simply refers to the medium of exchange function of the money commodity, waving aside the latter's nonmonetary uses but hardly providing any evidence of theoretical cartalism. In this chapter Law is in fact illustrating his proposal for reform, which is founded upon the metallist principles of money previously described. In the second paragraph, while explaining the superior properties of land as the standard, he manifestly compares it to other commodities. A cartalist interpretation would be at odds with the approach to the nature of money Law followed throughout his book: there is no single statement relating to that viewpoint.

Law's writings subsequent to 1705 further strengthen this rendering. Volume 1 of his *Oeuvres complètes* collects works that have theoretical relevance; the second and third volumes mainly deal with the defense of his "System." The opening of his 1706 *Mémoire* contains a most illuminating passage.

> Money does not receive its value from public authority, as M. Boissard pretends: the print marks its weight and titer; it makes it known that the coin is composed of such quantity of matter, of such fineness, but it does not give value: *it is the matter which makes it valuable*. . . .
>
> If the prince gave value to money, he could give the value of one *écu* to tin, lead or other metals made in pieces of one ounce, and could make them be used in trade, as silver money is used presently. But, when the prince would have given the mark and the name of *écu* to an ounce of tin, the individual would not hand over commodities worth one *écu* for the tin *écu because the matter it is made of is not worth it*. (1706, in Law 1934, 167, emphasis added)

The clear-cut character of these remarks needs no further comment.[11] In various tracts written after 1705 he repeats the main propositions of *Money and trade,* often inserting whole passages verbatim.[12] All in all there hardly is any compelling evidence for crediting Law with a cartalist theory of money. Out-of-context citation of a single sentence cannot corroborate that hypothesis.

11. A few pages later Law again states the same concepts: "But the mark does not give value to money, and its value is not imaginary, as MM. Locke and Boissard pretend. Money receives its value from the matters of which it is composed; and its value is more or less strong, according to the quantity as proportioned to the demand; *also its value is real, as the value of wheat, wines and other goods*" (1706, in 1934, 175, emphasis added).

12. The reader is especially referred to Law 1707, in Law 1934.

Galiani's view on the subject, although commonly interpreted as metallist,[13] appears in fact even more controversial than Law's. Actually he proceeds along the same argumentative lines laid down by Law but provides a more extensive and deeper treatment (1751, book 1, "Of the Metals"). For him the value of money depends upon the value of metals and cannot in any way be determined by the arbitrary will of man.[14] Having put forward his advanced theory of value (see note 13 above), he applies it to money, explaining the relationship between the price of money and the price of metals and its relevance to monetary theory.

> The just price of gold cannot, therefore, be known with any assurance in any other way than by asking how much it is generally worth, compared to all other things. It is necessary for me to linger over the discussion of the value of the metals without withdrawing the principles stated in the preceding paragraph, at least long enough to show another important truth. Namely, whether one observes the use made of the metals or their destruction, the metals will be seen to derive their value much more from their role as metals than their role as money. *Hence, one can conclude that they are used as money because they are valuable; they are not valuable because they are used as money.* It, therefore, behooves me to establish firmly the intrinsic value upon which every truth of this science is built. (1751, 40–41, emphasis added)[15]

An immediate corollary of these principles concerns the origin of

13. Showing Law's and Galiani's contributions to the paradox of value, Schumpeter incidentally contrasts their positions on the foundations of money in a way that, as maintained in the present section, is quite debatable: "John Law, in particular, in the tract quoted above (*Money and trade considered* . . . 1705), gave a short but excellent account of the matter [value]—actually using the examples of water and diamonds. However, we shall confine ourselves to the economist who carried this analysis to its eighteenth-century peak, Galiani. Unlike Law, he was so uncompromising a metallist that he felt compelled to inquire into the value of gold and silver considered as commodities and therefore into the value of all commodities. In doing so he displayed sure-footed mastery of analytic procedure and, in particular, neatness in his carefully defined conceptual constructions to a degree that would have rendered superfluous all the nineteenth century squabbles—and misunderstandings—on the subject of value had the parties to these squabbles first studied his text, *Della moneta,* 1751" (1954, 300–301).

14. In the opening page of his book Galiani states: "I shall begin by showing that all men have generally used the metals—principally gold and silver—as money; whence the value of the metals arises; that this originates, is determined and regulated neither by whimsey, nor by edicts of princes, and that money draws its value from the value of metals" (1751, 3).

15. In order to corroborate the hypothesis centered on the commodity value of money, Galiani provides a rudimentary estimate of the allocation of the silver stock in the kingdom of Naples, arguing that since the portion allotted to nonmonetary uses far exceeds the one making up the money supply (20 million versus 6 million ducats respectively), the value of money must depend on the value of metals (1751, 41–46).

money, which Galiani accounts for by referring to the special properties of metals, strongly rejecting the "consensus" view (1751, 48–49).[16] His treatment of the functions and properties of money is embedded in metallism. Having distinguished the unit-of-account and the medium-of-exchange functions, he stresses that while the former can also be performed by "ideal money," the latter can be carried out only by "real money," i.e., actual metallic money.[17] Real money, besides being easy to transport and to exchange, must be universally acceptable, which in turn requires that it have the following four "qualities": (1) an intrinsic value, (2) a true value easy to calculate, (3) insusceptibility to debasement by fraud, and (4) durability. His metallist stance could hardly be more clear. In particular, emphasizing the second point, he focuses on the uniform quality possessed by precious metals, the cornerstone of Law's approach. And, like Law, he attributes to coinage merely an information-producing role that raises the efficiency of the monetary system (1751, 49–57).[18]

Galiani's straightforward arguments notwithstanding, the analysis of book 2 on "the Nature of Money" wholly upsets his position. He describes an abstract model in which, in order to overcome the inconveniences of barter, individuals "live together" as in small communities, e.g., religious orders. However, in a large society a lazy person could defraud others by consuming more than he has produced. To solve this problem people can be given a receipt, or note, stating the quantity of goods they have stored in the public warehouse, thus acquiring the right to withdraw an equal amount of goods. The prince would establish the

16. Both Law and Galiani, it should be emphasized, refer to *market* not to *physical* characteristics of the money commodity, thus grasping the essential features of modern theory. In concluding his article Jones states that "the approach suggests that a very common good would emerge as a first commodity money in a barter economy. The important point is that this 'commonness' is *a market characteristic* of goods rather than an intrinsic physical characteristic such as portability, divisibility or cognizability" (1976, 775, emphasis added). For a detailed analysis regarding Galiani see Cesarano 1976.

17. Long before Galiani's time, frequent alterations in metallic currencies prompted the practice of expressing the price of goods in a hypothetical unit of account of a given weight and titer ("ideal money") in order to compute more easily the value of the coins effectively exchanged ("real money").

18. "It is certain that man will not risk concluding any contract except in situations he clearly understands without fear of deception. Since money intervenes in all contracts, it is most necessary that it be made of a substance that is easy to evaluate. But I have already demonstrated that nothing more appropriate or more secure than gold and silver will be found for this purpose. The Chinese nation demonstrates, by example, how easy it is to determine goodness and weight. Everyone there provides his own test and knows how to weigh gold and evaluate it perfectly well. In other, more learned nations, princes and republics have taken the trouble to determine the goodness and weight of the metals, and to insure these by their own imprint and on their own faith. In this manner, they have brought the use of the metals, as money, to perfection, as the book which follows will show. But this is not entirely necessary" (1751, 57). In the 1780 edition, the last sentence is more explicit and reads: "But coinage was not necessary for establishing money."

relative prices of commodities and would have the task of issuing the notes, so that counterfeiting would be disposed of. Yet such notes are nothing but money. Money is the means by which everyone's product is represented: it allows the "living together" of a large society where inconsistent claims on the common product are avoided by the pursuit of self-interest.

> I saw, and all can now see, that trade and money—its prime mover—have led us from a wretched state of nature in which each thinks only of himself, to a blissful communal life in which each thinks of and labors for all. We maintain ourselves in this latter state, not simply by the principles of virtue and piety, which where entire nations are envisaged are bonds that, by themselves, do not suffice—but by the self interest and comfort of each individual.
>
> *Coins are the notes discussed here, because in the end these are the representations of credit which one has against society, either directly, by reason of the work done by him, or indirectly because of coins donated to him by others.* In reality, there are no common warehouses among us, there are only private stores which correspond to them. Notes—really coins—are not paid to and collected from general custodians. With much greater wisdom, each person cares for his own labor and tries to fill his own store, giving up money which he receives by trading, or acquires by selling merchandise.
>
> In other words, virtue and faith are not needed by public warehousemen, nor is the vigilance of the prince required, because notes are not squandered. Everyone is reluctant to part with them since to give up money is to dispose of one's own arduous toil. Such a disadvantage which would not be sufficiently controlled by any virtue that is presumed to prevail in that first state, is taken care of in the present state perfectly by self interest, the force of which is always found in all of us, even the most vicious. (1751, 70, emphasis added)

Galiani's contribution has been given due prominence by several economists.[19] Notable anticipations of this view of money as a representation of labor can be found in the writings of nominalists such as

19. Einaudi (1953, 278–81) draws attention to the "methodology of successive approximations." Robbins, instead, refers to the relevance to the fundamentals of money and approvingly quotes Bousquet's appraisal (in his Introduction to Galiani 1955): "A great page of world economic literature" (Robbins 1968, 123). The importance of Galiani's model in relation to contemporary monetary theory is shown in Cesarano 1976, 384–87. Given the exhaustive treatment provided by the latter article, the present paper does not significantly add to the analysis of Galiani's work on the foundations of money, but looks at it from a different perspective.

Buridan, Oresme, and Biel (Gordon 1975, ch. 7). In the present context, Galiani's brilliant exposition is striking in that it sharply clashes with the metallist character of *Della moneta.* His cartalist model cannot be lightly cast aside, since it stands out in the structure of his work.[20] These opposite approaches might tentatively be reconciled by confining his metallism to the practical sphere while acknowledging his theoretical cartalism, following Schumpeter's assessment of Boisguillebert (1954, 293–94, n. 11). This interpretation is supported by the concluding passage of Galiani's cartalist model, where a metallic money is called for as an operational device to prevent fraud and inflationary policies.

> Finally, every disadvantage which notes might have, whatever material they might be made of, has been eliminated by metallic money. This quality, coinage, and structure of the latter provides for its intrinsic value a protection against private fraud, an abuse which even the prince might commit; for if the material did not have to contain the full value of the money, then the prince could always print an excessive number of notes. The doubt alone which he could cause in this way would be sufficient to take away from, or reduce their price, and inhibit their circulation. As for the material of which money is made, only God could increase it; and mining it or attempting to attract it from abroad would only give rise to as much expense as it is ultimately worth. Thus, nothing is gained by increasing it. Hence, it is of the greatest importance that money should be made of materials the whole value of which is natural and intrinsic and not imaginary. (1751, 71)

Nevertheless it seems farfetched to limit Galiani's metallism to the design of the standard, given the forceful exposition of his theoretical arguments. Apparently he had more than an intuition about a theory of fiat money, having developed a fully articulated model, but was not able to carry this analysis further (for reasons that will appear in section II).

But our interest here goes beyond the mere labeling of authors with their respective tags. The main question is to explain the late development of theoretical cartalism. Schumpeter (1954, 289, n. 5) points to the confusion between the historical origin of money—in which a highly saleable commodity likely plays a significant role—and its logic or essential functions, which have little to do with its physical characteristics. However, classic authors mostly keep their treatments of the origin

20. The model is included in the first chapter of book 2 on the nature of money. In book 1 he observes that "although money will be the object of my deliberations in the next book, as long as I have already approached it in this chapter, I will begin by stating its definitions, reserving their discussion, in turn, for the second book, thus establishing the entire discussion on a thoroughly well reasoned footing" (1751, 49).

of money quite distinct from those regarding its nature. A more relevant factor seems related to the failure to provide a rationale of the value of paper money. Drawing due attention to the quid pro quo restriction in the exchange process, the classic authors focused on the commodity, as they were unable to account for the value of token money.[21] Indeed that restriction is the basis of the Aristotelian tradition, emphasizing justice in exchange, which looms large in Law and Galiani. Detailed investigations by Langholm (1983, 1984) and Gordon (1975) have probed the subject much further, revealing a number of important elements from the analyses of the Schoolmen which have held the stage in the foregoing discussion. These elements, though not always unambiguously, drive towards theoretical metallism, thus exerting a remarkable influence in the general background of the authors considered here and corroborating the hypothesis I have advanced in this section.

II

Both Law's and Galiani's approaches to the standard contrast, in some degree, with their respective theoretical standpoints. Analysis of this antinomy, besides illustrating the authors' contribution, sheds light on the relationship between the foundations of money and the design of institutions. In general, theory bears upon the monetary system in at least two respects: first, by indicating the objectives to be aimed at, i.e., the arguments of the social welfare function; second, by defining the operational clauses of the standard or "rules of the game," i.e., the requirements that must be met in order to assure viability.[22] Thus the role of theory is to set a boundary within which the standard can be

21. Discussing the definition of money, Galiani states: "First of all, things which have conventional rather than intrinsic value are excluded from consideration. This is why it is surely less secure to have in hand a thing whose value depends on public faith and agreement than one which necessity and utility makes valuable to mankind. Generally speaking, such a thing cannot become money. For this reason, a country could never be satisfied for long to utilize notes or money made of leather. And although notes do circulate as money in many places, I do not know if when a country which now uses notes should fall under a nearby hostile neighbor, whether the conqueror would be content to continue to allow payments to be made with notes, or whether it would prefer that metallic money be used instead. Many and great are the differences between common belief and the public faith. The former is as immutable as it is universal. The latter does not extend any further than to persons and nations which have subscribed to some convention; it is subject to question, and often even to dissolution, by every little event. Consequently, people cannot for long use only representative money. Thus, that the value of the metals and their use as money rests on human convention is shown to be even more false" (1751, 55).

22. In contemporary literature Patinkin has formally analyzed the "minimum requirements of a monetary system," arguing that in order to avoid price-level indeterminacy, there should "be an exogenous fixing of (1) some nominal quantity and (2) some rate of return. . . . in an economy with both inside and outside money . . . it would suffice to fix the quantity of outside money and its rate of return (say, at zero)" (1961, 116).

developed but beyond which such development is constrained by the requirements of viability. These propositions are quite helpful in that they provide a benchmark for identifying the advances, as well as the limitations, of Law's and Galiani's work.

In accordance with these principles, Law's proposal in *Money and trade* (1705) strictly derives from his analytical framework.[23] The latter, described above in section I, focuses on the uniform quality of the money commodity, entailing a high information content and thus enhancing the functions of money. Following this approach, a substantial improvement in setting up the standard can be achieved by selecting goods that have a more stable price than silver. Law strongly criticizes the silver standard, pointing out its high variability in purchasing power due to public authorities' meddling with the currency and to eventual shifts in the demand for and supply of silver. Moreover, these changes in the value of currency occur even though both money and goods are certain in quality (1705, 59–64). Then two arguments, negative and positive respectively, enter Law's objective function: price level variability and "trade," i.e., a real variable like output or employment. Law identifies land as the commodity which, as it has a rather stable price and allows the issue of paper money against it, should be chosen as the standard in order to maximize social welfare. Given his mercantilist stance, he almost takes for granted the influence of money on income[24] but dwells at length upon price stability, which he approaches from two angles, relating to value and monetary theory. First, the price of land is not subject to wide variations given its fixed supply and its rather sticky demand, insofar as eventual shifts in tastes do not bring about variations in the total quantity of cultivated land. Second, since it is possible to issue paper against land, money supply can be changed as its demand changes, to stabilize the value of money (1705, 89–92).

> The Paper-money propos'd will be equal in value to Silver, for it will have a value of Land pledg'd, equal to the same Sum of Silver-money, that it is given out for. If any Losses should happen, one 4th of the Revenue of the Commission, will in all appearance be more than sufficient to make them good.

23. The present section concentrates on the theoretical aspects of monetary institutions and hence does not examine either Law's various projects or the writings dealing with them (see volumes 2 and 3 of his collected works edited by Harsin, 1934). The emphasis laid on theory stems from the following passage: "Considering the present state of Europe, France and Spain being Masters of the Mines. The other Nations seem to be under a necessity of setting up another Money. The only Reason can be given why it has not yet been done, is, that the nature of Money has not been rightly understood: Or they would not have continued buying Silver from Spain above its Value as a Mettal, when they had a more valuable Money of their own, and every way more fitted for that Use" (1705, 77).

24. The treatment of this topic is one of the least satisfactory in *Money and trade*.

> This Paper-money will not fall in value as Silver-money has fallen, or may fall: Goods or Money fall in value, if they increase in Quantity, or if the Demand lessens. But the Commission giving out what Sums are demanded, and taking back what Sums are offer'd to be return'd; this Paper-money will keep its value, and there will always be as much Money as there is occasion, or imployment for, and no more. (1705, 89)

Law's analysis, however, is not addressed to the demand for money to hold and fails to advance the notion of equilibrium cash balances. His important insight instead concerns the conception of money as a tool enabling the attainment of welfare objectives.[25] This interpretation is not new; Schumpeter recognized Law's work as giving "birth to the idea of Managed Currency" (1954, 322). But it should be emphasized because of its highly innovative character. In fact, in the mainstream of classical monetary economics the design of the standard is mainly considered as a technical problem not related to the optimal use of policy instruments. Stability of purchasing power is often stressed, but it was not conceived of as a goal within a discretionary policy framework until the end of the nineteenth century.[26]

Law's originality notwithstanding, his proposal is dominated by the concern—strictly related to his metallist theoretical stance—of assigning a value to the new paper money. References to this point are plentiful (1705, 83–84, 89, 92, 94–96, 100–4, 118). For example:

> The Practice of most Trading Nations confirms, that Paper is more Qualified for the Use of Money, than Silver; *providing it have a Value*. In Holland Silver is pledg'd, and Paper is used as Money. That Land pledg'd is a better Value than Silver pledg'd, is evident from what has been said. (1705, 94, emphasis added)

25. "Trade and Money depend mutually on one another; when Trade decayes, Money lessens; and when Money lessens, Trade decayes. Power and Wealth consists in Numbers of People, and Magazines of Home and Forreign Goods; these depend on Trade, and Trade on Money. So while Trade and Money may be affected directly and consequentially; that what is hurtful to either, must be so to both, Power and Wealth will be precarious.

"If a Money is establish't that has no intrinsick Value, and its extrinsick Value to be such, as it will not be Exported; nor will not be less than the Demand for it within the Country: Wealth and Power will be attained, and be less precarious. Money not being liable to be lessen'd directly, nor consequentially; and Trade not liable to decay consequentially. So the Power and Wealth of that Country will only be precarious, from what may be directly hurtful to Trade.

"The Paper Money propos'd being always equal in Quantity to the Demand, the People will be employ'd, the Country improv'd, Manufacture advanc'd, Trade Domestick and Forreign will be carried on, and Wealth and Power attained. And not being liable to be Exported, the People will not be set Idle, etc. And Wealth and Power will be less precarious" (Law 1705, 101–2).

26. Among the earliest examples of such an analysis are Wicksell 1898, 1906, and Fisher 1911. In the period following World War I important references are Keynes 1923 and Hayek's discussion of an "elastic" currency (1935, ch. 4).

This difficulty most clearly appears in his thought experiment regarding "an Island belonging to one man" (1705, 97–100), an abstract model which investigates the effects of a transition from a barter to a monetary economy upon the issue of paper money with the objective of employing "poor or idle" people. Concluding his exposition, Law again manifests his worries about the value of fiat money.

> This Money tho it has no value but what the proprietor [of the island] gives it, by receiving it in payments of his Rent; yet it will be esteem'd equal to the product payed before.
>
> If the Proprietor would give it a value in Land, computing after this Manner: An Acre of Land pays Number 100, at 20 years purchase worth Number 2000. And dispone the Property of Land for Paper at that value; Who would not be satisfied to receive or contract for that Money, since it not only bought the Product, but the Property of Land at a reasonable price[?] (1705, 100)

In this latter passage Law provides two answers to the question at stake: in the first paragraph he recurs to the notion of acceptability;[27] in the second, he assigns to notes a right to the property of land. He follows the latter, less suggestive, approach and compares, in much detail, land and silver as alternative monetary standards (1705, 100–1), thus strictly abiding by his views on the nature of money. He makes no advance on the problem of the value of fiduciary money—a question that would await a satisfactory answer for another two centuries—but perceives that a limit on the quantity of notes must be set. This is clearly indicated in his proposal of reform and in his island model (1705, 86, 89).[28]

In sum, Law's work on the fundamentals of money, upon which he builds, severely limits his cartalist approach to the standard. All the same, his theory provides the rationale of welfare objectives, e.g., price-level stability, which characterize the design of the monetary system. Thus as regards the first of the two benchmark principles stated at the beginning of this section, he does make some important contribution. But with respect to the second one, concerning the "rules of the game," he does not go very far, since he does not follow up his felicitous intuition focusing on acceptability.

Whereas Law stretches practical cartalism despite his metallist approach to the nature of money, Galiani displays just the opposite posture. In contrast with his penetrating analysis of a monetary economy embodied in the model of "living together" (see section I above), he

27. Notice, however, that he does not refer to *general* acceptability but to a more specific notion, confined to the proprietor of the island who bestows value upon the paper.

28. In later works, not considered in the present paper, Law also refers to convertibility of notes. See Nicholson 1915, 393, and Wasserman and Beach 1934, 649.

forcefully holds to a metallic standard. Hence our main task regarding his attitude towards the monetary system is not to demonstrate his relentless metallist view, but rather to account for his failure to carry out his model by developing a cartalist standard.

Before venturing an interpretation, we should consider the motivations mentioned by Galiani himself. Discussing the smooth working of a paper money in the English Colonies of North America populated by Quakers, he remarks that "such an event is very strange indeed" (1751, 236) and offers three explanations:

> I. The colonies of Pennsylvania have only savages for neighbors and, consequently, do not fear that their paper will be counterfeited; II. They only trade with England, which they can watch carefully and attentively. III. Finally, because extraordinary actions, which seem to exceed human strength, can truly be counselled by virtue. The only fanaticism (wretched condition!) is the obstinate duty by which some part of the group can make all the others follow faithfully. This is why false sects have followed some policies which Christians have admired, though they have in all honesty not been able to emulate them. Hence, the example of paper money cannot be taken from Quakers and imitated. (1751, 238)

This amusing exposition essentially boils down to considering the American case as a peculiar exception. However, Galiani does give some further rationales for his strong opposition to a fiduciary standard. (1) Although inconsistent with his model of "living together," several of his statements supporting theoretical metallism (see section I above) severely condition his approach to the standard. (2) In this connection, his treatment of paper money is revealing in that he defines notes as "representations of money."[29] (3) Last but not least is the strong impression left by the vicissitudes of Law's "System." This last topic is extensively dealt with in *Della moneta:* an entire chapter is dedicated to French monetary events of 1718 (1751, 191–98), and various sections on representative money specifically examine Law's experiences in France (1751, 242–45).

Galiani's assessment of Law—whom he refers to as an "artful planner" (1751, 187) and, a few pages later, as "a man of the rarest and most remarkable genius but one without virtue or religion" (242)—is highly critical and is based on Law's violation of the metallist principle. While recognizing the congruity of Law's measures aimed at retiring the *billets*

29. Fiduciary money is always referred to as representing full-bodied coins (1751, 42, 97). Furthermore, the chapter in which he extensively deals with the subject is entitled "The representations of money circulating in human commerce" (1751, 235–53).

d'état, Galiani faults him for having issued an excessive quantity of notes, the latter being "merely images of money" (244). This same argument is advanced in note xxx—added in the second (1780) edition of *Della moneta*—in order to explain the fall of the "System." He also estimates the volume of note issue which would have kept equilibrium in the money market and avoided the depreciation of paper.[30]

Commenting on the same episodes in the final chapter of part 3, dealing with the raising of money, Galiani emphasizes the relevance of the surprise element in successfully implementing an inflationary policy.[31] Indeed, his firm metallist standpoint notwithstanding, he favors inflation as a measure to be adopted only in exceptional circumstances when other policies are precluded. Thus his contribution relates more to the conduct of policy than to the design of the standard, although his treatments of bimetallism—calling for higher flexibility in the prices of metals—and of monetary reform deserve mention as examples of applied monetary analysis.

In terms of the two benchmark principles stated at the opening of this section, Galiani's search for measures to drive the economy towards an optimal path should be emphasized. Unlike Law and in line with classical tradition, he does not call for discretionary action but sees policy as an extraordinary instrument enabling the avoidance of heavy social costs in critical contingencies.

From discussion in this section we may draw some general lessons. The contrasting positions examined here are highly indicative of the uneven and difficult advancement of monetary economics.[32] The intricacy of the field can be seen not only in the persistence of weak theoretical hypotheses over substantial periods—the dominance of theoretical metallism being the most conspicuous example—but also in delays in bringing theory up to date with innovations spurred by market forces. In the course of monetary history, various developments in institutional arrangements have not received an adequate analytical treatment or have been downright misinterpreted. Notable instances are the multi-

30. Galiani follows a quantity theory approach and thus sets the limit to the issue of notes at the level which would have brought the total stock of money to that of 1698, a most prosperous year. Then he gives a conclusive judgment of Law's "System," again focusing on metallism: "Law made this blunder: that he thought that all State debts could be extinguished with notes, and thus he created them in proportion to the mass of all the debt of the French crown. A very serious and unexcusable mistake to so great a man; because one thing has nothing to do with the other; because it is not either useful or feasible to extinguish all State debts; finally because, if that could be done, justice requires that it is done with real money, and not with the imposture of paper, which represents nothing effectively existing and nothing probable in the future" (1751, 342; translated from A. Caracciolo's edition, since this note does not appear in Toscano's translation).

31. Galiani's analysis of inflation is thoroughly discussed in Cesarano 1976. See also Cesarano 1983.

32. In this regard see Hicks's pregnant observations in his *Critical essays* (1967, v–vii).

plicative process of deposit creation and the viability of a paper standard. The complexity of monetary phenomena brings about a lag in theoretical developments which may have momentous implications.

Even today, innovations in the monetary scenario may be accompanied by a theoretical vacuum. The recent diffusion of nontangible means of payment has prompted a lively debate that has touched on both theoretical and institutional issues.[33] One main point in that debate is intimately related to discussion here. So far as it concerns an accounting system of exchange, the problem of minimum requirements—stemming from the familiar Wicksellian phenomenon of price-level indeterminacy (see note 22 above)—is far from being settled,[34] since its solution may well be at odds with the one that holds for an economy with tangible money and may prove to be elusive.

III

This paper has presented a novel hypothesis on John Law's work on the fundamentals of money and has contrasted that with Galiani's viewpoint. The apparently schizophrenic attitude of these authors—Law embraced theoretical metallism but headed towards practical cartalism, whereas Galiani succeeded in building a model of theoretical cartalism while firmly standing by practical metallism—sheds light on several important issues. The quid pro quo requirement in classical conceptions of the exchange mechanism has long played a crucial role in the dominance of theoretical metallism. Both Law and Galiani suffered from this influence, although Galiani developed a detailed model of cartalism.

In this connection, the question of the value of fiat money affects the analysis of a fiduciary standard, whose design Law attempted to advance. His ingenious insight about a managed currency was matched by his failure to draw the appropriate "rules of the game." The factual counterpart of the latter was the collapse of his "System," which had a devastating impact and likely held back the implementation of Galiani's substantial contribution to theoretical cartalism.

This paper has benefited from the perceptive comments made by two anonymous referees. The usual caveat applies.

33. This literature has been synthetically labeled "new monetary economics," following Hall 1982b. The main references include Black 1970, Fama 1980, Hall 1982a, 1982b, and Greenfield and Yeager 1983. A critical assessment can be found in White 1984 and McCallum 1985. An exchange of notes between Greenfield and Yeager, and White can be found in the September 1986 issue of the *American Economic Review*. Cowen and Krozner (1987) have analyzed the subject from a history of economics standpoint.

34. McCallum (1985, 34–35) criticizes Greenfield and Yeager (1983) for failing to cope with price-level determinacy in their proposal.

References

Alchian, Armen. 1977. Why money? *Journal of Money, Credit, and Banking* 9 (February): 133–40.

Black, Fischer. 1970. Banking and interest rates in a world without money: the effect of uncontrolled banking. *Journal of Bank Research* 1 (Autumn 1970): 9–20.

Brunner, Karl, and Allan H. Meltzer. 1971. The uses of money: money in the theory of an exchange economy. *American Economic Review* 61 (December): 784–805.

———. 1985. The "new monetary economics," fiscal issues, and unemployment. *Carnegie-Rochester Conference Series on Public Policy* 23:1–12.

Cesarano, Filippo. 1976. Monetary theory in Ferdinando Galiani's *Della moneta*. *HOPE* 8 (Fall): 380–99.

———. 1983. The rational expectations hypothesis in retrospect. *American Economic Review* 73 (March): 198–203.

———. 1988. Ferdinando Galiani. In *The new Palgrave: a dictionary of economic theory and doctrine*. Edited by J. Eatwell, M. Milgate, and P. Newman. London: Macmillan.

Cowen, Tyler, and Randall Krozner. 1987. The development of the new monetary economics. *Journal of Political Economy* 95 (June): 567–90.

Einaudi, Luigi. 1953. Galiani economista. In *Saggi bibliografici e storici intorno alle dottrine economiche*. Rome: Edizioni di storia e letteratura. First published in German in *Schweizerische Zeitschrift für Volkswirtschaft und Statistik* 81, no. 1 (1945).

Fama, Eugene F. 1980. Banking in the theory of finance. *Journal of Monetary Economics* 6 (January):39–57.

Fisher, Irving. 1911. *The purchasing power of money*. New York: Macmillan.

Friedman, Milton. 1986. The resource cost of irredeemable paper money. *Journal of Political Economy* 94, part 1: 642–47.

Galiani, Ferdinando. [1751] 1977. *On money*. Translated by Peter R. Toscano. Ann Arbor: University Microfilms International.

———. 1955. *De la monnaie*. Partial translation by G.-H. Bousquet and J. Crisafulli. Paris: Rivière.

Gambino, Amedeo. 1956. John Law, banker and economist. Banca Nazionale del Lavoro, *Quarterly Review* 9 (September): 100–110.

Gordon, Barry. 1975. *Economic analysis before Adam Smith*. London: Macmillan.

Greenfield, Robert L., and Leland B. Yeager. 1983. A laissez-faire approach to monetary stability. *Journal of Money, Credit, and Banking* 15 (August): 302–15.

———. 1986. Competitive payments systems: comment. *American Economic Review* 76 (September): 848–49.

Hall, Robert E. 1982a. Explorations in the gold standard and related policies for stabilizing the dollar. In *Inflation: causes and effects*. Chicago: University of Chicago Press, 1982.

———. 1982b. *Monetary trends in the United States and the United Kingdom:* A review from the perspective of new developments in monetary economics. *Journal of Economic Literature* 20 (December): 1552–56.

Hamilton, Earl J. 1968. John Law. In *International encyclopedia of social sciences*. Edited by David L. Sills. New York: Macmillan.

Hayek, Friedrich A. [1935] 1967. *Prices and production*. New York: Augustus M. Kelley. Reprint of the 2d ed., 1935.
Hicks, John R. 1967. *Critical essays in monetary theory*. Oxford: Oxford University Press.
Jones, Robert A. 1976. The origin and development of media of exchange. *Journal of Political Economy* 84, no. 4, part 1 (August): 757–75.
Keynes, John Maynard. 1923. *A tract on monetary reform*. London: Macmillan.
King, Robert G., and Charles I. Plosser. 1986. Money as the mechanism of exchange. *Journal of Monetary Economics* 17 (January): 93–115.
Langholm, Odd. 1983. *Wealth and money in the Aristotelian tradition*. Bergen: Universitetsforlaget.
———. 1984. *The Aristotelian analysis of usury*. Bergen: Universitetsforlaget.
Law, John. 1705. *Money and trade considered with a proposal for supplying the nation with money*. Edinburgh: Anderson. Reprinted New York: Augustus M. Kelley, 1966.
———. 1934. *Oeuvres complètes*. Edited by P. Harsin. Paris: Sirey.
McCallum, Bennett T. 1985. Bank deregulation, accounting systems of exchange, and the unit of account: a critical review. *Carnegie-Rochester Conference Series on Public Policy* 23:13–46.
Menger, Carl. 1892. On the origin of money. *Economic Journal* 2 (June): 239–55.
Monroe, Arthur E. 1923. *Monetary theory before Adam Smith*. Cambridge: Harvard University Press.
Nicholson, J. S. 1915. A chapter in the life of John Law. *Economic Journal* 25 (September): 389–94.
Patinkin, Don. 1961. Financial intermediaries and the logical structure of monetary theory. *American Economic Review* 51 (March): 95–116.
Rist, Charles. 1951. *Histoire des doctrines relatives au crédit et à la monnaie depuis John Law jusqu'à nos jours*. 2d ed. Paris: Sirey.
Robbins, Lionel. 1968. *The theory of economic development in the history of economic thought*. London: Macmillan.
Schumpeter, Joseph A. 1954. *History of economic analysis*. Oxford: Oxford University Press.
Vickers, Douglas. 1960. *Studies in the theory of money 1690–1776*. London: Owen.
Wasserman, Max J., and Frank H. Beach. 1934. Some neglected monetary theories of John Law. *American Economic Review* 24 (December): 646–57.
White, Lawrence H. 1984. Competitive payments systems and the unit of account. *American Economic Review* 74 (September): 699–712.
Wicksell, Knut. [1898] 1965. *Interest and prices*. New York: Kelley. 1st German ed., 1898; 1st English trans., 1936.
———. [1906] 1935. *Lectures on political economy*. Vol. 2. London: Routledge. 1st Swedish ed., 1906.

[10]

JES
30,5

Defining fundamental disequilibrium: Keynes's unheeded contribution

Filippo Cesarano
Banca d'Italia, Roma, Italy

Keywords *Keynesian economics, Agreements, Monetary policy*

Abstract *The Bretton Woods agreements set up the post-war monetary order on the basis of fixed exchange rates and autonomous national economic policy. Changes in parity were allowed in the case of fundamental disequilibrium, but this concept was not defined, promoting a lengthy but sterile debate. This paper, after reviewing the main features of the discussion, analyzes Keynes's overlooked contribution, which helps to clarify the issue at stake.*

The Bretton Woods agreements laid the foundations of the international monetary system after the failures and disorders of the inter-war period. In the mid-1920s, Britain's ephemeral return to gold was accompanied by deflation and unemployment. The pound was eventually forced off the gold standard in September 1931, triggering off an irreversible crisis of the world's centuries old commodity-based monetary arrangements. As the Second World War unfolded, then, the reconstruction of the international monetary system posed an intellectual challenge. For the first time in history, a monetary order was arrived at neither through the imposition of an imperialistic power, as in the Roman-Byzantine era, nor through a historical process like the gold standard, but was designed by experts[1].

The task was not an easy one. Keen to avoid the problems of the 1930s, such as exchange controls and beggar-thy-neighbor devaluations, the architects of Bretton Woods sought to provide for both exchange rate stability and an autonomous economic policy centered on full employment. These features were reflected in the *modus operandi* of the system (Bordo, 1993, p. 37; Williamson, 1985, section I). In the short run, countries would use their own reserves and Fund financial facilities to cope with temporary payments imbalances. In the medium term, a correction of economic policies was required in the case of conflict between external and internal balance, while capital controls would prevent speculative attacks and create leeway for domestic policy action. Finally, a change in parity would be allowed in the case of a "fundamental disequilibrium". However, the IMF Articles of Agreement left this notion undefined, leading to a heated debate over its precise meaning. As Mikesell

Thanks are due to two anonymous referees for their useful comments. The usual caveat applies.

Journal of Economic Studies
Vol. 30 No. 5, 2003
pp. 474-492
© MCB UP Limited
0144-3585
DOI 10.1108/01443580310492790

(1994, p. 18) recalls in his memoir on the Bretton Woods negotiations: "Indeed, fundamental disequilibrium has never been defined in fewer than ten pages."

Much of this squabble would have been avoided if Keynes's view of the subject had been accorded due consideration. Keynes had played a crucial role in the talks leading to the Bretton Woods conference. In November 1940, he was consulted by the British government about post-war monetary arrangements and began to draft a reform proposal that eventually became the Keynes plan of April 1943, the end-product of three decades of reflections. Here, he investigated the conditions under which a change in parity should be admitted. The present paper illustrates the debate on the definition of fundamental disequilibrium and then analyzes Keynes's unheeded contribution.

The debate on fundamental disequilibrium

The term "fundamental disequilibrium" appeared in the first mimeographed draft of the White Plan of April 1942 as the undefined condition allowing a change in parity, subject to the consent of four-fifths of member votes. In the published version of July 1943, the required majority was lowered to three-fourths, but the condition remains undefined. It is only in the "Joint Statement" of British and American experts at the basis of the Bretton Woods conference that we find the qualification, later included in the IMF Articles of Agreement, whereby "the Fund shall not reject a requested change [in parity] necessary to restore equilibrium because of domestic social or political policies of the country applying for a change" (Horsefield, 1969, p. 133).

The overriding concern of the Bretton Woods architects was to re-establish a viable fixed exchange rate regime, admitting parity adjustments in exceptional circumstances only. The US Treasury's commentary on the Joint Statement, issued shortly before the conference, was that parities should not be altered "unnecessarily or when there are other satisfactory means of restoring equilibrium in a country's international balance of payments" (Horsefield, 1969, p. 155). In this connection, Viner (1943, p. 204) noted that the 80 percent of the majority requirement set in the first draft of the White Plan was so strict as to make any parity change virtually unfeasible, since each country would be interested in avoiding devaluation by any other, making the system much more rigid than the gold standard. This was a sensitive issue, in that the dramatic experience of the Great Depression spotlighted the working of monetary arrangements in relation to full employment. Until the end of the 1920s, only a few critics of the gold standard, and Keynes (1923) in particular, had called for an economic policy aimed at price and output stabilization. Afterwards, when the role of the gold standard in propagating the depression was perceived[2], the state of the art underwent a major change and Keynes's unorthodox position became the majority view. The analytical framework of the *General Theory* made the case for activist policy a compelling one. Consequently, the design of the monetary system had to be turned upside-down in order to introduce, in contrast with the gold standard, rules flexible enough to attain domestic targets[3]. However, this development in the direction of greater flexibility can potentially clash with fixed exchange rates: while full employment requires autonomous demand policies, adherence to a fixed-rate regime subjects those policies to the constraint of maintaining parity. Essentially, the difficulty of defining fundamental disequilibrium is bound up with this latent conflict.

The notion of fundamental disequilibrium generally relates to inadequacies of the adjustment mechanism. Indeed, owing to the depression and the influence of Keynes's (1973, 1964) writings, skepticism about the self-adjusting nature of the economy was widespread in the profession[4], and this was reflected in the attempt to define fundamental disequilibrium. Purchasing power parity theory would have answered the purpose, providing a ready analytical tool. However, despite the popularity it enjoyed after the First World War, the theory was widely criticized in the 1930s and eventually fell into disrepute. Even an economist close to the classical tradition like Haberler (1948, p. 387) pointed to the difficulties of calculating purchasing power parity, arguing that this "should not be regarded as a definition but rather as one symptom (indicator) among others of exchange equilibrium or its absence". Given the imprecision of this indicator, attention should focus directly on the flow of international reserves (Haberler, 1945, p. 313). A necessary condition for fundamental disequilibrium, in his view, was a balance-of-payments deficit, and currency devaluation should be allowed only if the deficit persisted after the implementation of corrective policies. An actual payments deficit thus provided "an objective, unambiguous, and observable criterion" to interpret fundamental disequilibrium (Haberler, 1948, p. 392). As Haberler recalled, this criterion is set also in the Keynes plan. In fact, Keynes (1930) definitely abandoned purchasing power parity theory in the *Treatise* and, in his article on "The future of the foreign exchanges," (Keynes, 1982a) took up the balance-of-payments criterion[5].

While interpreting the Bretton Woods agreements, economists aimed to supply an operational definition of disequilibrium and soon became entangled in details concerning the items of the capital account to be included in the definition, the size of the unbalanced position, and the relevant time span. Yet, it was not the controversy on these specific questions that fueled the debate, because a common view of disequilibrium eventually emerged, identifying it with the impossibility of achieving basic balance over the medium term[6]. Instead, the main disputes turned on the efficacy of devaluation to correct a payment deficit and the limitations of the common view. The first is an empirical issue relating to the Marshall-Lerner condition. The skeptical attitude towards the self-adjusting property of the economy fostered elasticity pessimism (Hansen, 1948, pp. 379-80) partly corroborated by the pioneeristic econometric work of Tinbergen (1946). But the evidence was not unambiguous

(Polak, 1947) and quite a few authors (Bloomfield, 1947, pp. 312-13; Haberler, 1948, pp. 392-3) followed Marshall's conjecture in support of an equilibrating effect of devaluation. Metzler (1948, pp. 232-3) related the question to the relevant time span and hypothesized smaller and greater elasticities in the short and long run, respectively. Hence, in the early stage of the debate the issue remained undecided.

The second point regards the emergence of fundamental disequilibrium even if the country's international position is balanced. An obvious instance is given by the presence of exchange controls, a common state of affairs at the time. But the main argument consists in the fall in output and employment caused by an overvalued currency. Many writers (Haberler, 1948, p. 388; Hansen 1948, p. 379; Nurkse, 1944, p. 125, 1945, pp. 10-11; Robinson, 1947, p. 103) cited the UK experience during the ephemeral return to gold from 1925 to 1931, when the balance of payments was in equilibrium and yet, given the overvaluation of the pound, the country suffered depression and unemployment. After 1931, an analogous situation was observed in Belgium (Triffin, 1947, pp. 76-7). These stylized facts undermined the balance-of-payments criterion and led to a more articulated conception of equilibrium in which the state of employment is essential. Currency misalignments can be easily detected in a full employment situation in which parity change is the correct solution. In conditions of unemployment, though, attention should be focused on internal factors and on alternative policies, i.e. temporary exchange controls to counter price competition deriving from cyclical fluctuations, or an increase in investment to stimulate sluggish aggregate demand. On the other hand, a persistent payments deficit deriving from an unbalanced structure of production can be met by reshaping of the import and export structure (Hansen, 1948, pp. 380-2). In the effort to capture the various situations giving rise to fundamental disequilibrium, many writers indulged in cataloguing different causes and circumstances that eventually proved unsuccessful. Eschewing such taxonomies, Robinson, 1947, p. 103, italics in the original) took a more systematic approach:

> [T]here is no one rate of exchange which is the equilibrium rate corresponding to a given state of world demands and techniques. In any given situation there is an equilibrium rate corresponding to each rate of interest and level of effective demand, and any rate of exchange, within very wide limits, can be turned into the equilibrium rate by altering the rate of interest appropriately. Moreover, any rate of exchange can be made compatible with any rate of interest provided that money wages can be sufficiently altered. The notion of *the* equilibrium exchange rate is a chimera. The rate of exchange, the rate of interest, the level of effective demand and the level of money wages react upon each other like the balls in Marshall's bowl, and no one is determined unless all the rest are given.

Hence, there is no hard and fast criterion to identify the fundamental disequilibrium since the exchange rate is one variable of a general equilibrium system. Furthermore, the rejection of the self-adjusting property of the economy entails the pursuit of active economic policies to bring aggregate demand to the full employment level. Balance-of-payments disequilibrium, therefore, is neither a necessary nor a sufficient condition of fundamental disequilibrium:

> Just as a mere balance of payments deficit is not conclusive evidence of a fundamental disequilibrium, the absence of such a deficit is not conclusive proof of a fundamental equilibrium in a country's international position. In the absence of compensatory action by the monetary authorities, a fundamental disequilibrium may fail to be reflected in any balance of payments deficit, owing to the prompt transmission of external deflationary pressures to domestic prices and incomes (Triffin, 1947, p. 76).

The difficulties of pinning down the notion of fundamental disequilibrium thus stemmed from the rejection of the classical paradigm. The employment level had become a policy target, so equilibrium was no longer a matter of adjustment driven by market forces but a question of policy design to achieve internal and external balance. This issue would eventually find a solution in Mundell's (1962) analysis of the assignment problem. But until then economists were groping to find away out of the taxonomic riddle, attempting to define the conditions of a change in parity.

Some critical contributions, however, throw light on this often sterile discussion. Viner (1944, p. 235) considers parity adjustments as an almost inevitable consequence of the "domestic social or political policies" contemplated by the Articles of Agreement, called for a more severe attitude towards parity changes. With the benefit of hindsight, his concern proved irrelevant because the post-war monetary order eventually evolved into a fixed rate dollar standard. Since full employment policies could hardly be consistent with a fixed exchange rate regime, the coherence of the monetary system was made up by a reduced autonomy of domestic policies. In this regard, Machlup (1958) offered a more substantive critique to the normative character of considering the employment target in the definition of fundamental disequilibrium. Proposing to put the analysis back on positive grounds, he contrasted the analytical usefulness of the notion of free market price with the lack thereof on the full employment concept. The latter, he held, is related to the criterion of a desirable level of activity which depends on value judgments and, hence, is an impediment in economic theory:

> [I]f a proper balance of payments is defined as one that does not prevent the country from having the employment level it desires at the wage rate it desires, then it all depends on what is desired, and every country in the world may have a balance of payments problem at the same time; the deficit countries, because they have deficits; the surplus countries, because they put up with unsatisfactory levels of activity. People or nations who cannot earn and borrow as much as they spend run into cash deficits and will have payments difficulties. People or nations who merely would like to spend more than they earn and borrow, but actually refrain from doing so, have no cash deficits; to say that people or nations have payments problems because *if* they did what they wanted they *would* have trouble does not seem to me useful, at least not in economic analysis (Machlup, 1958, p. 138, italics in the original).

Arguing for a positive analysis of balance-of-payments problems, Machlup rejected definitions based on a desirable level of employment, thus steering the debate towards an equilibrium approach. This different theoretical perspective would have cleared up most of the definitional ambiguities, but there was still widespread skepticism about the self-adjusting property of the economy and, in particular, the efficacy of international adjustment. The Keynesian adjustment mechanism considered was not at all effective, in that the increase in imports following an output expansion in the reserve-gaining country might not eliminate the trade surplus. As Metzler (1948, p. 220) noted in his survey: "[T]he new explanation, as we have seen, normally accounts for only a part of the adjustment and thus constitutes a theory of disequilibrium as well as a theory of equilibrium". On the other hand, the classical specie-flow mechanism was rejected because, in the presence of price and wage rigidity, the decrease in money supply in a deficit country entailed a fall in output and employment[7]. Also the central bank could sterilize gold flows, as in the early 1930s, impairing the effectiveness of the adjustment process.

With respect to the inadequacy of adjustment mechanisms, however, Keynes's followers went much further than Keynes, as is clear from an analysis of a related, hotly debated topic in post-war international finance, i.e. the dollar scarcity. Dollar scarcity was a corollary of the hypothesis underlying the ineffectiveness of international adjustment. The US payments surplus was viewed as an intractable phenomenon, in that equilibrating forces were either inefficacious or fraught with unacceptable consequences. Dissenting voices were not absent, but despite their authority they had little impact on the mainstream opinion. Haberler (1948, pp. 431-32), Keynes (1946), and Viner (1944, p. 240) cast serious doubt on the existence or the insolubility of dollar scarcity and eventually rejected both outright. This result is important in that, by denying the inefficacy of the adjustment mechanism, it helped to fix the boundaries of the notion of fundamental disequilibrium. Much of the controversy arose from the failure to distinguish between short- and long-run analysis and to consider the different policy targets – output, employment, and the price level – in their respective time horizons. Keeping these planes of inquiry separate would have helped to bring the definition of fundamental disequilibrium into focus. A related and most relevant matter was the limited effectiveness of employment policies relative to the structural deficiencies of the economy that do not respond to those policies and, hence, are not amenable to quick correction. These aspects were considered by Keynes, whose work clarifies most of the intricacies of the problem.

Keynes's view of fundamental disequilibrium

The international monetary system was one of the main interests of Keynes throughout his academic career, from his first book, *Indian Currency and Finance* (Keynes, 1971, to his last published article on the dollar shortage

(Keynes, 1946). All his writings in this field are linked by a unifying thread, namely the fundamental critique of the gold standard whose rigid rules prevented control of the money supply and thus imposed enormous welfare costs, particularly in deflationary periods. More flexibility in monetary arrangements was needed in order to stabilize prices and employment. The ceaseless quest to shed the shackles of the gold standard is the leitmotiv of Keynes's contributions to the subject. In his House of Lords speech about the Joint Statement (23 May 1944), he remarked:

> If I have any authority to pronounce on what is and what is not the essence and meaning of a gold standard, I should say that this plan is the exact opposite of it. The plan in its relation to gold is, indeed, very close to proposals which I advocated in vain as the right alternative, when I was bitterly opposing this country's return to gold. The gold standard, as I understand it, means a system under which the external value of a national currency is rigidly tied to a fixed quantity of gold which can only honourably be broken under *force majeure*; and it involves a financial policy which compels the internal value of the domestic currency to conform to this external value as fixed in terms of gold . . . The plan not merely confirms the de-thronement [of gold] but approves it by expressly providing that it is the duty of the Fund to alter the gold value of any currency if it is shown that this will be serviceable to equilibrium. In fact, the plan introduces in this respect an epoch-making innovation in an international instrument, the object of which is to lay down sound and orthodox principles. For instead of maintaining the principle that the internal value of a national currency should conform to a prescribed *de jure* external value, it provides that its external value should be altered if necessary so as to conform to whatever de facto internal value results from domestic policies, which themselves shall be immune from criticism by the Fund. Indeed, it is made the duty of the Fund to approve changes which will have this effect. That is why I say that these proposals are the exact opposite of the gold standard. They lay down by international agreement the essence of the new doctrine, far removed from the old orthodoxy (Keynes, 1980b, pp. 17-19).

Keynes's several proposals to reshape the international monetary system evolved in parallel with his contributions to economic analysis. His research program, dwelling at first on the classical model, culminated in its rejection in the *General Theory* (Keynes, 1964), which laid the foundations of full employment policy[8].

Although calling for more flexible monetary arrangements consistent with an activist policy design, Keynes always rejected floating exchange rates. As Moggridge (1986, pp. 66-7) remarks: "By the time Keynes came to draft his proposals for the post-World War II monetary system, he had at one time or another recommended almost every exchange rate regime known to modern analysts except completely freely floating exchange rates". In fact, in an early draft of the Keynes plan "the idea that a freely fluctuating exchange would discover itself a position of equilibrium" was considered a "false approach" (Keynes, 1980a, p. 22). The preferred solution was to widen the gap between the gold points in order to discourage capital movements and allow the implementation of monetary policy. This view had been discussed at length in the last three chapters of the *Treatise*, emphasizing the need to balance the rules of an international standard with "a reasonable measure of local autonomy" (Keynes, 1930, Vol. II, p. 306). In this connection, a main reason for rejecting the high capital mobility characterizing a fixed exchange rate regime was the presence of frictions and rigidities, which heightens instability[9].

The widening of the exchange rate fluctuation band then became a key feature of Keynes's various reform proposals. In the *Treatise* (Keynes, 1930, Vol. II, pp. 398-9), the band was set equal to 2 percent, and in *The Means to Prosperity* (Keynes, 1972a, p. 362) to 5 percent. The latter booklet drew a detailed scheme anticipating the Bretton Woods agreements in several respects[10]. The central idea was again to maneuver the interest rate instrument to sustain employment, although an increase in public expenditure is needed to trigger output expansion. The important novelty was that changes in parity were cautiously admitted, although the conditions were not specified. An effort in this direction can be found in a subsequent article (Keynes, 1982a, p. 363) where, having defined equilibrium exchange rates in accordance with the balance-of-payments criterion (see [5]), short-run fluctuations and "persistent disequilibrium" were discussed. As regards the former, Keynes argued that central banks should be required to hold a sufficient gold stock and to cooperate in the foreign exchange market. A number of technical contrivances, such as widening the gap between gold points and capital controls, would make short-run exchange rate stabilization feasible. In any case, in contrast with the gold standard rules, interest rate variations should be aimed at internal rather than international targets. Coherently with this approach, Keynes answered the second question by admitting parity changes in the event of major shocks, whether domestic or foreign in origin. In fact, the classical recipe of monetary restriction, which works through a fall in employment and then in money wages, could hardly be accepted and those, like the BIS Council, who "contemplate . . . a return to a régime of fixed gold parities . . . are living in an unreal world, a fool's world" (Keynes, 1982a, p. 367):

> It is realized today, as it was not realized formerly, that the instrument of Bank rate and credit contraction can only be successful as a means of remedying a *fundamental international maladjustment*, so far as it diminishes employment and, if the unemployment thus caused is sufficiently intense and prolonged, eventually forces a reduction of money wages. As a result of this better understanding of its *modus operandi*, I do not believe that it will ever be used again for this purpose (Keynes, 1982a, pp. 367-8, italics added).

Devaluation, however, should not be used to acquire a competitive advantage, but only in particularly severe conditions. In any case, no hard and fast rule should be established. Finally, the introduction of exchange media alternative to gold, like sterling or a BIS bank money, was deemed impracticable (Keynes, 1982a, p. 368).

Keynes's research program developed in the inter-war period through the progressive introduction of flexible elements in the rigid gold standard. Until the onset of the depression, this was a minority approach, but it then gained momentum, emphasizing the employment target and some innovative technical aspects of monetary arrangements. Keynes had the occasion to put his ideas to work and substantially expand them in November 1940, when he was consulted by the Treasury about the reconstruction of the international monetary system. The starting-point was to extend the "principle of banking" or bank clearing to the international economy, in order to avoid the contractive pressures characteristic of commodity standards. In the domestic context, this principle had already been introduced by classical economists. Mill (1848, p. 524) investigated the "ideal case" in which currency is entirely eliminated and all payments are made by check; likewise, Wicksell (1906, pp. 87-126) analyzed an "ideal banking system". Keynes's aim was to overcome the monetary disorders of the inter-war years – bilateral trade, competitive devaluations, lack of control of the money stock, asymmetry in the adjustment process – and allow each country to enact autonomous policies with a view to full employment. Most of these features were already incorporated in the first draft of the Keynes plan of September 1941, which opened with a devastating critique of the classical adjustment mechanism[11]. In particular, it was argued, the latter's asymmetrical character entailed a deflationary bias that could be overcome by the Clearing System.

With specific regard to the issue discussed in the present paper, countries with a debit balance exceeding a quarter of their quota were to be allowed to reduce the exchange rate by up to 5 percent per year, while those exceeding half of their quota could be *required* to do so; *mutatis mutandis*, these provisions applied for countries showing a credit balance (Keynes, 1980a, pp. 35-6). The dry aspect of these clauses, which remained substantially the same in the final version of the plan (Horsefield, 1969, pp. 23-4), was explained in the third draft (December 1941) with the same argument put forward in the 1935 article, i.e. the inadvisability of precise rules[12]. In fact, in a preceding section of the same document, Keynes clarified the meaning of disequilibrium and the possible solutions in general terms:

> If, indeed, we lack the productive capacity to maintain our standard of life, then a reduction in this standard is not avoidable. If our price levels are hopelessly wrong, a change in the rate of exchange is inevitable. But if we possess the productive capacity and the difficulty is the lack of markets as a result of restrictive policies throughout the world, then the remedy lies in expanding opportunities for export by removal of restrictive pressure, not in contracting imports (Keynes, 1980a, p. 77)[13].

Prices and wages, therefore, must be considered in relation to potential output so that a change in parity, albeit justified when their level is misaligned, should not be implemented when productive capacity is slack. In this instance, an increase in the demand for exports is the right solution, and this means involving creditor countries in the adjustment process. Indeed, symmetry was a basic property of the Keynes plan[14], helping to prevent the accumulation of disequilibrium. In case of payments imbalances, the remedy did not consist in monetary restriction, which would bring unemployment, or in trade controls, which would attack the symptom and not the cause, but in reshaping economic policies ((Keynes, 1980a, pp. 76-7). As Keynes (1980a, pp. 105-6) makes clear in answer to criticisms of the third draft by Richard Hopkins, permanent secretary of the Treasury, exchange rate change is an ultimate measure to solve structural, not temporary, problems and should be resorted to only if the country's productive capacity is lacking:

> I myself greatly doubt the utility of sudden exchange depreciations to meet sudden developments. Broadly speaking, the factor governing the exchanges in the long run is the level of money wages relatively to efficiency in one country as compared with another. This is not as a rule anything which changes very suddenly. The causes of sudden difficulties are very rarely, I should have thought, properly dealt with by exchange depreciation, which may easily do more harm than good.

Keynes dealt with the issue at stake very succinctly, both in the various versions of his plan and in the 1935 article where he already referred to "a rise of money wages not offset by increased efficiency" (Keynes, 1982a, p. 366) as a factor of exchange rate disequilibrium. This idea was developed at some length in his comment on von Hayek's (1943) article making the case for a commodity reserve currency. The latter would maintain the advantages of the gold standard – the creation of an international standard without submitting countries to an international authority, the automaticity and thus predictability of monetary policy, the stabilizing property of money stock variations – while avoiding its main defect, i.e. the slow adjustment of gold supply to changes in demand. Von Hayek's paper was not very original, but it gave Keynes the chance to clarify the essence of his plan and, particularly, the conditions justifying a parity change.

According to Keynes's own interpretation, the International Clearing Union would resolve two of the main shortcomings of the gold standard in stabilizing the price level. The first, i.e. the uncontrollable behavior of the money stock, had been tackled by various schemes (i.e. Marshall's tabular standard, Fisher's compensated dollar, von Hayek's commodity reserve currency), which operated through the volume of money. The Clearing Union, instead, would act on the velocity of circulation by substantially decreasing both the transactions and the precautionary demand for international money. In this way it "would deal with the quantity of international money by making any significant quantity unnecessary" (Keynes, 1943, p. 185). The second problem, less tractable, was the rise in unemployment consequent to restraining the wage trend from increasing beyond the limit set by the money stock. The control of the money supply was a necessary but not sufficient condition for price level stability, which could only be accomplished "by first stabilizing the relation of money-wages (and other costs) to efficiency" (Keynes, 1943, p. 185). Countries should aim at this target but, in contrast with the gold standard, must also be allowed to follow different wage and price policies in order to avoid deflationary pressures. This policy design, however, could not be pursued endlessly, since the wages and prices of any country cannot permanently deviate from the rest of the world. The solution required a correction of policies; if this should prove unfeasible, however, the only possible way out would be a change in parity:

> Thus the more difficult task of an international currency scheme, which will only be fully solved with the aid of experience, is to deal with the problem of members getting out of step in their domestic wage and credit policies. To meet this it can be provided that countries seriously out of step (whether too fast or too slow) may be asked in the first instance to reconsider their policies. But, if necessary (and it will be necessary, if efficiency wage-rates move at materially different rates), exchange rates will have to be altered so as to reconcile a particular national policy to the average pace. If the initial exchange-rates are fixed correctly, *this is likely to be the only important disequilibrium for which a change in exchange rates is the appropriate remedy* (Keynes, 1943, p. 186, italics added).

Even though Keynes focused on price level differentials as the main factor behind exchange rate changes, Keynes's position was at odds with classical theory. In fact, he called for autonomous price policy, motivated by the rejection of classical equilibrium hypothesis. Activist employment policies might then lead, if the country's productive capacity remained feeble, to a widening of the price differential. According to the *General Theory* (Keynes, 1964, ch. 21), an increase in the money stock raises output, as long as there is unemployment; when full employment is attained, it raises prices. This result, based on an L-shaped aggregate supply curve and on highly simplifying assumptions, is qualified by the introduction of a number of complicating factors[15] which, bringing about various kinds of bottlenecks, make prices and wages increase before full employment is reached. But this is a short-run analysis. In the long-run context relevant to the present paper, liquidity preference tends to settle around a uniform value, thus entailing a stable money-income ratio, and long-run price stability depends "on the strength of the upward trend of the wage-unit (or, more precisely, of the cost-unit) compared with the rate of increase in the efficiency of the productive system" (Keynes, 1964, p. 309).

This theoretical framework provided the foundation for analyzing exchange rate disequilibrium, both in the preparatory writings to the Keynes plan and in the comment to von Hayek. The starting-point was the rejection of the self-adjusting nature of the economy (Keynes, 1973) which squared with the case for a more flexible monetary system. In a commodity standard, equilibrium can be maintained in exceptional circumstances only, such as those prevailing during the historical period ending with the First World War. Owing to the balance of forces, overall purchasing power remained stable; investment activity was sufficient to keep unemployment low and the increase in the wage-unit was matched by a parallel increase in efficiency of production. However, the price trend has historically been upward, since, given stronger frictions in downward adjustment, the way out of deflationary pressures has usually been found not in a decrease in the wage-unit but in a change of the monetary standard[16]. In this regard, the International Clearing Union can be viewed as Keynes's ambitious attempt to offer a definitive solution by allowing countries sufficient domestic policy autonomy while maintaining a symmetric fixed exchange rate system. The Clearing Union was the last stage in his research program, which had always aimed to overcome the tight rules of the gold standard in order to improve social welfare:

> [A]n international currency scheme can work to perfection within the field of maintaining exchange stability, and yet prices may move substantially. If wages and prices double everywhere alike, international exchange equilibrium is undisturbed. If efficiency wages in a particular country rise 10 percent more than the norm, then it is that there is trouble which needs attention. The fundamental reason for thus limiting the objectives of an international currency scheme is the impossibility, or at any rate the undesirability, of imposing stable price-levels from without. The error of the gold-standard lay in submitting national wage-policies to outside dictation. It is wiser to regard stability (or otherwise) of internal prices as a matter of internal policy and politics. Commodity standards which try to impose this from without will break down just as surely as the rigid gold-standard (Keynes, 1943, pp. 186-7).

Keynes's position – in favor of independent economic policy with domestic targets and restricting exchange rate adjustments to a specific instance of long-run disequilibrium[17] – clearly shows that he never entirely parted with equilibrium methodology. Otherwise his construction, founded on fixed rates, could hardly be viable. Conclusive evidence is provided by Keynes (1946) in his last published article where, rejecting the widely held thesis of an intractable dollar shortage, he revindicates some fundamental tenets of classical economics and, in particular, the effectiveness of the specie-flow adjustment mechanism to tackle structural problems. This is no surprise. Rather, it is the confirmation of Keynes's multi-faceted, ingenious personality as an economic theorist who confronted complex problems in full awareness of the dangers of encapsulating social science in any rigid, single scheme. As Haberler (1948, p. 434) quipped, "Whatever one's view there is always a Keynes to whom one can look for support!".

It is a commonplace that little of the Keynes plan was left in the final Bretton Woods agreements, which mostly reflected the US proposals[18]. The new monetary arrangements, while sharing many properties with the gold exchange standard, introduced changes in parity as a characterizing feature. However, against the spirit of the treaty the system evolved into a fixed-rate dollar standard (McKinnon, 1993, pp. 12-15), so the question of defining fundamental disequilibrium necessarily lost importance and the debate eventually petered out. From a theoretical point of view, however, the issue cannot be definitely disposed of since, despite the predominance of flexible exchange rates in the last quarter-century, innovative proposals have revived fixed exchange rates (McKinnon, 1988; Mundell, 2000). Although the pendulum has long since swung back to the classical approach, major shocks or inadequacies in the adjustment mechanism would put a fixed exchange rate regime under pressure. Hence, barring the sudden multiplication of fully-fledged and viable currency unions, the reconsideration of fixed exchange rates makes Keynes's contribution to fundamental disequilibrium still topical.

Conclusions

The difficulty of defining fundamental disequilibrium in the Bretton Woods system related to the latent inconsistency between full employment policy and fixed exchange rates. The depression resulted in economists' rejection of the classical equilibrium hypothesis, with unemployment now added to payments imbalances as a sign of fundamental disequilibrium. However, far from clearing up the issue, extending the analysis in this direction led analysts to consider a multiplicity of cases in the search for a precise, operational definition. The proliferation of taxonomies kept the debate away from positive analysis, directing it to a dead-end. Widespread skepticism about the efficacy of adjustment mechanisms, Keynesian or classical, distracted the economists from studying policy effectiveness in relation to different time horizons and to aggregate supply conditions.

Keynes did not neglect these aspects and followed a more general approach. Refraining from hard and fast rules for a change in parity, he related fundamental disequilibrium to productive capacity. If capacity is large, the solution to payments imbalances should be an increase in exports; if it is scarce, a structural price and wage misalignment will impose devaluation. To control the price level, countries must stabilize the relation of money wages to efficiency, but should also pursue independent price and wage policies. When disequilibrium emerges, corrective policies are necessary. Only if the latter fail, parity is allowed to vary; this, in fact, is the ultimate measure when potential output remains feeble.

Keynes's approach, although based on the *General Theory*, was rather pragmatic in that, instead of delivering an exact solution to maintain both the stability of the monetary system and the autonomy of domestic policies, it advocated appeal to "the aid of experience". While aggregate demand policies to sustain employment remained essential, a country's output potential was a necessary condition for long-run equilibrium. Keeping cyclical and structural disequilibria on different analytical planes, Keynes did not attempt a punctilious definition of fundamental disequilibrium but posed the problem in more general terms, showing an ingenuity and a detachment from dogmatic attitudes not always found in his followers.

Notes

1. According to Mundell, it is the latter characteristic that makes the Bretton Woods monetary order unique. "When we look back over the past twenty centuries and ask how the monetary order has been manifested in actual institutions, we are startled to find that the Bretton Woods system is unique. For there are only two previous periods in history when it could be

said that a monetary order existed. One was during the Roman-Byzantine era, from the time of Julius Caesar to the fall of Constantinople; the other was the period of the international gold standard as it operated in the nineteenth century. ... The gold standard was never formalized in international law. The first agreement of a comprehensive and binding sort in modern times was the Bretton Woods agreement of 1944. Not since the absurdly long stability of the Byzantine system could it be said that we had an international monetary 'order' until the IMF was set up. It is here that the uniqueness of the Bretton Woods agreements lies" (Mundell, 1972, pp. 97-8). Contrasting the gold standard with the successive monetary systems up to the present, McKinnon (1993, p. 3) notes: "[For] the pre-1914 gold standard ... there was no collective 'founding treaty' nor major regime changes. Countries opted unilaterally to follow similar rules of the game that proved remarkably robust".

2. "The full severity of the disturbance is by no means revealed by the change in the price level. There was a competition among all countries on the gold standard in the compression of the consumers' income. Each had to keep pace with the others. Each was confronted with the shrinkage of demand caused by the action of the others, and had to compress its consumers' income and outlay to the point at which it did not attract an excess of imports" (Hawtrey, 1932, p. 217). "If the 'debt-deflation theory' is correct, the infectiousness of depressions internationally is chiefly due to a common gold (or other) monetary standard and there should be found little tendency for a depression to pass from a deflating to an inflating, or stabilizing, country. A study has been made to test the last named hypothesis and it has been found to be substantially correct. For instance, it was found that, in the depression of 1929-1935, when one gold standard country had a depression with a rising value of gold, all gold standard countries were practically sure to catch the contagion, because prices fell alike in all. But silver standard countries and countries with a managed paper currency escaped, as their price levels were rising or stable" (Fisher, 1945, p. 133). Hawtrey (1932, p. 221) thought the crisis of the early 1930s to be international in character also in another sense, emphasizing the role of foreign creditors in setting off banking panics.

3. "The classical doctrine of the automatic standard was thus opposed by the conception of a managed currency. More and more economists were accepting the principles of the new school. At present Keynes appears to have the greatest number of adherents; according to him the gold parity should be changed from time to time. Foreign-exchange quotations should fluctuate within limits broader than those of the gold point, for instance within 5 percent of a given parity. The issue of bank notes should be severed from gold movements and controlled only from the point of view of stabilizing the purchasing power of money as the most important consideration. Without going into technical details, and without discussing the shortcomings or advantages of the new doctrine, it can be stated that it is a complete reversal of the Ricardian theory and hence quite revolutionary with regard to the classical doctrine" (Mlynarsky, 1937, p. 272).

4. Metzler (1948, p. 253) draws a clear picture of the cultural climate of time. "Historically, the interwar period will probably be remembered as a period of retreat from the price system, when all sorts of temporary or provisional measures were adopted to regulate economic activity. The market mechanism had broken down and no one seemed to know quite why or just what to do about it. This was perhaps even more true of the international mechanism than of domestic markets, and to a very great extent the theoretical developments reflected the empirical".

5. An often-quoted passage runs as follows: "We have to consider, on the one hand, a country's balance of payments on income account on the basis of the existing natural resources, equipment, technique and costs (especially wage costs) at home and abroad, a normal level of employment, and those tariffs, etc., which are a permanent feature of national policies; and, on the other hand, the probable readiness and ability of the country in question to borrow or lend abroad on long term (or, perhaps, repay or accept repayment of old loans), on the average of the next few years. A set of rates of exchange, which can be established without

undue strain on either side and without large movements of gold (on a balance of transactions), will satisfy our condition of equilibrium" (Keynes, 1982a, p. 361).

6. Mikesell (1947, pp. 503-04), who was an economic advisor at the Bretton Woods Conference, remarked: "Although fundamental disequilibrium is not defined in the Fund's *Articles of Agreement*, it was evident from the discussions which preceded the formal drafting of the agreement that the term refers to a sustained imbalance in a member's current international accounts. Properly interpreted, such an imbalance would be one which was not offset by long-term borrowings and would be accompanied by a sustained loss of international reserves or continued borrowings from the Fund or from other sources of short-term credits". And, in a footnote appended to this passage, he further pointed out: "From a study of the unpublished minutes of the pre-Bretton Woods negotiations, . . . it is clear that the principal criterion for rate alterations in the minds of the authors of the text of the Fund agreement was the existence of a disequilibrium in the current international accounts of the member requesting a change" (Mikesell 1947, p. 503).
7. "For a country in which money wages do not readily yield to the pressure of unemployment the gold standard can be maintained, in an era of rapid change, only by means of recurrent periods of severe unemployment, and it is the realisation of this fact which has in recent years so much impaired the popularity of the gold standard" (Robinson, 1947, p. 103).
8. A general survey of Keynes's work on the international monetary system is beyond the scope of the present paper. In this respect, the reader is referred to the excellent studies by Meltzer (1988, 1989), Moggridge (1986), and Williamson (1983).
9. "If we deliberately desire that there should be a high degree of mobility for international lending, both for long and for short periods, then this is, admittedly, a strong argument for a fixed rate of exchange and a rigid international standard. What, then, is the reason for hesitating before we commit ourselves to such a system? Primarily a doubt whether it is wise to have a Currency System with a much wider ambit than our Banking System, our Tariff System and our Wage System. Can we afford to allow a disproportionate degree of mobility to a single element in an economic system which we leave extremely rigid in several other respects? If there was the same mobility internationally in all other respects as there is nationally, it might be a different matter. But to introduce a mobile element, highly sensitive to outside influences, as a connected part of a machine of which the other parts are much more rigid, may invite breakages" (Keynes, 1930, Vol. II, pp. 334-5).
10. The role assigned to gold, involving "a qualified return to the gold standard" (Keynes, 1972, p. 362), induced some commentators to charge Keynes with having shifted his position. Keynes (1982bb, p. 186) firmly denied this accusation, in a letter to *The Economist*.
11. "To suppose that there exists some smoothly functioning automatic mechanism of adjustment which preserves equilibrium if only we trust to methods of *laissez-faire* is a doctrinaire delusion which disregards the lessons of historical experience without having behind it the support of sound theory" (Keynes, 1980a, pp. 21-2).
12. This is revealing of how sterile the debate actually was on the operative definition of fundamental disequilibrium described in Section 1. "Changes in the value of the national currencies of member states stand in a different category. For the real significance of such changes is to be found not in relation to gold itself but in relation to the values of other national currencies. . . . It would be undesirable, if it can be avoided, to lay down precise rules in advance, since it is difficult to distinguish by means of a rigid formula the cases in which a change in the rate of exchange will assist the restoration of equilibrium and is the right remedy from those cases where some other type of measure is more appropriate" ((Keynes, 1980a, p. 86). This paragraph was included, virtually unmodified, in a Treasury memorandum on External Monetary and Economic Problems (Keynes, 1980a, p. 129).

13. In the Treasury memorandum cited in the previous footnote, the same paragraph ends with a different sentence which reads: "There is great force in the contention that, if active employment and ample purchasing power can be sustained in the main centres of world trade, the problem of surpluses and unwanted exports will largely disappear, even though under the most prosperous conditions there may remain some disturbances of trade and unforeseen situations requiring special remedies" (Keynes, 1980a, p. 116).
14. In the first draft of his plan, Keynes, after emphasizing the asymmetrical character of the inter-war monetary system, noted: "The object of the new system must be to require the chief initiative from the creditor countries, whilst maintaining enough discipline in the debtor countries to prevent them from exploiting the new ease allowed them in living profligately beyond their means" (Keynes, 1980a, p. 30).
15. The complications considered by Keynes (1964, p. 296) include: effective demand does not change in proportion to the quantity of money; diminishing returns occur because resources are not homogeneous; conditions of inelastic supply are reached even in the presence of unemployed resources since the latter are not interchangeable; the wage-unit tends to rise before full employment is attained; factor remunerations do not change all in the same proportion.
16. "[I]f the quantity of money remains very deficient for a long time, the escape will be normally found in changing the monetary standard or the monetary system so as to raise the quantity of money, rather than in forcing down the wage-unit and thereby increasing the burden of debt. Thus the very long-run course of prices has almost always been upward. For when money is relatively abundant, the wage-unit rises; and when money is relatively scarce, some means is found to increase the effective quantity of money" (Keynes, 1964, p. 307). In the *Tract*, Keynes interpreted the resort to debasement in the Middle Ages as an efficacious solution to the inconveniences of "scarcity of currency": "No doubt some of the debasements were helped by the fact that they profited incidentally a necessitous Exchequer. But they may have been, nevertheless, the best available expedient for meeting the currency problem. We shall look on Edward III's debasements of sterling money with a more tolerant eye if we regard them as a method of carrying into effect a preference for stability of internal prices over stability of external exchanges, celebrating that monarch as an enlightened forerunner of Professor Irving Fisher in advocacy of the 'compensated dollar', only more happy than the latter in his opportunities to carry theory into practice" (Keynes, 1923, pp. 162-3).
17. Although not referring to the von Hayek-Keynes exchange in the *Economic Journal*, Harrod (1971, p. 642) accurately points out Keynes's view of the criterion underlying parity variations at the time of the Washington talks. "The adjustment of exchange rates was only designed to correct a tendency towards long-run disequilibrium, due, for instance, to secular changes in the rates of interchange of goods between nations or to gradual divergences in the rates of increase of efficiency of labour". Other biographers do not consider the matter, but this is no reproach to them since the issue at stake was a rather technical one, analyzed in a three-page note.
18. A discordant voice is Eichengreen (1989, pp. 263-7) who argues that Britain, despite the American dominance of the Bretton Woods negotiations, was able to wring a number of concessions, namely less strict procedures for exchange rate changes and controls on capital movements.

References

Bloomfield, A. (1947), "Foreign exchange rate theory and policy", in Harris, S.E. (Ed.), *The New Economics. Keynes's Influence on Theory and Public Policy*, Alfred A. Knopf, New York, NY.

Bordo, M.D. (1993), "The Bretton Woods international monetary system: a historical overview", in Bordo, M.D. and Eichengreen, B. (Eds), *A Retrospective on the Bretton Woods System*, The University of Chicago Press, Chicago, IL.

Eichengreen, B. (1989), "Hegemonic stability theories of the international monetary system", in Cooper, R.N., Eichengreen, B., Randall Henning, C., Holtham, G. and Putnam, R.D. (Eds), *Can Nations Agree? Issues in International Economic Cooperation*, The Brookings Institution, Washington, DC.

Fisher, I. (1945), *100% Money*, The City Printing Company, New Haven, CT, originally published in 1935.

Haberler, G. (1945), "The choice of exchange rates after the war", *American Economic Review*, Vol. 35, June, pp. 308-18.

Haberler, G. (1948), "Dollar shortage", in Harris, S.E. (Ed.), *Foreign Economic Policy for the United States*, Harvard University Press, Cambridge, MA.

Hansen, A.H. (1948), "Fundamental disequilibrium", in Harris, S.E. (Ed.), *Foreign Economic Policy for the United States*, Harvard University Press, Cambridge, MA.

Harrod, R.F. (1971), *The Life of John Maynard Keynes*, Avon Books, New York, NY, originally published in 1951.

Hawtrey, R.G. (1932), *The Art of Central Banking*, 1970 ed., Frank Cass, London.

Horsefield, J.K. (1969), *The International Monetary Fund 1945-1965: Twenty Years of International Monetary Cooperation*, Documents Vol. 3, International Monetary Fund, Washington, DC.

Keynes, J.M. (1923), *A Tract on Monetary Reform*, Macmillan, London.

Keynes, J.M. (1930), *A Treatise on Money*, Macmillan, London.

Keynes, J.M. (1943), "The objective of international price stability", *Economic Journal*, Vol. 53 No. 210, pp. 185-7.

Keynes, J.M. (1946), "The balance of payments of the United States", *Economic Journal*, Vol. 56, June, pp. 172-87.

Keynes, J.M. (1964), *The General Theory of Employment, Interest and Money*, Macmillan, London, originally published in 1936.

Keynes, J.M. (1971), *Indian Currency and Finance, The Collected Writings of John Maynard Keynes*, Vol. I, Macmillan, London, originally published in 1913.

Keynes, J.M. (1972), *The Means to Prosperity, The Collected Writings of John Maynard Keynes*, Vol. IX, Macmillan, London, originally published in 1933.

Keynes, J.M. (1973), "Poverty in plenty: is the economic system self-adjusting?", in Moggridge, D. (Ed.), *The Collected Writings of John Maynard Keynes*, Macmillan, London, originally published in 1934.

Keynes, J.M. (1980a) Moggridge, D. (Ed.), *Activities 1940-1944. Shaping the Post-war World: The Clearing Union, The Collected Writings of John Maynard Keynes*, Vol. XXV, Macmillan, London.

Keynes, J.M. (1980b) Moggridge, D. (Ed.), *Activities 1941-1946. Shaping the Post-war World: Bretton Woods and Reparations, The Collected Writings of John Maynard Keynes*, Vol. XXVI, Macmillan, London.

Keynes, J.M. (1982), "Letter to The Economist, 20 March 1933", in Moggridge, D. (Ed.), *The Collected Writings of John Maynard Keynes*, Vol. XXI, Macmillan, London, originally published in 1933.

Keynes, J.M. (1982a), "The future of the foreign exchanges", in Moggridge, D. (Ed.), *The Collected Writings of John Maynard Keynes*, Vol. XXI, Macmillan, London, originally published in 1935.

McKinnon, R.I. (1988), "An international gold standard without gold", in McKinnon, R.I. (Ed.), *The Rules of the Game: International Money and Exchange Rates*, The MIT Press, Cambridge, MA.

McKinnon, R.I. (1993), "The rules of the game: international money in historical perspective", *Journal of Economic Literature*, Vol. 31, No. 1, pp. 1-44.

Machlup, F. (1958), "Comment to Bernstein", *Review of Economics and Statistics*, Vol. 50, pp. 137-40.

Meltzer, A.H. (1988), *Keynes's Monetary Theory: A Different Interpretation*, Cambridge University Press, Cambridge.

Meltzer, A.H. (1989), "Keynes on monetary reform and international economic order", in Capie, F. and Wood, G.E. (Eds), *Monetary Economics in the 1980s*, Macmillan, London.

Metzler, L.A. (1948), "The theory of international trade", in Howard, S.E. (Ed.), *A Survey of Contemporary Economics*, Blakiston, Philadelphia, PA.

Mikesell, R.F. (1947), "The role of the international monetary agreements in a world of planned economies", *Journal of Political Economy*, Vol. 55, December, pp. 497-512.

Mikesell, R.F. (1994), *The Bretton Woods Debates: A Memoir*, Princeton University, Princeton, NJ.

Mill, J.S. (1848), *Principles of Political Economy*, Ashley, W. (Ed.), 1987 ed., Augustus M. Kelley, New York, NY.

Mlynarsky, F. (1937), "Proportionalism and stabilization policy", in Gayer, A.D. (Ed.), *The Lessons of Monetary Experience*, George Allen & Unwin, London.

Moggridge, D.E. (1986), "Keynes and the international monetary system 1909-46", in Cohen, J.S. and Harcourt, G.C. (Eds), *International Monetary Problems and Supply-side Economics. Essays in Honour of Lorie Tarshis*, Macmillan, London.

Mundell, R.A. (1962), "The appropriate use of monetary and fiscal policy for internal and external stability", *IMF Staff Papers*, Vol. 9, pp. 70-9.

Mundell, R.A. (1972), "The future of the international financial system", in Chant, J.F. and Prachowny, M.F.J. (Eds), *Bretton Woods Revisited*, Macmillan, London.

Mundell, R.A. (2000), "A reconsideration of the twentieth century", *American Economic Review*, Vol. 90, June, pp. 327-39.

Nurkse, R. (1944), *International Currency Experience. Lessons of the Inter-war Period*, League of Nations, Geneva.

Nurkse, R. (1945), "Conditions of international monetary equilibrium", in, *Readings in the Theory of International Trade*, The Blakiston Company, Philadelphia, PA.

Polak, J.J. (1947), "Exchange depreciation and international monetary stability", *Review of Economic Statistics*, Vol. 29, August, pp. 173-82.

Robinson, J. (1947), "The foreign exchange", in Ellis, H.S. and Metzler, L. (Eds), *Readings in the Theory of International Trade*, The Blakiston Company, Philadelphia, PA.

Tinbergen, J. (1946), "Some measurements of elasticities of substitution", *Review of Economic Statistics*, Vol. 28, August, pp. 109-16.

Triffin, R. (1947), "National central banking and the international economy", in, *International Monetary Policies, Postwar Economic Studies*, No. 7, Board of Governors of the Federal Reserve System, Washington, DC.

Viner, J. (1943), "Two plans for international monetary stabilization", *Yale Review*, Vol. 33, September, reprinted in Viner (1951).

Viner, J. (1944), "The Bretton Woods agreements", in Shields, M. (Ed.), *International Financial Stabilization, A Symposium*, reprinted in Viner (1951), Irving Trust Company, New York, NY.

von Hayek, F.A. (1943), "A commodity reserve currency", *Economic Journal*, Vol. 53, June-September, pp. 176-84.

Wicksell, K. (1906), *Lectures on Political Economy*, Vol. 2, 1935 ed., Routledge, London.

Williamson, J. (1983), "Keynes and the international economic order", in Worswick, D. and Trevithick, J. (Eds), *Keynes and the Modern World*, Cambridge University Press, Cambridge.

Williamson, J. (1985), "On the system in Bretton Woods", *American Economic Review. Papers and Proceedings*, Vol. 75, May, pp. 74-9.

Further reading

Bernstein, E.M. (1958), "Strategic factors in balance of payments adjustment", *Review of Economics and Statistics*, Vol. 50, pp. 133-7, February, Supplement.

Harris, S.E. (1948), *Foreign Economic Policy for the United States*, Harvard University Press, Cambridge, MA.

Horsefield, J.K. (1969), *The International Monetary Fund 1945-1965: Twenty Years of International Monetary Cooperation*, Chronicle Vol. 1, International Monetary Fund, Washington, DC.

Nurkse, R. (1947), "Domestic and international equilibrium", in Harris, S.E. (Ed.), *The New Economics. Keynes's Influence on Theory and Public Policy*, Alfred A. Knopf, New York, NY.

Viner, J. (1951), *International Economics*, The Free Press, Glencoe, IL.

[11]

The Origins of the Theory of Optimum Currency Areas

Filippo Cesarano

Robert Mundell is universally recognized as the founder of the literature on optimum currency areas. In his seminal work of 1961, Mundell posed the question of the appropriate domain of a currency area in order to attain both full employment and price stability. The solution suggested was to draw the borders according to the criterion of labor mobility, thus preventing the emergence of unemployment in the deficit region and inflation in the surplus region.

The basic principles of this theory, however, had actually been anticipated in the 1940s by Abba Lerner, following a period of intense discussion on the design of international monetary arrangements. In the interwar years, the difficulties of reinstating the gold standard and the disruptive shock of the Great Depression had prompted a wide-ranging debate on the international monetary system, whose defects were thought to have propagated the Depression worldwide. The end of Britain's ephemeral return to gold in September 1931 was a watershed in monetary history, marking the decline of commodity money after nearly three millennia. This epoch-making development posed the challenge of rethinking the design of the monetary system. Reflection on monetary reconstruction took a new turn

Correspondence may be addressed to Filippo Cesarano, Banca d'Italia, Ufficio Ricerche Storiche, Via Nazionale 191, 00184 Roma, Italy; e-mail: filippo.cesarano@bancaditalia.it.
Thanks are due to Robert Clower and two anonymous referees for their highly useful suggestions. The usual caveat applies.

History of Political Economy 38:4 DOI 10.1215/00182702-2006-017

after the outbreak of World War II with the Keynes and White plans that eventually led to the Bretton Woods agreements, the unprecedented enterprise of building a new monetary order from the ground up.

The Bretton Woods accord has always been described as a compromise in which the American position prevailed over the rather different British one. Yet this view disregards the impact of John Maynard Keynes's *General Theory* on the paradigm of economic analysis. Keynes's work was considered to have set off a Kuhnian revolution.[1] In fact, notwithstanding the differences between the Keynes and the White plans, both advocated fixed exchange rates and full employment policies, reflecting the influence of Keynes's contributions to international finance and economic theory. However, reconciling the two objectives became a most controversial issue.

It was in this context that Abba Lerner put forward some original but neglected ideas that were not developed into a full-fledged analysis but nonetheless anticipated Mundell's work on optimum currency areas. After the conference, the critical discussion of the Bretton Woods system gave rise to conflicting interpretations, especially over the conditions for exchange rate adjustments. Although the gold standard was now in utter disrepute, the specie-flow adjustment mechanism still represented the ideal type of fixed exchange rate regime as contrasted with a more flexible framework. The analysis of these distinct models set the stage for Lerner's contributions.

The problem of international adjustment remained at the center of the debate throughout the 1950s. Apart from the concern for Bretton Woods, the quest for economic integration in Europe stimulated further research. While tackling the subject from a different perspective, this research also captured the basic tenets underlying the theory of optimum currency areas. What is more important, this work independently elaborated Lerner's ideas in a direction that is suggestive of today's approach to optimality, opposite to that of Mundell's seminal article.

1. The Early Debate on Bretton Woods and the Adjustment Problem

The Bretton Woods architects wanted to remove the obstacles to multilateral trade and prevent the recurrence of the interwar monetary disorders

1. That opinion, always in dispute, has now been thoroughly criticized by David Laidler (1999).

by designing a symmetrical monetary system based on stable exchange rates, in which capital controls allowed activist economic policies and official parities could be varied in case of a fundamental disequilibrium. The spirit of the treaty was betrayed, however, and the Bretton Woods game was played with different rules, eschewing exchange rate flexibility. Ronald McKinnon (1993) accordingly distinguishes between the Bretton Woods Agreement in 1945 and the fixed-rate dollar standard of 1950–1970. To him, this shift in postwar monetary arrangements is "a major historical puzzle" (37) originating in the establishment of the European Payments Union in 1950, which introduced a clearing system with the dollar as unit of account, plus the determination of European countries and Japan to enhance the credibility of their anti-inflation policies (38). Two other factors, however, fostered the system's transformation: the central bankers' cultural background, still influenced by the success of the gold standard, and the overriding concern of the United States to discipline other countries to prevent the accumulation of external debt.[2] The system was therefore grounded on fixed exchange rates. This was implicitly at odds with the objective of full employment, but these conflicting aims were both deemed essential to monetary reconstruction.[3]

The antinomy between full employment and fixed exchange rates bears heavily on optimum currency areas. This potential conflict does not arise in the classical model, in which equilibrium forces see to the maintenance of full employment. As Mundell (1961, 662) remarks, for the classics the optimum currency area was the world, because they deemed stabilization policies totally irrelevant so that multiplying the number of currencies entailed only a cost. Thus, according to John Stuart Mill, it was a

2. This question worried the Americans throughout the negotiations. Thus, in his House of Lords speech on 18 May 1943, Keynes (1980a, 276) tried to reassure the Americans that his plan would not impose a large burden on them: "There is no foundation whatever for the idea that the object of the proposals is to make the United States the milch cow of the world in general and of this country in particular."

3. The case for activist monetary policy to smooth out income and employment in a context of stable exchange rates is paramount in Keynes's *Tract* (1923). Indeed, Keynes, the archcritic of the classical model at the basis of the gold standard, never called for exchange rate flexibility, retaining the two conflicting targets in his later works. Emphasizing Keynes's prolificacy in suggesting new monetary schemes, Donald Moggridge (1986, 66–67) notes: "By the time Keynes came to draft his proposals for the post-World War II monetary system, he had at one time or another recommended almost every exchange rate regime known to modern analysts except completely freely floating exchange rates." In fact, Keynes consistently rejects flexible exchange rates throughout his writings. In an early draft of his plan, he considers as a false approach "the idea that a freely fluctuating exchange would discover for itself a position of equilibrium" (Keynes 1980a, 22).

"barbarism . . . that almost all independent countries choose to assert their nationality by having, to their own inconvenience and that of their neighbours, a peculiar currency of their own" (quoted in Mundell 1961, 662). The "defining moment" of the Great Depression turned this conclusion on its head (Bordo, Goldin, and White 1998). Keynes's *General Theory* came to hold sway, stressing the need for full employment policies, with the immediate implication of waiving the rigid rules of commodity money.[4] In the debate on Bretton Woods, the clash between full employment and fixed exchange rates was immediately highlighted by George Halm (1944, 172) and, well before the signing of the agreements, by Frank Graham (1943, 21) in his critical appraisal of the British and American proposals:

> The primary defect of both the Keynes and the White plans, and of the compromise between them, is that their authors favor fixity of exchange rates in neglect of domestic monetary policies and, conscious of the disruptive effects to be expected in this situation, present measures of half-hearted coercion of such states as are recalcitrant in their adhesion to some undefined national monetary policy which, it is fondly hoped, will more or less miraculously emerge as the "norm."

Thus, unless all countries renounced their independence and conformed their monetary policies to the "norm"—that is, to the stance of the dominant country or "that country which, somehow, manages to corral the bulk of the world's gold"—the system was unstable (12). But Graham singled out a further, crucial weakness of fixed but adjustable exchange rates: the one-way bet offered to speculators. If monetary policies are not consistent with fixed exchange rates,

4. This point was made explicitly by Keynes (1980b, 18–19) in the House of Lords debate in May 1944 on the document to be discussed at Bretton Woods—the *Joint Statement by Experts on the Establishment of an International Monetary Fund*: "The plan not merely confirms the de-thronement [of gold] but approves it by expressly providing that it is the duty of the Fund to alter the gold value of any currency if it is shown that this will be serviceable to equilibrium. In fact, the plan introduces in this respect an epoch-making innovation in an international instrument, the object of which is to lay down sound and orthodox principles. For instead of maintaining the principle that the internal value of a national currency should conform to a prescribed *de jure* external value, it provides that its external value should be altered if necessary so as to conform to whatever *de facto* internal value results from domestic policies, which themselves shall be immune from criticism by the Fund. Indeed, it is made the duty of the Fund to approve changes which will have this effect. That is why I say that these proposals are the exact opposite of the gold standard. They lay down by international agreement the essence of the new doctrine, far removed from the old orthodoxy."

any attempt to establish fixity of rates accumulates disequilibria, offers a bonanza to speculators against weak currencies artificially maintained at levels beyond their inherent worth, shores up, for the time being, an essentially shaky international monetary structure, and results in ultimate collapse at the expense of any fund out of which credit has been provided in the effort to maintain the exchange values of certain currencies at levels above their evolving relative purchasing power in the domestic markets. Whatever the nostalgia for fixed exchange rates it cannot, in these circumstances, be safely indulged. (7–8)

In an earlier paper, Graham had expounded the same concept with reference to the lack of confidence in the currency's convertibility in the context of the gold standard.[5] Stressing the one-way bet as the "Achilles' heel" of monetary standards, he suggested widening the range of exchange rate flexibility about "a predetermined but unannounced norm" in order to increase uncertainty and enable the monetary authority to defeat speculators (Graham 1940, 21). Indeed, the factors underlined by Michael Bordo (1993, 83) as the main reasons for the demise of Bretton Woods—structural flaws such as the gold exchange standard and the adjustable peg, the U.S. failure to stabilize the price level after 1965, the industrial countries' reluctance to follow American policies, concentrating instead on their own goals—were all anticipated by Graham.

The inadequacy of the adjustment mechanism soon became a commonplace in analyses of Bretton Woods. Commenting on the scheme, Jacob Viner ([1944] 1951, 235) noted a certain ambiguity in setting the goal of exchange rate stability while sanctioning exchange rate variation "as a normal procedure for relieving pressure on international balance." John H. Williams ([1944] 1947), the proponent of the key currencies approach, feared that in the event of a dollar shortage the accord would put too heavy a burden on the United States. On a different interpretation, which eventually prevailed when the spirit of the treaty was abandoned, parity change was considered as an extraordinary measure and the burden of adjustment was placed on stabilization policies. But these were aimed at full employment, so forsaking exchange rate variations exposed the latent

5. "But when people are not sure of future, as well as present, convertibility, the drive against gold currencies becomes acute. Bear speculators are then presented with that rare, and greatly desired phenomenon, a 'sure thing' " (Graham 1940, 19). The circumstances giving rise to a one-way bet were also explained by Gustav Cassel ([1936] 1966, 240–41), Friedrich Lutz (1943, 13), and Milton Friedman (1953, 164).

inconsistency of the system.[6] With the disruptive shock of the Great Depression and the crisis of the classical paradigm, the stabilization argument had become overriding, and it eventually provided the main focus of Mundell's theory of optimum currency areas.

While policy makers hailed the agreements as the end of the interwar monetary disorder, in the academic world opinions were much more variegated. Simplifying in the extreme, we can distinguish three positions in the early stages of the debate. First, the few uncompromising critics of Bretton Woods, such as Frank Graham, deemed the system inherently inconsistent. Second, cautious supporters like Jacob Viner ([1944] 1951, 237), while objecting to some particular provisions such as exchange controls, approved the scheme with a view to monetary reconstruction. Third, more enthusiastic supporters—for example, Ragnar Nurkse—had no doubt that the postwar monetary order could allow countries to achieve both internal and external stability. Thus Nurkse (1945a, 14) viewed the Bretton Woods system as "the only one that is compatible at once with a national full employment policy and with a reasonable stability of exchange rates and freedom from severe exchange restrictions." In fact, like the majority of economists, he was confident that the provisions of the agreement could defuse the potential conflict between activist economic policies and stable exchange rates, failing to see the drawbacks of the adjustable peg.[7]

With the benefit of hindsight, it was the first of these three positions that proved correct. As we have seen, Graham, foreseeing the diffusion of a fixed exchange rate regime, emphasized both its incompatibility with independent economic policies and the one-way bet, which undermined the system's viability. Focusing on certain analogies between Bretton Woods

6. As Raymond Mikesell (1947, 502) noted, the adjustment mechanism could not be based either on price level changes as in the classical gold standard, because independent monetary policies would generally be pursued, or on the Keynesian multiplier effect, since domestic policies would be implemented to compensate for trade imbalances. Hence, he argued, aside from temporary and exceptional imbalances amenable to corrective policies, "there exists no dependable mechanism by means of which deep-seated maladjustments in the structure of world trade can be removed." In this connection, Walter Gardner (1945, 284–85) of the Federal Reserve Board, ruling out exchange rate variations except in extreme circumstances not otherwise resolvable, stressed monetary and fiscal policies as the appropriate adjustment tool. In reply, Ragnar Nurkse (1945b, 291) criticized the use of anti-inflation policies, in place of devaluation, because of their depressive effects.

7. A glaring example is the following: "The object of the International Monetary Fund is to keep exchange rates stable in the short run but to permit step-by-step adjustments of rates from time to time, as and when the trend of international payments requires it. The method of exchange adjustment can under the new system be used in a way entirely compatible with the objectives of internal as well as external equilibrium" (Nurkse 1947, 575). The background of Nurkse's ideas can be found in his monograph on the interwar currency experience (Nurkse 1944).

and the Tripartite Agreement of 1936, he restated the inconsistencies that tainted the new monetary institutions, drawing attention to the dominating support of fixed exchange rates.

> It would seem that, after all this, we might have learned that we cannot both have our cake and eat it. We should know that we must either forgo fixed exchange rates *or* national monetary sovereignty if we are to avoid the disruption of equilibrium in freely conducted international trade or the system of controls and inhibitions which is the only alternative when the internal values of independent currencies deviate—as they always tend to do—from what was, perhaps, a correct relationship when the fixed rates of exchange were set up. Yet the old error was, to all intents and purposes, again repeated in the International Monetary Organization which did not much curtail national monetary sovereignty. It is true that some concessions were made to the consequent demand for flexibility in exchange relationships. But there is, nevertheless, a strong bias in the statute toward the ideal of rates maintained unchanged for an indefinitely lengthy period, and not even the slightest provision for the adoption, by the various participating countries, of the congruent monetary policies without which a system of fixed exchange rates simply does not make sense. (Graham 1949, 6)

Indeed, the shift to a fixed-rate standard after 1950 precluded the main channel of long-run adjustment envisaged by the Bretton Woods agreements, thus giving rise to a thorny problem for postwar monetary arrangements. The actual solution was to use fiscal policy to balance savings and investment and keep each country's current account deficit or surplus small to avoid the need for large-scale capital transfers (McKinnon 1993, 24). On the other hand, notwithstanding Keynes's (1946) revivification of the price-specie-flow mechanism as a solution to the dollar shortage, after the Depression the classical adjustment model was in utter disrepute.[8] Hence, in the Bretton Woods monetary order, maintaining internal and external balance emerged as a complex, stubborn problem.

8. In this connection, Moggridge (2001) has recently dispelled allegations that Keynes's disciples suggested suppressing the publication of his last paper. Certainly, Keynes's wholehearted vindication of classical theory might have looked surprising, yet it can be explained by his unyielding quest for creative, original thinking (Cesarano 2003). As Roy Harrod wrote to E. A. G. Robinson: "The point is that Maynard knew quite well that many experts differed from his conclusions. That was his main reason for wanting to publish the article" (quoted in Moggridge 2001, 822). A further explanation of Keynes's position may be related to the need to show that an adjustment mechanism existed in a fixed exchange rate regime, which Keynes had continuously called for and which was at the basis of the Bretton Woods monetary order.

2. The Contributions of Abba Lerner

When Mundell's classic paper appeared in 1961, the postwar monetary system was definitively operating on fixed exchange rates, the only changes in parity having been the devaluations of the French franc in 1957 and 1958. And even afterward parity changes were rather exceptional, the main episodes being the deutsche mark revaluation of 1961 and the sterling devaluation of 1967. Before 1950, however, the resort to exchange rate variations to adjust structural imbalances had been considered a key provision of the treaty.[9] This was an essential innovation in that, waiving the gold standard's restoration rule, which imposed the reestablishment of the official parity after a suspension, it turned the nature of monetary arrangements on its head, emphasizing the pursuit of domestic targets, in particular full employment. Thus, reflecting the cultural climate of the time, in his *Economics of Control* (1944) Abba Lerner analyzed the gold standard not as a realistic solution but on purely abstract grounds. The book's subtitle, *Principles of Welfare Economics*, is more indicative of the true nature of the work, a treatise applying contemporary economic theory to a wide range of topics.[10] In the preface, Lerner, who had studied at the London School of Economics and Cambridge in the 1930s, acknowledged his intellectual debt to such former teachers as Robbins, Hayek, Hicks, and Robertson, as well as to Kahn and Joan Robinson, adding: "Mr. J. M. Keynes's influence is of course seen throughout, as in practically all modern writings" (Lerner 1944, viii).

In dealing with the monetary aspects of international economics, Lerner draws attention to the greater difficulties of maintaining full employment in the open economy. In the gold standard, the advantages of an unvaried official parity—"a simple rule for the management of the currency" (370)—in conducting foreign trade and insulating the central bank from political

9. Keynes (1943, 186), clarifying the salient features of his plan in a comment on an article by Hayek, considered a parity change necessary when domestic wage and price policies gave rise to a misalignment in the country's efficiency wages, impervious to a revision of policies. "If the initial exchange-rates are fixed correctly, this is likely to be the only important disequilibrium for which a change in exchange rates is the appropriate remedy."

10. In his review, Milton Friedman ([1947] 1953, 319) criticized many analytical and institutional arguments. Though recognizing "Lerner's very considerable gifts—his acuteness as a theorist and dialectician, his skill and patience in exposition, his flexibility of mind, his profound interest in social welfare, and his willingness to accept and courage to state what seems to him right social policy, regardless of precedent or accepted opinion," Friedman concluded that "these gifts have been imperfectly realized because they have been employed in a vacuum and have not been combined with a realistic appraisal of the administrative problems of economic institutions or of their social and political implications."

interference must be set against the drawbacks of monetary restriction to stop a gold drain. To this effect, raising the interest rate works through three channels:

1. It keeps idle funds at home and draws them from abroad.
2. It makes investment fall, thus decreasing output, consumption, and imports, and raises unemployment until external equilibrium is reestablished.
3. Because of the fall in economic activity and employment, it lowers the price of exports, bringing about an increase in exports and output until full employment is restored.

However, Lerner notes, the economy may get stuck in stage two for a lengthy period indeed, as in the case of Britain's return to gold in 1925–31, a "strange situation in which the maintenance of full employment is sacrificed to the relatively insignificant consideration of stabilizing the value of gold or of foreign currencies" (373).[11]

Following the Keynesian paradigm, Lerner's theoretical framework centers on the persistence of the fall in output and employment, drawing attention to an inadequacy in the adjustment process. The immediate impact of monetary tightening is not on prices and wages, which would eliminate the imbalance, but (via investment) on economic activity. Prices and wages, instead, are the last variables to change under the pressure of increasing unemployment. Thinking of a possible remedy, the resort to a general tariff together with a subsidy for exports would dam the gold drain without impairing employment and international trade, but this would be tantamount to devaluation; in short, an overt, formal currency depreciation would be a more transparent policy (374).

At this point Lerner raises a key question: within a country the region hit by an adverse shock suffers unemployment, yet adjustment is smooth

11. This analysis recalls Keynes's ([1925] 1972, 218) critique of the return to the gold standard, envisaging the effects of deflationary policy on unemployment, and then on wages and prices, to make them consistent with the prewar parity. "Our problem is to reduce money wages and, through them, the cost of living, with the idea that, when the circle is complete, real wages will be as high, or nearly as high, as before. By what *modus operandi* does credit restriction attain this result? *In no other way than by the deliberate intensification of unemployment.* The object of credit restriction, in such a case, is to withdraw from employers the financial means to employ labour at the existing level of prices and wages. The policy can only attain its end by intensifying unemployment without limit, until the workers are ready to accept the necessary reduction of money wages under the pressure of hard facts." The roots of Keynes's position are to be found in his earlier works, especially the *Tract*, an extensive and penetrating analysis of monetary arrangements (Cesarano 2003, sec. 1).

even though devaluation is obviously impossible. To account for these seemingly contrasting propositions, he puts forward the basic principles underlying the theory of optimum currency areas.

> If this [adjustment mechanism] works out satisfactorily within a country, the gold standard advocate can argue, why can it not operate internationally? Does not our argument for flexible exchanges also logically commit us to a demand for currency autonomy for every region, district, and village?
>
> The answer is that the region within the country differs from an independent country in the important respect that it enjoys the free movement of goods, of people, and of investment into the other regions of the same country. An import balance that causes money to flow out of one region means an export balance in another region where money is flowing in, and economic activity is at an unusually high level. The inhabitants of the first region can move without restriction into the prosperous region. This does not mean that there cannot be depressed areas within a country, but it does mean that these are not likely to be very serious if it is easy to get a job by moving into the other area, and in any case the depressed area will be recognized as a responsibility of the country as a whole. (375–76)

Mundell reached the same conclusion, although from a different perspective, focusing on the possible failure of exchange rate adjustments to restore equilibrium, since the regions hit by shocks do not necessarily coincide with nations. In his clarifying example, if Canada and the United States are divided into two regions, the East producing cars and the West producing lumber, a productivity increase in the automobile industry brings about excess demand for lumber and inflationary pressures in the West, and an excess supply of cars and unemployment in the East (Mundell 1961, 659–60). An expansionary monetary policy does not restore equilibrium in both regions because it would eliminate unemployment in the East but not inflation in the West; and conversely in the event of a restriction. However, redrawing national borders in such a way that East and West replaced Canada and the United States, a depreciation of the Eastern dollar would reestablish equilibrium. Exchange rate flexibility, therefore, is an effective equilibrating mechanism between areas, inside each of which factors of production are highly mobile.

To arrive at this solution, Lerner and Mundell start from two distinct points, relating to the dual nature of the issue at stake: the smoothness of adjustment *within* a country (Lerner) and the possible failure of exchange rate flexibility to reestablish equilibrium *between* countries (Mundell). Mundell focuses on the conceivable impotence of economic policy to attain both full employment and price stability, singling out labor mobility as an exogenous feature of the economy, on the basis of which borders must be redrawn to achieve the optimum. Lerner, instead, takes the national border as given, arguing that while an equilibrium mechanism enhances domestic adjustment, the border hinders factor mobility and leads to tariffs, quotas, and other trade barriers.[12] As the next section shows, these different perspectives, though leading to identical results, suggest alternative theoretical approaches and policy implications of the optimality hypothesis.

After the war, the positive appraisal of the Bretton Woods system grew in parallel with the spread of Keynesian economics, prevailing over skeptics and critics. At the meeting of the American Economic Association in January 1947, Ragnar Nurkse (1947, 569), investigating how the Bretton Woods institutions "can be operated so as to agree rather than conflict with the domestic objective of stability at full employment," contended that the pursuit of internal equilibrium, defined analogously to the modern concept of NAIRU, does not contrast with external equilibrium, which can be maintained through a panoply of policy instruments: the buffer of external reserves, commercial policies, and exchange rate adjustment. Nurkse's rather optimistic view of the operation of Bretton Woods, failing to detect the flaw of the adjustable peg and calling for "compensatory" expansionary domestic policies in case of a fall in exports (575–76), appears untenable nowadays, but reflects the postwar intellectual climate.[13] Indeed, in his comment, Abba Lerner (1947, 592–93) noted

12. If these obstacles were removed, the gold standard would provide an optimal solution. "Tariffs and quotas interfere with trade, and the movement of people from country to country is seriously limited. It is only because of these restrictions that a rigid enforcement of fixed exchange rates between the values of the currencies of different countries can be so very harmful. If there were complete freedom of movement of goods, investment, and people, an international currency system would be as sound as a single monetary system for a country within which the three freedoms of movement are realities, and a properly managed gold standard system might be one way of arranging this" (Lerner 1944, 376).

13. In the same session, "Domestic versus International Economic Equilibrium," Arthur Smithies (1947) contributed an essay titled "Multilateral Trade and Employment." The wide-ranging discussion by Bloomfield, Wood, Mikesell, Ellis, and Lerner examined several other issues: from the distinction between the defensive and aggressive use of adjustment policies to the definition of fundamental disequilibrium, and, particularly relevant in this context, the choice between exchange rate variations and trade controls in balance-of-payments adjustment.

the substantial consensus on rejecting the classical assumption of full employment: "The outstanding feature of this session is the extent of agreement. . . . The agreement between Mr. Smithies, Mr. Nurkse, and nearly all the other discussants stems from the recognition of this error [that somehow full employment was being maintained all the time] and the integration of the free trade issue with the employment problem. As such it has great promise for future public policy."

Although there was little progress in solving the conflict between internal and external equilibrium, Elmer Wood (1947, 584), the only discordant voice in the Keynesian-oriented session, pointed out the disruptive effects of trade restrictions and exchange rate changes on international price relationships and trade flows, which would bring internal disequilibrium and unemployment. Hence, while avoiding ruinous deflation, countries should contribute to international monetary stability by a consistent price level policy, relying on the flexibility of the domestic economies, as in industries and regions inside a country.

> It was a great accomplishment for the world to renounce the use of severe deflationary pressure, whether to meet the requirements of the international standard or for any other reason, and we do not want to go back to the old copybook maxims. But under any price system there must be some flexibility in individual industries and in particular areas. Large areas under one sovereignty have this problem. Surely the different sections of the United States would not gain in economic prosperity if they were to acquire local monetary autonomy and freedom to apply import restrictions against other sections. (584)

Underlying Wood's argument is the claim of effectiveness for the classical adjustment mechanism in expanding international trade and maintaining equilibrium, as well as a criticism of the ephemeral benefits of exchange restrictions, which are only apparent and encourage retaliation by other countries, leading to the reciprocal destruction of export markets. Envisaging the scenario that emerged in 1950 with the fixed-rate dollar standard, Wood argued for an integrated world economy under the economic leadership of the United States, required to pursue a rigorous economic policy strategy (586–87).

Wood's bold criticism, grounded in the classical paradigm, exposed the inconsistency of the postwar monetary system, aiming at both full employment and stable exchange rates. This reminds one of Graham's critique, although his proposed solution was exchange rate flexibility while Wood

(1947, 586) called for a highly integrated world economy, not necessarily based on gold, provided that the dollar was "anchored to a stable economy." More important, Wood's emphasis on the effectiveness of adjustment within a country prompted Lerner's explanation of this stylized fact. Having warned against the great cost of maintaining fixed exchange rates, Lerner (1947, 594) restated the hypothesis underlying optimum currency areas from what would correspond to Mundell's viewpoint, looking at the adjustment process between countries.

> If it is good for a country to be able to adjust its exchange rate, why is this not good for a state, county, city, village, or even family? This is a very powerful argument and reminds one of the free traders' argument on the same lines against protection. The only way this attack can be met is by giving a satisfactory principle which would show where the possibility of exchange adjustment is desirable and where it is not.
>
> There is such a principle. Where there is mobility of labor, and for this purpose it is real and not just legal mobility which is relevant, there is no need for an exchange adjustment to restore equilibrium between a deficit area and a surplus area. This is because the unemployed in one area where there is a depression can go to the other area, where there is a boom, and get a job.

If labor mobility is lacking and exchange rates remain fixed, adjustment could be brought about only through changes in the price level, depression, or trade controls. Calling the first channel of adjustment unlikely, Lerner excludes the other two as indefensible, thus indicating exchange rate flexibility as the right solution of structural disequilibrium. On the other hand, trying to trigger the conditions for optimality by fixing exchange rates would be futile.[14]

In his analysis of the adjustment mechanism, Abba Lerner grasped the essential principles underlying the optimality of currency areas, yet he did not elaborate these principles to develop a full-fledged theory like Mundell. Lerner did not discuss the implications of increasing the number of currencies, that is, the trade-off between the costs of waning money

14. The same concept is expressed in his book. To set up a single monetary system, "the first step . . . is to remove the hindrances to movement," thus making exchange rate changes less necessary for maintaining full employment. "But to try to establish [exchange stability] before the underlying conditions of stability (that is, the freedoms of movement) have been established is certainly to attempt to establish world unity by decreeing one of its symptoms—like attempting to establish good health by commanding everybody to display a glowing complexion" (Lerner 1944, 376–77).

functions and the benefits of stabilization policies. This problem is inherent in the optimality question, and Mundell examines it in section 5 of his paper, citing two further factors that raise the costs of currency multiplication: a thinner foreign exchange market, which could enable speculators to affect the market price, and the vanishing of money illusion, which would make exchange rate adjustments to overcome price and wage rigidity totally ineffective.

In general, while Lerner answered a specific question, namely, the reason for smooth adjustment inside a country, Mundell tackled the topic from a different point of view, showing the conditions under which, if exchange rate flexibility failed to reestablish equilibrium, the optimum could be attained by redrawing the borders of currency areas. This assessment is not meant to detract from Lerner's brilliant intuition, but simply to put it into perspective relative to Mundell's more far-reaching contribution.

3. Monetary Unions and Optimality

After World War II, the movement for economic and political unification in Europe caused interest in the theoretical aspects of monetary union (Maes, Smets, and Michielsen 2002). Actually, economists' interest revived periodically every two decades: in the 1950s when the first European institutions were set up, in the 1970s with the Werner report, and in the 1990s with the Maastricht Treaty instituting the Economic and Monetary Union. Here our focus is on the first stage, preceding the publication of Mundell's article.

The analysis of monetary unions raises the same analytical problems as the theory of optimum currency areas, only viewed from a reverse perspective. Where the latter searches for the optimality principles to trace the currency area, the former takes national borders as given and inquires into the optimality of a monetary area on the basis of the same principles. Hence, early studies of monetary union focused on the mechanism of adjustment between members, and specifically on the conditions ensuring interregional equilibrium. James Meade and Tibor Scitovsky investigated these issues thoroughly, starting, like Lerner, from the smoothness of adjustment within a country.

In his lectures on economic union at the University of Chicago, James Meade (1953, 38–43) argued that the introduction of a common currency would mitigate the hardships of the gold standard adjustment mechanism by lengthening the adjustment period, depriving member countries of domestic stabilization policies, and creating a central authority responsible for monetary policy. To make a monetary union viable, however, fiscal policy too needs to be centralized.[15] Furthermore, factor mobility was essential to the success of a common currency; freedom of trade alone is not sufficient to equalize the marginal product of labor and other factors (chapter 3). Analogously, Scitovsky (1957, 24–32), after noting the higher labor mobility between regions, stressed the key role of an integrated capital market to redistribute savings, thus strengthening interregional adjustment (see also Ingram 1959), and of stabilization policies to maintain full employment. Of course, this concern reflected the Keynesian paradigm, yet the working of a monetary union was accounted for by the classical model of the balance of payments. This may seem paradoxical, or even schizophrenic, but it simply shows the emphasis on the smoothness of intranational adjustment as contrasted with the international specie-flow mechanism.

Both Meade (1957, 385–87) and Scitovsky (1957, 19–21) therefore argue that, while under the gold standard deficit countries suffer unemployment, inside a country this is avoided by effective interregional adjustment through a variety of channels—chiefly, goods and factor mobility, fiscal and monetary policies, and regional development measures. Penelope Hartland (1949) had already corroborated this hypothesis empirically, showing that in the 1930s factor mobility and fiscal transfers by the federal government had tempered the disruptive impact of the Great Depression in the United States. At the theoretical level, the main principles underlying monetary union had been anticipated by Milton Friedman (1953, 193 n. 16) in his discussion of fixed exchange rates between the members of the sterling area as contrasted with the different regions within a country.

> The key difference for present purposes between the different states of the United States, on the one hand, and the different members of the sterling area, on the other, is that the former are, while the latter are not, all effectively subject to a single central fiscal and monetary authority—the federal government—having ultimate fiscal and monetary powers. In addition, the former have, while the latter have not,

15. This proposition has always been controversial and still is. While Meade (1953, 42; 1957, 388), Scitovsky (1958, 98), and Erik Lundberg (1972, 129) called for a supranational fiscal authority, Lutz (1972) and Robert Triffin (1972) thought it unnecessary.

effectively surrendered the right to impose restrictions on the movements of goods, people, or capital between one another. This is a major factor explaining why a central monetary authority is able to operate without producing serious sectional strains.

Hence, the basic tenets of the theory of optimum currency areas had been set out by a few distinguished economists—Lerner, followed by Friedman, Meade, and Scitovsky—in analyzing the effectiveness of interregional adjustment. This hypothesis, however, was explicitly rejected by Mundell, who simply assimilated intranational adjustment to international adjustment in the gold standard.[16] This feature helps to capture the peculiarities of his theory. For Mundell labor mobility, the optimality criterion, is an exogenous characteristic of the economy. Thus, the optimum does not result from an equilibrium process but requires a policy action—that is, redrawing the country's borders—like the solution of a static problem in economic policy design (Tinbergen 1952). By contrast, for Lerner and the others the optimality criteria are the product of an equilibrium mechanism. Indeed, while Mundell's Keynesian analysis is static and centered on disequilibrium (price and wage rigidity is a key assumption), the classical theory behind interregional adjustment is its mirror-image opposite. As Scitovsky (1957, 19) remarked, "The classical theory . . . is a dynamic equilibrium theory; dynamic, because it deals with a process of adjustment over time; equilibrium, because it asserts the existence of a tendency toward balance-of-payments equilibrium."

Though they shared the same theoretical framework, Meade and Scitovsky suggested opposite strategies for European monetary unification. Meade (1953, 82–85) saw the introduction of a common currency as the final stage of economic integration, a challenging goal to be achieved gradually, not by a single constitutional change. Restating these points in his presidential address to the British Association, he emphasized the great powers with which the union's authorities would have to be endowed and the political difficulties that would have to be

16. "If the gold standard imposed a harsh discipline on the national economy and induced the transmission of economic fluctuations, then a common currency would be guilty of the same charges; interregional balance-of-payments problems are invisible, so to speak, precisely because there is no escape from the self-adjusting effects of interregional money flows. . . . Today, if the case for flexible exchange rates is a strong one, it is, in logic, a case for flexible exchange rates based on *regional* currencies, not on national currencies. The optimum currency area is the region" (Mundell 1961, 660).

overcome.[17] Scitovsky (1957, 34–36) viewed the establishment of a common European currency as the means for fulfilling the conditions of economic integration, although like Meade he emphasized the sizable share of sovereignty that would have to be surrendered. In this context, however, the interesting point does not concern the subtleties of Meade's and Scitovsky's different opinions, but Mundell's assessment of them. After weighing the two positions, he reduced the dispute to an empirical question about the degree of factor mobility in Europe (Mundell 1961, sec. 4). In his conclusion he confirms that the optimality criteria are exogenous, thus a negation of equilibrium forces, contrasting with the analysis of interregional adjustment in monetary unions grounded in the classical model. The latter is suggestive of the modern equilibrium approach to optimum currency areas, a recent development based on the teachings of the new classical macroeconomics, in which optimality becomes entirely endogenous (Cesarano 1997; Frankel and Rose 1998; Alesina and Barro 2002).

The view of monetary unification held by Lerner and the other distinguished economists after him differs from the experience of the Economic and Monetary Union, which introduced the euro as single currency without centralized fiscal policy, let alone a supranational authority. This essentially reflects the fact that the underlying strategy was to use monetary union to accelerate political union. However, the maintenance of national borders is patently at odds with the equilibrium approach to optimum currency areas. Actually, a common currency for a group of sovereign states might be the worst of all possible worlds, with an ineffective interregional adjustment mechanism and, at the same time, the impossibility of monetary policy at a national level.

17. Specifically, Meade (1957, 387–88) said: "The integration approach thus involves—in addition to the formation of a common market for goods and for factors of production and the provision of much greater international liquidity for European monetary authorities—a very extensive range of powers for what would amount to a single European government. Such a government would have to be able to control central-bank monetary policy and governmental budgetary policy throughout Europe, to determine a single European commercial and exchange-rate policy *vis-à-vis* third countries, and to carry out an effective special-area policy for depressed regions in Europe. This is in my opinion ultimately desirable; let us hope that it will prove ultimately practicable; but it is not a starter at the moment, and it would be a great shame to sacrifice the present real political possibilities of building a commercial free-trade area to this ideal of simultaneous monetary and budgetary integration." Meade's arguments entirely reflect Lerner's analysis (see footnote 14 above).

4. Conclusions

Mundell will still be remembered as the originator of the theory of optimum currency areas, notwithstanding Lerner's anticipation. The two arrived at the optimality principle of factor mobility by different routes. Mundell set the problem in terms of the geographical area to be drawn in order to achieve the optimum, whereas Lerner focused on the properties and effectiveness of intranational adjustment, an interesting approach in the light of recent work. Certainly, Lerner did not put forward an elaborated, full-fledged theory as did Mundell, but by dwelling on the adjustment model of the gold standard he anticipated the analysis of monetary union of the 1950s.

A last, important question is whether Mundell was aware of Lerner's contribution. It seems that he was not. While it can be conjectured that Mundell had come across *The Economics of Control*, the key passages on the international adjustment mechanism might have escaped his attention, so that Lerner's original yet incidental observations went unnoticed. In fact, while Mundell referred to Meade and Scitovsky, he did not mention Lerner. Indeed, to my knowledge, Lerner's writings are never cited anywhere in the literature on optimum currency areas of the past half century.[18] Furthermore, examining the early debate on European monetary integration, Mundell (1961, sec. 3) totally disregarded Meade's and Scitovsky's argument for the efficiency of interregional adjustment vis-à-vis the costly specie-flow mechanism of the gold standard, which was also Lerner's argument, and instead considered the two adjustment mechanisms to be alike and both very costly. Lerner, however, may have encouraged Mundell to pursue with confidence the optimum currency areas issue, as evidenced by an interesting episode revealed by Mundell himself. During his stay at Stanford in 1958–59, he presented a paper, "The Theory of International Adjustment and Optimum Currency Units" (a draft of Mundell 1960), at a faculty seminar attended by several economists of note, Abba Lerner among them. As Mundell (1997, 31) recounts: "I spent most of my time at the seminar explaining the dynamic model and the adjustment mechanism under fixed and flexible exchange rates. After the seminar, Lerner chided me for not having talked enough about optimum currency areas, but with his great intellect, it was easy for him to grasp my basic idea in a few sentences."

18. A referee recalls that Abba Lerner discussed with his colleagues many variations of the idea underlying currency area optimality, such as introducing money by sectors to allow price flexibility by sector, but nobody picked up these suggestions.

References

Alesina, Alberto, and Robert J. Barro. 2002. Currency Unions. *Quarterly Journal of Economics* 117:409–36.

Bordo, Michael D. 1993. The Bretton Woods International Monetary System: A Historical Overview. In *A Retrospective on the Bretton Woods System*, edited by Michael D. Bordo and Barry Eichengreen. Chicago: University of Chicago Press.

Bordo, Michael D., Claudia Goldin, and Eugene N. White, eds. 1998. *The Defining Moment: The Great Depression and the American Economy in the Twentieth Century*. Chicago: University of Chicago Press.

Cassel, Gustav. [1936] 1966. *The Downfall of the Gold Standard*. New York: Augustus M. Kelley.

Cesarano, Filippo. 1997. Currency Areas and Equilibrium. *Open Economies Review* 8:51–59.

——. 2003. Keynes's Revindication of Classical Monetary Theory. *HOPE* 35.3:491–519.

Frankel, Jeffrey A., and Andrew K. Rose. 1998. The Endogeneity of the Optimum Currency Area Criteria. *Economic Journal* 108:1009–25.

Friedman, Milton. [1947] 1953. Lerner on the Economics of Control. In *Essays in Positive Economics*. Chicago: University of Chicago Press.

——. 1953. The Case for Flexible Exchange Rates. In *Essays in Positive Economics*, by Milton Friedman. Chicago: University of Chicago Press.

Gardner, Walter R. 1945. The Future International Position of the United States as Effected by the Fund and Bank. *American Economic Review: Papers and Proceedings* 35.2:272–88.

Graham, Frank D. 1940. Achilles' Heels in Monetary Standards. *American Economic Review* 30.1, pt. 1:16–32.

——. 1943. *Fundamentals of International Monetary Policy*. Essays in International Finance, no. 2. Princeton, N.J.: Princeton University, International Finance Section.

——. 1949. *The Cause and Cure of "Dollar Shortage."* Essays in International Finance, no. 10. Princeton, N.J.: Princeton University, International Finance Section.

Halm, George N. 1944. The International Monetary Fund. *Review of Economic Statistics* 26:170–75.

Hartland, Penelope. 1949. Interregional Payments Compared with International Payments. *Quarterly Journal of Economics* 63:392–407.

Ingram, James C. 1959. State and Regional Payments Mechanisms. *Quarterly Journal of Economics* 73:619–32.

Keynes, John M. 1923. *A Tract on Monetary Reform*. London: Macmillan.

——. 1943. The Objective of International Price Stability. *Economic Journal* 53:185–87.

——. 1946. The Balance of Payments of the United States. *Economic Journal* 56:172–87.

——. [1925] 1972. The Economic Consequences of Mr. Churchill. In vol. 9 of *The Collected Writings of John Maynard Keynes*. London: Macmillan.

——. 1980a. *Activities 1940–1944: Shaping the Post-War World; The Clearing Union*. Vol. 25 of *The Collected Writings of John Maynard Keynes*, edited by Donald Moggridge. London: Macmillan.

——. 1980b. *Activities 1941–1946: Shaping the Post-War World; Bretton Woods and Reparations*. Vol. 26 of *The Collected Writings of John Maynard Keynes*, edited by Donald Moggridge. London: Macmillan.

Laidler, David. 1999. *Fabricating the Keynesian Revolution: Studies of the Inter-war Literature on Money, the Cycle, and Unemployment*. Cambridge: Cambridge University Press.

Lerner, Abba R. 1944. *The Economics of Control: Principles of Welfare Economics*. New York: Macmillan.

——. 1947. Discussion of "International Monetary Policy and the Search for Economic Stability" by Ragnar Nurkse. *American Economic Review: Papers and Proceedings* 37.2:592–94.

Lundberg, Erik. 1972. Discussants on Professor Lutz' Paper. In Machlup, Gutowski, and Lutz 1972.

Lutz, Friedrich A. 1943. *International Monetary Mechanisms: The Keynes and White Proposals*. Essays in International Finance, no. 1. Princeton, N.J.: Princeton University, International Finance Section.

——. 1972. Foreign Exchange Rate Policy and European Economic Integration. In Machlup, Gutowski, and Lutz 1972.

Machlup, Fritz, Armin Gutowski, and Friedrich A. Lutz. 1972. *International Monetary Problems*. Washington, D.C.: American Enterprise Institute for Public Policy Research.

Maes, Ivo, Jan Smets, and Jan Michielsen. 2002. EMU from a Historical Perspective. In *Economic Thought and the Making of European Monetary Union: Selected Essays of Ivo Maes*. Cheltenham: Edward Elgar.

McKinnon, Ronald I. 1993. The Rules of the Game: International Money in Historical Perspective. *Journal of Economic Literature* 31.1:1–44.

Meade, James E. 1953. *Problems of Economic Union*. London: George Allen and Unwin.

——. 1957. The Balance-of-Payments Problems of a European Free-Trade Area. *Economic Journal* 67:379–96.

Mikesell, Raymond F. 1947. The Role of the International Monetary Agreements in a World of Planned Economies. *Journal of Political Economy* 55.6:497–512.

Moggridge, Donald E. 1986. Keynes and the International Monetary System, 1909–46. In *International Monetary Problems and Supply-Side Economics: Essays in Honour of Lorie Tarshis*, edited by Jon S. Cohen and G. C. Harcourt. London: Macmillan.

——. 2001. "Maynard would not have wished"? Second-Guessing the Author of "The Balance of Payments of the United States." *HOPE* 33.4:815–24.

Mundell, Robert A. 1960. The Monetary Dynamics of International Adjustment under Fixed and Flexible Exchange Rates. *Quarterly Journal of Economics* 84:227–57.

——. 1961. A Theory of Optimum Currency Areas. *American Economic Review* 51.4:657–65.

——. 1997. Updating the Agenda for Monetary Union. In *Optimum Currency Areas: New Analytical and Policy Developments*, edited by Mario I. Blejer, Jacob A. Frenkel, Leonardo Leiderman, and Assaf Razin, in cooperation with David M. Cheney. Washington, D.C.: International Monetary Fund.

Nurkse, Ragnar. 1944. *International Currency Experience: Lessons of the Inter-War Period.* Geneva: League of Nations.

——. 1945a. *Conditions of International Monetary Equilibrium.* Essays in International Finance, no. 4. Princeton, N.J.: Princeton University, International Finance Section.

——. 1945b. Discussion of "The Future International Position of the United States as Effected by the Fund and Bank" by Walter R. Gardner. *American Economic Review: Papers and Proceedings* 35.2:291–94.

——. 1947. International Monetary Policy and the Search for Economic Stability. *American Economic Review: Papers and Proceedings* 37.2:569–80.

Scitovsky, Tibor. 1957. The Theory of the Balance of Payments and the Problem of a Common European Currency. *Kyklos* 10:18–44.

——. 1958. *Economic Theory and Western European Integration.* London: George Allen and Unwin.

Smithies, Arthur. 1947. Multilateral Trade and Employment. *American Economic Review, Papers and Proceedings* 37.2:560–68.

Tinbergen, Jan. 1952. *On the Theory of Economic Policy.* Amsterdam: North-Holland.

Triffin, Robert. 1972. Discussants on Professor Lutz' Paper. In Machlup, Gutowski, and Lutz 1972.

Viner, Jacob. [1944] 1951. The Bretton Woods Agreements. In *International Economics: Studies.* Glencoe, Ill.: Free Press.

Williams, John H. [1944] 1947. After Bretton Woods. In *Postwar Monetary Plans and Other Essays.* New York: Knopf.

Wood, Elmer. 1947. Discussion of "International Monetary Policy and the Search for Economic Stability" by Ragnar Nurkse. *American Economic Review: Papers and Proceedings* 37.2:583–87.

[12]

The History of Economic Analysis in Perspective*

In the last half century, neglect of the history of economic analysis has progressively increased, together with the diffusion of formal modelling. Mathematical economics has a long tradition, dating back at least to Cournot's pathbreaking *Recherches* (1838), but it did not become embedded in mainstream economics until the publication of Hicks' *Value and Capital* and Samuelson's *Foundations* one hundred years later. Subsequently, the spread of innovative analytical tools accelerated sharply, achieving a critical mass deemed to have given rise to the formalist revolution: 'a revolution that is more profound than the Keynesian' (Ward 1972, 40; Blaug 1999). It reshaped economic theorising in an essential way and fostered momentous contributions.[1] Using the same tools as the hard sciences, economists felt they were overcoming the inferiority complex of 'physics envy' and achieving their dream of making economics almost like physics. In some fields, such as finance, mathematical methods have actually advanced to match, if not surpass those employed by physicists.[2] The evolution of economics was thus regarded as cumulative, made of ever more refined and general theories. Indifference towards the history of economics was a natural consequence of these developments. This paper takes this view to task, arguing that, however paradoxical it may appear, the formalist revolution implies a greater not a lesser role for the history of economic analysis.

* I would like to thank Benjamin Friedman, Nicola Giocoli, Geoffrey Harcourt, Samuel Hollander and David Laidler for their perceptive comments. The usual caveat applies.

1 Samuelson highlighted this significant transformation: 'Shortly after 1930 economics burst out into new life. At least four revolutions erupted: the *monopolistic competition* revolution, the *Keynesian macro* revolution, the *mathematicization* revolution, and the *econometric inference* revolution' (1987, 52). For a concise reconstruction of the main factors behind these developments, see Mirowski (2002). The expression 'formalist revolution' is used here as a shorthand, without entering into the question of whether or not it is appropriate. For a discussion of this and related issues, see the symposium on formalism in economics hosted by the *Economic Journal* (November 1998) and Giocoli (2003, 6).

2 Economists' propensity to follow physicists' achievements is described by Debreu: 'Before the contemporary period of the past five decades, theoretical physics had been an inaccessible ideal toward which economic theory sometimes strove. During that period, this striving became a powerful stimulus in the mathematization of economic theory' (1991, 2).

Notwithstanding the profession's general lack of interest, the history of economic theory has flourished in recent decades, witness the foundation of several journals, the number of new books and the establishment of academic societies, whose membership has substantially increased (Vaughn 1993, 175; Blaug 2001, 145–6). Yet, this is no reason to rejoice because ostracising historians offers a gloomy prospect. Looking for a way out, Margaret Schabas boldly called for the history of economics to break away from economics and join the history of science. This opinion, however, has been disputed (see the comments on her paper) and Schabas herself noted that, though historians of science had considered a variety of fields, including the human sciences, they had totally ignored economics (1992, 192–3). The history of economic analysis is therefore left in limbo.

This situation reflects the special position of economics, a rigorous social science bordering on the hard sciences. As Samuelson put it: 'Economics is in between belles lettres and cold sciences' (1987, 53). This seems an innocuous platitude, but helps to clarify several peculiarities of the state of the art, which are important for the role of the discipline's past. Economists of the generation of the formalist revolution were well-read in the classics, not out of mere intellectual curiosity but because they clearly perceived the importance of such knowledge for the advance of economic theory. Hicks and Samuelson, themselves protagonists of the revolution, are striking examples, but quite a few twentieth century giants could be added to the list. The monograph-sized Supplementary Notes of Patinkin's treatise (1956, 373–478) are an outstanding case of intertwining the contributions of the classics with modern theory. Subsequently, this approach lost ground inasmuch as the diffusion of formal methods led to neglect of the distinctive characteristics of economics as a social science. When these characteristics are considered, however, they show that mathematical modelling, far from implying that the history of economics should be disregarded, heightens its usefulness for the modern theorist.

The case for the history of economics has been made on several grounds – cultural, pedagogical, rhetorical (Blaug 1991) – but seldom on theoretical grounds, with knowledge of past theories seen as a means of fostering research. This is a challenging task, and yet it is worth pursuing because it would effectively contribute to bringing the field out of limbo. This paper revisits the case for the history of economic analysis from this perspective, some decades after a first attempt (Cesarano 1983). After examining the implications of the formalist revolution on the state of the art (section 1), the characteristics of economics as a social science are investigated (section 2), showing that the history of the discipline can play an important role in furthering the progress of economic theory (section 3).

1. Language and knowledge in economics

In the title-page of Samuelson's *Foundations*, Willard Gibbs' motto 'Mathematics is a Language' catches the eye. A few years later, Samuelson propounded a shorter dictum – 'Mathematics *is* language' – to point out that, in principle, mathematics cannot be worse or better than prose: 'For in deepest logic – and leaving out all tactical and pedagogical questions – the two media are strictly identical' (1952, 56). Thus, for the sake of argument, he contended that a literary proof of Euler's theorem on homogeneous functions could be provided (1952, 58–9). This is no longer an issue, so that debating it today would be as anachronistic as arguing for horse-drawn transportation in the age of spaceships. Formal modelling unquestionably constitutes a major advance in economics: none of the arguments put forward in this paper conflicts with this proposition. The purpose of this section is simply to bring the contributions of the formalist revolution into focus in order to assess the role of the history of economics.

As a means of communication, language can be more or less precise, rigorous, efficient. In this respect, mathematics is patently advantageous but it is no guarantee of a better theory.[3] Language is just a tool and should not be confused with the object of analysis, i.e. knowledge. Formal modelling brought many important results – the Slutsky equation, the Bickerdike condition and Haavelmo's balanced-budget theorem, to name a few textbook examples that immediately come to mind. Yet, equally momentous contributions have been developed in simple prose, e.g. Hume's specie-flow adjustment mechanism, Ricardo's principle of comparative advantage and Tiebout's hypothesis concerning the efficient provision of public goods. On a first approximation, therefore, the advancement of economic theory is independent of the means of communication – knowledge is independent of language.

This proposition can be viewed as a corollary of Samuelson's equivalence of literary and mathematical languages. Good, or bad, economics can be done either in prose or with formal models. Only valuable works survive the test of time, whatever language they use. Thus, Ramsey's (1928) seminal article on optimal growth is still referred to while hundreds of other mathematical papers are ignored. Likewise, students still read Hume's essay on money, but have never heard of many eighteenth century pamphleteers

3 Having illustrated the advantages of mathematical symbolism in avoiding mistakes in logic, Samuelson observed: 'Logic is no protection against false hypotheses; or against misinterpretation of reality; or against the formulation of irrelevant hypotheses. I think it is one of the advantages of the mathematical medium – or, strictly speaking, of the mathematician's customary canons of exposition of proof, whether in words or symbols – that we are forced to lay our cards on the table so that all can see our premises. But I must confess that I have heard of card games – in fact I have participated in them myself – where, knowingly or unknowingly, we have dealt cards from the bottom of the deck. So there are no absolute checks against human error' (1952, 64).

on the same subject. In fact irrelevant, even silly things can be expressed in a sophisticated language and pathbreaking contributions made in simple prose: the Coase Theorem was stated in plain English but, as far as the progress of economics is concerned, it is far more important than the countless mathematical theorems published in today's journals.

These are straightforward propositions. Nonetheless, as the spread of the new techniques fuelled the formalist revolution, the change in language tended to be equated with advancement in knowledge, lending support to the idea of a cumulative evolution of economics. Even in the hard sciences, however, the instrument of mathematics has never been mistaken for the theory's results nor thought to bring about cumulativeness or convergence in the growth of knowledge (Cesarano 1983, section 3). A further consequence of the revolution was the temptation to mould theory to the most attractive technique, with the risk of formulating weak hypotheses.[4]

A century after Walras, general equilibrium theory has made considerable progress, with substantial gains in generality (Debreu 1991, 4). Yet, while in physics the language of mathematics remained a tool at the service of theory, this was not always the case in economics. Acknowledging the different relationship of mathematics with economics and physics, Debreu noted that physics was never subordinated to mathematics, whereas economics was.

> The benefits of that special relationship [between physics and mathematics] were large for both fields; but physics did not completely surrender to the embrace of mathematics and to its inherent compulsion toward logical rigor. The experimental results and the factual observations that are at the basis of physics, and which provide a constant check on its theoretical constructions, occasionally let its bold reasonings to violate knowingly the canons of mathematical deduction.
>
> In these directions, economic theory could not follow the role model offered by physical theory. . . . Being denied a sufficiently secure experimental base, economic theory has to adhere to the rules of logical discourse and must renounce the facility of internal inconsistency.
>
> (1991, 2)

4 The target-zone model is a case in point. Despite the elegant mathematics borrowed from financial economics, the theory was falsified by many empirical tests. As Mark Taylor (1995) showed in his excellent survey, a rehabilitation of the model was subsequently attempted by removing the assumption of perfect credibility. However, after the experience of Bretton Woods and especially that of the European Monetary System, marked by eleven realignments in the first eight years, it is ironic that a theory of target zones should have been built on such an assumption, patently in contrast with Friedman's well-known critique, anticipated by Cassel and Frank Graham (Cesarano 2006b, 115), stressing the one-way bet nature of such exchange rate arrangements.

Efficient scrutiny for logical errors allowed economics to arrive at rigorous results, enabling 'researchers to build on the work of their predecessors and to accelerate the cumulative process in which they are participating' (Debreu 1991, 3). By the axiomatic method, the conditions under which a hypothesis holds could be strictly defined, thereby eliminating loose or incorrect propositions.[5]

Nevertheless, this method does not lend itself to all topics. In some instances, the gain in rigour may well be accompanied by a loss of relevance, both theoretical and empirical. Thus Robert Clower, though finding 'no logical flaw in any aspect of Arrow-Debreu theory', argued that 'as a foundation for applied economics, Arrow-Debreu theory is empirically vacuous and conceptually incoherent' (1995, 317). The point is that, faced with the limitations of experimentation in economics, Debreu paradoxically called for even stricter logical rigour, thus further narrowing the focus of analysis rather than shaping the model to a more complex, elusive object of inquiry. But, if the axiomatic approach fails to increase the truth content of theories, it becomes sterile as a tool of analysis, while giving the false impression of a solid contribution.

Not all mathematical economists, however, are exposed to this critique. Maurice Allais is an eloquent example. Allais was trained as an engineer, not as a mathematician like Debreu. This is no trifling difference and it clearly shows in their antithetic positions. Applying the experimental methods of physics, Allais (1989, 6) contended that economic phenomena must first be probed and understood in order to formulate hypotheses, which must stand the ultimate test of experience. The mathematical structure of the model is an intermediate stage that ensures the rigorous and consistent development of a theory, but is the least important.

> All science is based on models, whether descriptive, explanatory, forecasting, or decision making, and every scientific model entails three distinct stages: start with well specified hypotheses, deduce from these hypotheses all their implications and nothing but these implications, and confront the implications with observed data. Of these three stages, only the first and the third – establishing hypotheses, and confronting

5 Considering the labour theory of value, for example, Hahn noted: 'Whether you take Smith's hunters, or Ricardo's industry agriculture model, or indeed dear Marx, it is now crystal clear that a theory which claims that in an orderly economy goods exchange in the ratio of their direct and indirect labour input can only be correct if (a) there is a linear production structure, (b) labour is the only non-produced input, (c) there is no joint production and (d) production does not take time, or the rate of profit is zero or the ratio of the value of produced input to labour is the same everywhere. This is a theorem. As far as I can see it is also the end of the matter. It is a very special kind of economy which is being discussed and what is more it is a very special version of G.E. [General Equilibrium] The habit of thought which G.E. has instilled has, I am arguing, the great advantage that it efficiently disposes of theoretical cul de sacs' (2005, 8).

> results with reality – are of interest to the economist. The second stage is purely logical and mathematical, that is tautological, and is of mathematical interest only.
>
> The model and the theory it represents are accepted, at least temporarily, or rejected, depending on the agreement or disagreement between observed data and the model's hypotheses and implications. *When neither the hypotheses nor the implications of a theory can be confronted with the real world, that theory is devoid of scientific interest.* Mere logical, or even mathematical deduction, remains worthless in terms of the understanding of reality if it is not clearly linked to reality.
>
> (1989, 12)

Allais (1989, 11), perhaps over-stretching the parallelism between economics and physics, emphasised that formal modelling is a tool, not an end in itself, thus taking fellow economists to task for distorting the use of mathematics.[6] Among the many holding this view, Morishima put the case in a telling way and drew an interesting parallel with the evolution of mathematics in Japan.[7] As Roger Backhouse argued, the problem is not with formalism *per se*, but with how and in what context formalism is resorted to.[8] The quotations in the last three footnotes (apologies to readers for their

6 'While mathematics is an instrument whose mastery is extremely precious, it is, and can only be, an instrument. One cannot be a good physicist or economist simply because one has some ability and skill in mathematics. For almost forty five years contemporary economic literature had developed too often in a totally erroneous direction with the construction of completely artificial mathematical models detached from reality; and too often it is dominated more and more by a mathematical formalism which fundamentally represents an immense regression. . . . Axiomatization may be necessary, but it is secondary to the confrontation of its implications in relation to experimental data. Paradoxically, from the scientific viewpoint, incomparably more care is brought today to the mathematical elaboration of models than to the discussion of their structure, their hypotheses, and their results from the viewpoint of analysis of facts' (Allais 1989, 13).

7 'Unlike physics, economics has unfortunately developed in a direction far removed from its empirical source, and GET [general equilibrium theory] in particular, as the core of economic theory, has become a mathematical social philosophy. In spite of its scientific presentation, the Arrow–Hahn book may remind us of Baruch Spinoza's *Ethica Ordine Geometrico Demonstrata*. . . . Japanese mathematics (or *wasan*) in the Tokugawa period, though it had attained a high level of sophistication, came to a wretched end due to its total absence of interaction with natural science. It turned into a technique for the setting of puzzles, and the *wasan* scholars were reduced to being the playmates of culture-loving samurai and members of the newly risen merchant class, just like the masters of the tea ceremony, of flower arrangement and of the *haiku*. At the same time, the mathematics itself regressed' (Morishima 1991, 69–70).

8 Pointing out the potential misuse of formalism, Backhouse and Harcourt quote the following passage by John von Neumann: 'As a mathematical discipline travels far from its empirical source, or still more, if it is a second and third generation only indirectly inspired by ideas coming from "reality", it is beset with grave dangers. It becomes more and more

length) clearly show that distinguished mathematical economists, and no less a mathematician than John von Neumann, criticised the habit of considering mathematics not as an instrument but as an object of economic theorising. This confusion may well lead to degenerating research programmes in the sense of Lakatos (1978, 33–4).

Elucidating the functions and limits of mathematics clarifies its effective contribution to the advancement of economics. To take an example from a different subject, a theory of political change could be built on the basis of the nature and magnitude of shocks affecting political equilibrium. This hypothesis could be developed using sophisticated models of dynamic optimization, but there is no guarantee that they would improve on an analysis in plain prose grounded in the tenets of Machiavelli's five-century-old *Prince*; indeed, they could actually be weaker. Hence, focusing on language as an end in itself mistakes the tool for the object of research and can lead astray. In any field, progress is propelled by the thrust of original ideas, developed through a suitable language. In the arts, minor painters and musicians remain unknown while great masters and major composers make their mark in history not just owing to their command of technique, but above all owing to their unique ability to innovate: the mere familiarity with technique does not ensure the production of a masterpiece. Likewise, in economics the uncritical shaping of hypotheses on available mathematical methods does not guarantee a lasting contribution and actually inverts the logic of discovery. Novel ideas, not the means of communicating them, are the prime mover of scientific knowledge.

The ideal of physics drove the evolution of economics in the last half century, but has been interpreted in quite different ways, witness the clashing views of Allais and Debreu. Besides, other economists argued for

purely aestheticizing, more and more purely *l'art pour l'art*. This need not be bad, if the field is surrounded by correlated subjects, which still have closer empirical connections, or if the discipline is under the influence of men with exceptionally well-developed taste. But there is a grave danger that the subject will develop along the line of least resistance, that the stream, so far from its source, will separate into a multitude of insignificant branches, and that the discipline will become a disorganised mass of details and complexities. In other words, at a great distance from its empirical source, or after much "abstract" inbreeding, a mathematical subject is in danger of degeneration' (quoted in Backhouse 1998, 1856 and Harcourt 1995, 216). In the same vein, Bruno de Finetti stressed that the axiomatic method does not contrast with but complements other, less abstract approaches. 'The evil does not lie in abstraction, which, through the rigour of limpid axiomatic approaches, demonstrates the possibility of grandiose constructions independent of extraneous notions, both empirical and metaphysical. The evil lies in considering these two aspects – internal rigour and external fecundity – to be in opposition rather than complementary. Purification and isolation from the remnants of ideas and external realities meet vital needs at the moment of abstraction and are an essential conquest in this respect, but they do terrible harm if they degenerate into purism and isolationism, in other words into a suicidal reason for permanent enclosure. Would a person be a surgeon who, after duly sterilising the scalpels, were to refrain from operating to keep them sterilised? . . . The ivory tower of the "end in itself" is full of traps that lead to a fall into aberration' (1963, 4–5, author's translation).

methodological eclecticism, calling for a plurality of approaches because, otherwise, the advancement of many fields of economics, especially the applied ones, would be precluded. Thus Baumol observed:

> There can hardly be any argument with the proposition that the use of mathematical methods has not solved all problems in economic analysis, and that some problems lend themselves more readily to statistical, experimental, historical or other lines of attack. While formal mathematical theory has made invaluable contributions in fields where its success might have caused considerable surprise in an earlier day – fields such as public finance and industrial organisation – each of these areas surely still leaves considerable scope for other research procedures. And there are still other areas, for example, labour economics, in which this is probably even truer.
>
> (1991, 2)

In the same vein, Frank Hahn (1991, 47–9), acknowledging the inability of pure theory to tackle new problems without resorting to psychological, sociological and historical postulates, foresaw the development of economics as a 'softer' science. The finite but large number of equilibria brings path dependence in the analysis, weakening the sway of pure theory.

> Not only will our successors have to be far less concerned with the general (leave alone the 'generic') than we have been, they will have to bring to the particular problems they will study particular histories and methods capable of dealing with the complexity of the particular, such as computer simulation. Not for them the grand unifying theory of particle physics which seems to beckon physicists. Not for them, or at least less frequently for them, the pleasures of theorems and proof. Instead the uncertain embrace of history and sociology and biology.
>
> (1991, 50)[9]

Venturing a prophecy is highly risky. But abandoning the language of mathematics seems most unlikely in the near future. Even putting aside for a moment the rarefied analyses of the axiomatic approach, the strong appeal of rigorous and clear-cut results will ensure formal modelling continues to dominate economic research. Mathematical models may not suit all topics

9 Hahn's warning about the limited ability of economic theory to reach the peaks of physics parallels Debreu's scepticism. Yet Debreu drew the opposite conclusion, calling for greater resort to the axiomatic approach in order to tackle specific problems. '[A] Grand Unified Theory will remain out of the reach of economics, which will keep appealing to a large collection of individual theories. Each one of them deals with a certain range of phenomena that it attempts to understand and to explain. When it acquires an axiomatic form, its explicit assumptions delimit its domain of applicability and make illegitimate overstepping of its boundary flagrant' (Debreu 1991, 3).

and may not foster progress in all branches of economics, but these deficiencies are unlikely to alter the current trend.[10] In this connection, paraphrasing Irving Fisher's dictum that 'There is no place you can go by railroad that you cannot go afoot', Samuelson dropped the equivalence of literary and mathematical languages and noted that 'To get to some destinations it matters a great deal whether you go afoot or ride by a train' (1952, 56, 64). In principle, however, neither statement can be accepted. Inasmuch as the properties of languages differ, their efficacy also differs, depending on the nature of the topic. The simple point is that, since language is an instrument, the choice of language and its effectiveness depend on the object to be pursued: using a hammer would not do where a screwdriver is needed. A more appropriate technique can be decisive in untangling hitherto unsolved problems, but there is no one technique that is always superior in analysing all topics.[11] Returning to Samuelson's analogy, beyond a certain grade a train cannot travel, but you can go afoot. Also, to reach the top of a mountain, a cableway would serve the purpose and a helicopter be even faster, but it is only by climbing that many awkward spots can be reached and the landscape enjoyed from diverse perspectives.

Hence, all languages, including the axiomatic method, can help to advance the state of the art with varying degrees of effectiveness according to the nature of the problem.[12] This is particularly the case of economics, which, lying at the border between hard and soft sciences, involves topics having very different characteristics. Thus, fixed point theorems are essential to prove the existence of equilibrium in the Walrasian model, while the

10 Commenting on the poor quality of econometric research, Milton Friedman noted: 'By now there is wide agreement that GIGO (garbage in, garbage out) is a real problem. But I suspect the reaction will be like that which Keynes anticipated in a highly critical note on Tinbergen's use of a system of simultaneous multiple regressions to test business cycle theories (one of the first comprehensive econometric models of the economy). Said Keynes (1939, p. 568), "I have a feeling that Prof. Tinbergen may agree with much of my comment, but that his reaction will be to engage another ten computors and drown his sorrows in arithmetic" (needless to say, Keynes meant human computers not electronic marvels)' (1991, 36).

11 In this regard, Baumol noted: 'There surely is no philosopher's stone in economic method – no one approach whose unqualified success and power mean that it deserves to replace all (or even any) of its rivals. *Every* method used in the social sciences has its glaring shortcomings which one can only hope to ameliorate by recourse, as a supplement, to other approaches' (1991, 2).

12 A striking illustration of this proposition is provided by Friedman and Schwartz's *Monetary History of the United States* together with Friedman's (1968) AEA presidential address, which, though entirely eschewing formal methods, fatally undermined the 'Keynesian revolution.' As Laidler remarked: 'Anachronistic in approach and technique even at its time of publication, it [the *Monetary History*] nevertheless broke the influence of the so-called "Keynesian consensus" about how market economies functioned in general, and had functioned in particular during the 1930s, and it reoriented economists' attention towards the power of monetary forces in a way that still marks the discipline. . . . It was narrative history, rather than state-of-the-art theory and econometrics, that so profoundly changed the views of economists in the 1960s and 1970s' (2003, 20–1). In this connection, Pareto

narrative approach is most appropriate to analyse the implementation of monetary policy in various monetary regimes. As the many branches of knowledge stretch over a wide range – from mathematics to literature and the arts – economics, having features typical of both hard and soft sciences, displays a kaleidoscope of topics that can suitably be analysed with different methods. Without doubt, formal modelling has acquired a dominant position. This development should not be complained about, as long as its limits are taken into account. These relate to the nature of economics as a social science, which is especially important for the evolution of the subject and the role of the history of economic analysis.

2. Economics as a social science

The shift from literary to mathematical language is an eloquent sign of the peculiar position of economics in the range of knowledge. Samuelson's argument (1952, 63–4), stressing the quantitative nature of economic problems and thus the greater efficiency of formal analysis, seems a platitude today. It was not fifty years ago and it is indeed puzzling that, for centuries, mathematical modelling was eschewed and even disparaged. As late as the mid-1930s Keynes, certainly an original and iconoclastic thinker by no means ignorant of mathematics, bluntly remarked:

> Too large a proportion of recent 'mathematical' economics are mere concoctions, as imprecise as the initial assumptions they rest on, which allow the author to lose sight of the complexities and interdependencies of the real world in a maze of pretentious and unhelpful symbols.
> (1936, 298)

This view was widely held[13] and, though it now looks like a relic of a bygone age, it does highlight the distinctive features of economics as a social

observed: 'Disputes about "the method" of political economy are useless. The goal of the science is to know the uniformities of phenomena. Consequently, it is necessary to employ all procedures and utilize all methods which lead us toward that goal. The good and bad methods are discovered by trial. One which leads us to the goal is good – at least as long as a better one has not been found. History is useful in that it extends the experience of the past into the present and supplies experiments which we are unable to make; hence the historical method is good. But the deductive method, or the inductive method, which is applied to present facts, is no less worthy. Where ordinary logic is adequate in deductions, we are satisfied with it; where it is not we replace it, without any qualms, by the mathematical method. In short, if an author prefers such or such a method, we will not quibble about it. We will simply ask him to show us the scientific laws, without caring too much about how he came to know them' (1909, 18–19).

13 In the same vein, an economist as intellectually distant from Keynes as Hayek noted: 'In the past, periods of monetary disturbance have always been periods of great progress in this branch of Economics. The Italy of the sixteenth century has been called the country of the worst money and the best monetary theory. If recently that has not been true to the same

science. Not by chance, the context of Keynes's and Hayek's rejection of mathematical modelling was the same – the analysis of the effects of changes in money supply – an intricate topic defying straightforward explanations. More important, their common position was based on similar reasoning: in a nutshell, formal models, focusing on a limited number of variables, leave out many complicating, interdependent factors, thus weakening the model's explanatory power.[14] To some extent this criticism applies to the social sciences as a whole, shedding light on their distinctive features *vis-à-vis* the physical sciences.

This partition has often been related to specific characteristics of social phenomena – the changing historical and institutional setting, the impossibility of controlled experimentation, the voluntary element in human behaviour, and the like – and has therefore been considered a matter of kind and not of degree. These features, however, are not peculiar to the social sciences (Samuelson 1952, 61–2) and are mere symptoms of a more general characteristic – the complexity of social phenomena – a concept displaying several dimensions. Thus Hayek talks about the '*essential* complexity' of the social sciences (1989, 4) and, in particular, of economics because the structures it deals with can be analysed by models that involve a myriad of actors. This aspect, related to methodological individualism, is highly relevant in studying the actual operation or malfunctioning of economic systems but, if excessively stretched, may verge on theoretical nihilism. At a higher level of abstraction, the main concern is not about the number of agents but about the number of interdependent forces that affect economic phenomena.

Although physical phenomena may appear obscure and impenetrable, their intrinsic nature is seldom complex in that hypotheses hinge on a few variables. The difficulty is to capture the core idea underlying the structure and the relationships linking its elements but, once these are correctly intuited, a 'simple', clear-cut model is readily built. In the social sciences, the situation is the diametrically opposite one. The main determinants of social phenomena are promptly perceived, very easy to grasp. As Samuelson recounted, when challenged by the noted mathematician Stanislaw Ulam to

extent, the reason seems to me to lie in a certain change of attitude on the part of most economists in regard to the appropriate methodology of economics, a change which in many quarters is hailed as a great progress: I mean the attempt to substitute quantitative for qualitative methods of investigation' (1935, 2–3).

14 'It is a great fault of symbolic pseudo-mathematical methods of formalising a system of economic analysis . . . that they expressly assume strict independence between the factors involved and lose all their cogency and authority if this hypothesis is disallowed; whereas, in ordinary discourse, where we are not blindly manipulating but know all the time what we are doing and what the words mean, we can keep "at the back of our heads" the necessary reserves and qualifications and the adjustments which we shall have to make later on, in a way in which we cannot keep complicated partial differentials "at the back" of several pages of algebra which assume that they all vanish' (Keynes 1936, 297–8).

'name . . . one proposition in all of the social sciences which is both true and non-trivial', it took him thirty years to find an appropriate answer: Ricardo's principle of comparative advantage (1969, 9). Stemming from plain tenets, economic models are actually easy to build, and yet they deal with complex structures, involving a large number of variables linked by relationships, mutable with respect to both effectiveness and timing. This would not in itself be an unsurpassable complication as long as the variables left out in the construction of the model exerted a negligible influence, but this is not always the case. Economic phenomena are therefore characterised by an 'inherent complexity' (Cesarano 1983, 67–71, 76–9).

An immediate implication is the multiplicity of modelling strategies. Of course, in any field theorists endeavour to abstract the key determining factors from a manifold reality, sometimes arriving at competing theories. However, while in the physical sciences those theories that do not repeatedly stand the test of falsification die off and can thus be excluded, in the social sciences this may not obtain. Excludability is indeed crucial in distinguishing these realms of knowledge (Cesarano 2006c, section 2).

Compared to other social sciences, economics tackles relatively less complex structures, but complexity increases along the overall range of topics and so does the number of potentially important variables left out by the model. Hence, hypotheses progressively lose explanatory power and the probability of falsifying them increases. In this regard, price theory appears to be closest to the physical sciences, yielding accurate predictions and perhaps displaying an analogous state of advancement; by contrast, business cycle theory and growth theory tend towards the opposite extreme. Theorists are presented with several choices for modelling a specific problem, and yet only one state of the world will be observed afterwards. Several hypotheses will then be falsified, but cannot be excluded because they may be corroborated under different conditions.[15] A graphic instance is Keynes's liquidity trap, a once disparaged and totally forgotten theory that has been successfully revived in the past decade to analyse monetary developments in Japan. An even better example is Hawtrey's analysis of the credit deadlock, contending that monetary expansion could pull the economy out of the

15 As Hicks noted: '[S]ince it is a changing world that we are studying, a theory which illumines the right things now may illumine the wrong things another time. . . . Accordingly, while we are right to allow ourselves to become wrapped up in those theories which are useful now, we are unwise if we allow ourselves to forget that the time may come when we shall need something different. We may then be right to reject our present theories, not because they are wrong, but because they have become inappropriate. Things which we formerly left unnoticed (more or less deliberately unnoticed) may rise up and become essential; we shall have to bring them in, even if that means averting our attention from things we thought important before. That is the *special* reason why economics is prone to revolutions — revolutions which appear, while they are occurring, to be steps in advance, though from a different point of view they may take on quite another character' (1976, 208).

depression, however severe it was, because of a limit to the amount of money held idle. Hawtrey's theory, albeit dating back to the early 1930s, is much better than modern theory at accounting for some important effects of monetary policy, with particular regard to the Japanese experience (Laidler 2004, 37–9).

This argument bears no relationship to the relativistic tenets of the historical school. The historical and institutional setting is just one dimension of complexity, impinging on theory together with many other forces. Actually, even a slight change in assumptions can lead to a totally different hypothesis and very different implications.[16] As complexity increases, the degree of excludability falls, to the point that several theories can coexist for centuries with the prevalent one alternating. This is the case of monetary economics, which advanced along parallel strains of thought, opposing the Currency School to the Banking School, classics to Keynesians, New Classical to New Keynesian Macroeconomics.[17]

The concept of a 'true' model in economics must thus be used with great care. As David Laidler noted, 'If we treat the History of Economic Thought with any degree of seriousness, . . . at no time in the past have economists ever provided a single model with an undisputed claim to embody the truth' (2003, 18). The concept can better be viewed as a theoretical benchmark which, upon weighing the main complicating factors and the interplay among them, can be adapted to the specific state of the world. A certain dose of intuition and eclecticism is essential in order to detect these factors and

16 A telling example was recently given by Mundell at a conference organised by the University of Bologna, in his dinner speech discussing the controversial effects of issuing paper money under a commodity standard. According to Hume and Smith, the issue of fiat money causes an equal amount of specie to flow abroad while, for Thornton, it increases the world price level. The solution, Mundell argued, depends on whether the small country assumption holds or not. This question has enormous implications for the analysis of the evolution of the international monetary system (Cesarano 2006b, 27–8; Chapter 8, section 1). Keynes's contention that under the gold standard the Bank of England was the 'conductor of the international orchestra' clashes with the modern monetary approach, whose followers, such as McCloskey and Zecher, consider the Bank of England a 'triangle player', assuming that the United Kingdom was too small a part of the world economy to control the world price level. On the other hand, the position of the United States in the Bretton Woods monetary order was rather different. As the centre country of a system that was progressively becoming a fiat money standard, and thus operating with rules quite different from those of the gold standard, the United States played a key role in line with Thornton's hypothesis.

17 In this connection, Schumpeter, discussing the contraposition between real analysis and monetary analysis, stressed their alternate dominance in diverse epochs from Aristotle to our days: 'Such spirals of advance are, I believe, not uncommon: theories that it is an achievement to displace may return to displace those by which they had been displaced, and both the displacement and the return may benefit that strange thing, scientific knowledge' (Schumpeter 1954, 288). In 1980, discussing a draft of an article of mine (Cesarano 1983) over lunch, Paul Samuelson also suggested the idea of a 'spiral' to describe the growth of economic knowledge, though interpreting it as a cumulative process, thus quite differently from Schumpeter.

shape the hypothesis accordingly, with a view to obtaining correct predictions.[18] The substantial progress in formal modelling and econometric techniques has, in fact, not been matched by equal progress in economic theory. Accounting for this divergence, Stiglitz has pointed to the inability of these advanced methods to distinguish between diverse hypotheses and overcome differences in ideological positions.[19] At the basis of this contrast, however, there is the complexity of the subject, which makes most hypotheses non-excludable. If the object of inquiry were less complex, a difference in approach or in the economist's 'vision' would not result in many conflicting theories because falsified hypotheses could be excluded. This is not the case of economics.

Excludability is a less clear-cut notion than falsifiability and should not be viewed as a criterion of demarcation. Besides, as there are different degrees of falsifiability, there are different degrees of excludability. To take an example from outside the physical and social sciences, in the scramble to discover the structure of DNA several models were envisaged, and especially a three-chain helix (Watson 1980, 93). Watson and Crick eventually came up with the double helix, which passed the falsification test while other hypotheses did not, paving the way for the rise of molecular biology. The structures studied by biology are actually complex, yet models show a high degree of excludability, thus arriving at solid results. This is conducive to a comprehensive view of knowledge, not divided into water-tight compartments but displaying gradually differentiated characteristics.

The non-excludability of hypotheses weakens the notion of cumulative progress in economics. Although the use of formal modelling encouraged the belief that economics could come closer to physics, the mere mimicking of the methods of hard sciences is no guarantee of reaching equally solid results. That predicting the price of a company's share or the exchange rate is far from being as accurate as predicting particle trajectories in nuclear collisions raises many doubts about economists' achievements *vis-à-vis* those of physicists. In this connection, the gulf separating physics from

18 To this end, Schumpeter assigned an important role to economic history, as supplying 'an adequate command of historical *facts* and an adequate amount of historical *sense* or of what may be described as *historical experience*' (1954, 13). For a detailed analysis, see Cesarano (2006c).

19 '[I]n spite of these methodological triumphs, the subject does not bear all the hallmarks of some of the other sciences. Most strikingly, while economists of many persuasions may agree about the tools to be employed, there is no agreement about the basic economic model for describing the economy: while in many circles, the competitive model, with perfectly informed agents, rational consumers and value maximising firms, is believed to provide the foundations for understanding both the aggregative behaviour of the economy and its components, in other circles, that model is viewed with some circumspection. Evidently, the tools are not strong enough to discriminate among fundamentally different hypotheses, or at least not strong enough to overcome differences in prior beliefs, beliefs which are often influenced by ideological concerns' (Stiglitz 1991, 134).

economics may well widen in the future since the former, tackling relatively simpler structures, will continue to supply solid theories, thus outpacing the latter's slower progress. Moreover, there are several economic questions that defy mathematical treatment. For instance, the huge differences between China and Russia in the transition from a centralised to a market economy cannot simply be accounted for by growth models – neoclassical, endogenous or otherwise – but rather by resorting to Hayek's analysis of market economies *vis-à-vis* planned economies and North's approach emphasising the role of institutions.

When faced with complex topics, the economist weighs the impact of several interdependent factors but, in building the model, he must necessarily neglect most of them. The formalist revolution heightened this feature of economics. When economists used literary language, they could keep many balls in the air, whereas, resorting to mathematical language, they have to confine the analysis to a small number of variables. The two languages, however, are just different tools and, thus, should be employed for different objectives; as in hunting, different types of game require different weapons, such as the shotgun (short but wide range) and the rifle (long but narrow range). The tardy diffusion of formal methods reflects these differences. From the very beginning, economists, both practical men like Cantillon and Ricardo and philosophers like Hume and Smith, focused on comprehensive analyses of major topics while, as the subject progressed, more attention was given to specific, detailed issues. In any case, formal models were long eschewed, even by those who had sufficient mathematical competence. Alfred Marshall is a clear example. In the mathematical appendix to the *Principles*, Marshall first criticised but then, showing an open-minded attitude, argued for mathematical modelling, because otherwise progress would be hampered.

> [W]hile a mathematical illustration of the mode of action of a definite set of causes may be complete in itself, and strictly accurate within its clearly defined limits, it is otherwise with any attempt to grasp the whole of a complex problem of real life, or even any considerable part of it, in a series of equations. For many important considerations, especially those connected with the manifold influences of the element of time, do not lend themselves easily to mathematical expression: they must either be omitted altogether, or clipped and pruned till they resemble the conventional birds and animals of decorative art. And hence arises a tendency towards assigning wrong proportions to economic forces; those elements being most emphasized which lend themselves most easily to analytical methods. No doubt this danger is inherent in every application not only of mathematical analysis, but of analysis of any kind, to the problems of real life. It is a danger which more than any other the economist must have in mind at every turn. But to avoid it altogether, would be to abandon the chief means of scientific progress: and in

> discussions written specially for mathematical readers it is no doubt right to be very bold in the search for wide generalizations.
>
> (1890, 850–1)

Several decades later, Marshall's call for innovative methods was definitively embraced, reversing the old stance. The triumph of the formalist revolution, however, also blurred and eventually blotted out the perception of the limits of the new tools. In particular, dealing with complex structures, mathematical models narrow the focus of analysis, leaving out a number of potentially important factors, which weakens their explanatory and predictive power and lowers the degree of excludability. This reasoning does not suggest reverting to prose in economic theorising, but simply to be aware of the limits of formal methods in order to appreciate their true analytical capabilities.

Mathematical modelling and econometric techniques brought a substantial improvement in the box of tools, fostering progress and giving a new turn to economics. However, language is no substitute for knowledge: ultimately, it is novel ideas that spark theoretical advancement. The theorist's creative effort precedes model building, which is simply the translation of the intuitive scheme into an effective analytical language. In the early stage of theorising, a wider perspective is conducive to original intuitions, helping to arrive at an innovative theory. The formalist revolution, narrowing the focus of analysis, heightened this opportunity. Of course, the ultimate test of theories is empirical relevance. New hypotheses will compete with the mainstream, possibly providing better explanations if they captured the factors disregarded by the received view. In general, any piece of information that can further the economist's analytical horizon enhances research. Just as economic history enlarges the perception of stylised facts, the interaction among current dominating factors and future developments, the history of economic analysis widens the economist's theoretical background and suggests alternative modelling strategies.

3. Economic theory: past and future

The distinctive characteristics of economics as a social science run counter to the cumulative evolution of economic theory. This does not mean that there is no progress in economics. Even if the development path of the field is not monotonically increasing, the long-run trend is, because more efficacious analytical tools have deepened our knowledge of traditional topics and new insights have broadened our understanding of a variety of issues, from the role of information to the strategic nature of economic behaviour. However, the multiplicity of modelling strategies and the low degree of excludability of most hypotheses present the theorist with a pervasive uncertainty. In this respect, the history of economic analysis plays an important role, not by supplying ready-made alternative theories but by throwing light on hidden analytical aspects and suggesting new research paths.[20] The historian's objective must not be to revive heterodox currents of thought, an approach that would relegate the history of economics in a ghetto, but to offer useful materials in order to tackle complex issues from different perspectives and formulate novel hypotheses. To take a cursory example, the monetary approach to the balance of payments, which puts the money market and the law of one price at the centre of the stage, has an intellectual ancestry very close to Hume's specie-flow model (Cesarano 1998). This feature has been stressed by its proponents in order to challenge other modern approaches. A sure command of the classics and the ability to recognize and link concealed theoretical hints in a coherent framework can suggest innovative hypotheses. This is no easy task, and yet distinguished economists often possess and greatly benefit from these skills. A few examples will be given in this section.

What follows may give the impression of overrating the profession's performance because 'original' theories are often defective. However, the object here is not the theories' novelty as such but the process of formulating them and, in particular, how knowledge of classic works can foster this process. This emerges above all in the analysis of policy issues, where the lower level of abstraction heightens the impact of complicating factors on the modelling strategy with major consequences. Policy mistakes can indeed have disruptive effects, as in the Great Depression, a glaring example of the misunderstanding and mishandling of a crisis, which turned into an economic catastrophe.

In the aftermath of World War I, the difficulty of restoring the gold standard led to a major transformation of the international monetary order. In the *Tract*, Keynes (1923, Chapters 4 and 5) had clearly described the shift to a managed money and the dominant role of the Fed, since he deemed

20 As Negishi observed: 'To develop our science in the right direction, I believe more theoretical resources should go into the study of the history of economics from the point of view of the current theory. This of course does not mean to cut or stretch a past theory into a Procrustean bed for the current theory. The history of our science should be used as a mirror in which the current theory reflects the knowledge of how it failed to succeed in the past. To learn from past theories does not impede the progress of our science. Progress often means, however, sacrificing something old. To make sure that we are going in the right direction, it is always necessary to see whether we have sacrificed something in error' (1992, 228). Pointing out the need to focus on a small number of explanatory factors in order to discover general patterns, Hicks noted: 'What we want, in economics, are theories which will be useful, practically useful. That means that they must be selective. But all selection is dangerous. So there is plenty of room for criticism, and for the filling in of gaps, building some sort of bridge between one selective theory and another. There is plenty of room for academic work, doing that sort of a job. Much of it, I am well aware, works in its own "blinkers", seeing the mote that is in one's brother's eye but not the beam that is in one's own. That, I am afraid, is the nature of the case. Still, one could learn a little humility" (1976, 218).

cooperation not to be feasible.[21] Yet, most policymakers did not fully perceive the implications of these momentous changes and stuck to the pre-war rules of the game (Cesarano 2006b, Chapter 3). In the early 1930s, the sharp fall of the money supply in the United States and its international propagation through the gold exchange standard (Fisher 1934; Eichengreen 1992) shattered the world economy. Had policymakers absorbed Keynes' lesson, the depression might have been tackled at an early stage, thereby avoiding its most severe and lasting consequences.

Keynes, far ahead of his time, argued for activist monetary management in order to stabilise the price level, as well as output and employment (1923, 137–40; 153–33), and put forward 'the proposal – which may seem, but should not be, shocking – of separating entirely the gold reserve from the note issue' (1923, 154).[22] Keynes' felicitous intuitions, paving the way for modern monetary policy, built upon a deep knowledge of classical monetary theory, which served to bring the implications of the change in the rules of the game into focus and to predict future developments.[23]

After the disruptive shock of the Great Depression, the *General Theory* provided the foundation for widening the scope of economic policies in order to smooth business cycles and prevent major contractions. A few decades later, this paradigm was attacked, especially by Milton Friedman. In his classic paper on the role of monetary policy, Friedman (1968, 100–5) exploded two widely held tenets – the pegging of interest rates and the reduction of unemployment in the long run – by focusing on the Fisher effect of expected inflation on the interest rate and extending the Wicksellian distinction between natural and market interest rates to the unemployment rate. Dwelling upon these principles, he arrived at an innovative yet controversial hypothesis, which was then corroborated by the stagflation of the 1970s, definitely making the pendulum swing in the opposite direction. This story is well known. But the point to be emphasised here is that Friedman's shrewd combination of elements of theories, introduced much earlier by other distinguished economists, was essential to his pathbreaking contribution.

These examples clearly show that, as Blaug (2001, 156–7) stressed, the

21 'I see grave objections to reinstating gold in the pious hope that international co-operation will keep it in order. With the existing distribution of the world's gold, the reinstatement of the gold standard means, inevitably, that we surrender the regulation of our price level and the handling of the credit cycle to the Federal Reserve Board of the United States' (Keynes 1923, 139).

22 This proposal was anticipated by Wicksell (1898, 193), who also argued, together with Marshall and several others, for activist monetary management (Laidler 1991, Chapter 6).

23 To give just one example, Keynes (1923, 125) answered the thorny question of whether or not to resume the pre-war parity by recalling Ricardo's suggestion of doing so if the depreciation rate was within 5 per cent, since otherwise this measure would be unsuitable and useless because, to maintain the credibility of the gold standard, the restoration rule must be precisely applied: 'It is of the essence of the argument that the *exact* pre-war parity should be recovered' (1923, 122).

full potential of the history of economic analysis is never exhausted. This is an immediate implication of the distinctive features of economics as a social science, dealing with complex structures that are analysed by hypotheses with a high degree of excludability. The history of economics, therefore, draws attention to theoretical clues that cast light on unsolved issues. The cases just expounded provide an *ex post* illustration of this proposition. Many other examples could easily be added, but it is more interesting to show the same proposition from an *ex ante* perspective, focusing on current, hitherto unsettled debates.

Mundell's (1961) seminal paper on optimum currency areas has been a cornerstone of international economics for almost half a century. Mundell showed the possibility of exchange rate flexibility failing to achieve internal and external balance under the Keynesian assumption of price and wage rigidity, and proposed the innovative solution of redrawing national borders in accordance with labour mobility. Spurred by projects of monetary unification in Western Europe, research on the topic gained momentum, leading to the introduction of further optimality criteria – openness to trade, product diversification, similarity of inflation rates and several others. All these criteria related to given characteristics of the economy and were therefore exogenous. In the last decade, an alternative approach, tackling the subject from the equilibrium perspective of the new classical macroeconomics, stressed the endogeneity of optimality criteria (Cesarano 1997; Frankel and Rose 1998). On the basis of the Lucas critique, the equilibrium approach emphasizes the impact of fixing the borders of a currency area on agents' behaviour and the institutional and legal framework, thus enhancing the adjustment mechanism inside the monetary area.

In the context of this paper, the important point is the close relationship between the modern equilibrium approach and the literature of the 1950s on monetary unions, which, in contrast with Mundell, considered labour mobility and other optimality criteria as the outcome of a highly effective adjustment mechanism within a country (Cesarano 2006a, section 1; 2006d). Albeit lacking the analytical apparatus of the new classical macroeconomics, this literature, to which Meade and Scitovsky were major contributors, viewed the optimality criteria as the result of domestic adjustment forces and, thus, essentially endogenous.

This story is eloquent evidence of the role that the history of economics can play in fostering research: not pre-packaged hypotheses, but useful insights for building new theories. This requires a heedful, intuitive reading of classic works in order to stimulate novel patterns of analysis, which is neither easy nor immediate.[24] The equilibrium approach to optimum

24 Adding a personal note, it did not occur to me to think of the early post-war literature on monetary unions while working on the equilibrium approach to currency areas (Cesarano 1997), although my acquaintance with that literature dated back to my student days. It was only a decade later that I saw the relationship between the two strands of thought (Cesarano 2006d).

currency areas is grounded on the tenets of modern macroeconomics, and yet the literature of the 1950s contained the essential principle – the endogeneity of optimality criteria – that has turned the traditional approach upside down. These different views have contrasting policy implications, so that choosing between them has momentous consequences. While under the traditional approach optimality is related to the actual existence of exogenous criteria and therefore reduces to an empirical question, under the equilibrium approach political union, by removing national borders, sets in motion adjustment forces that enhance optimality. Needless to say, embracing one or the other approach is of paramount importance for assessing the viability of Europe's Economic and Monetary Union.

A last example, currently of great interest, is the heated debate on the revaluation of the Chinese currency. In the United States, the widespread call for revaluing the yuan in order to redress 'global imbalances' has been disputed by Ronald McKinnon (2006). Drawing an analogy with the recent Japanese experience, McKinnon stresses the narrowing of the wage differential as the main channel of adjustment in a fixed exchange rate regime and points to the impact of the negative risk premium in interest rates and wage growth on the interest rate on Chinese assets under floating rates. In the event of financial liberalization, the expectation of ongoing appreciation of the yuan could give rise to a liquidity trap and severe deflationary pressures. The right policy action, McKinnon argues, would be to stick to fixed exchange rates and implement aggregate demand policies in order to redress imbalances stemming from a very high savings rate in China and a very low one in the United States.

The contraposition between the elasticity approach and the absorption approach underlying this controversy again highlights the multiplicity of modelling strategies in economics, leading to quite opposite policy recipes, with potentially major consequences. In general, inasmuch as theory bears on policy, the impact of the history of economics extends to the future. The future will write the epilogue of the last two stories and determine which hypothesis is eventually falsified. The fate of EMU is going to be decided by the many effects of maintaining national borders, and the related lack of federal economic policies, on the optimality criteria and on long-run adjustment, the crux of the theory of optimum currency areas. Analogously, the question of revaluing the yuan will be decided by the prevalence of one or another approach.

The history of economic analysis simply makes economists less ignorant, helping to build better models and take right policy decisions. The frequent reference to the 'true' model of the economy is misleading in that, dealing with complex structures, the impact of complicating factors may significantly alter the model, with momentous policy implications. The knowledge of past theories is therefore not mere erudition but part of the box of tools because, by helping to capture those factors, it ultimately raises the predictive power of the model. The study of the past is instrumental to the development of the future. As Enrico Barone remarked:

> Deduction, use of that special logic of quantities that is mathematics, graphical illustration, statistical induction, historical research, and comparison of economic facts with other facts of social life all contribute to discovering the uniformities that are present in economic *facts*. Only petty spirits can believe, for example, that a well conducted historical enquiry does not make a notable contribution to the knowledge of those uniformities, the search for and logical concatenation of which are the subject of science, and only such spirits can assert that intelligently reconstructing the history of economic doctrines, facts and principles is not political economy! Almost as if *today* is not the result of *yesterday* and the preparation of *tomorrow*!
>
> (1908, IV–V, author's translation)[25]

4. Conclusions

The challenge for historians of economics is to attract the interest of fellow economists, by showing that revisiting the classics can help foster progress in economic theory. The case for the history of economics can of course be made on other grounds – cultural, pedagogical or even for its own sake – but these approaches would not rescue the discipline from neglect. Moreover, considering the history of economic thought mere history of science would confirm its total irrelevance to our profession, as in the hard sciences. This paper takes issue with these positions, arguing that the formalist revolution makes the study of past theories more, not less, relevant to current research.

The spread of mathematical modelling substantially enhanced the rigour of economic analysis, but gave the impression that economics could progress in a cumulative fashion. Economics has gone a long way towards becoming a matter for specialists ('like dentistry', Keynes 1931, 332). Due to their

25 In the following passage, Allais takes the same position as Barone, showing their common intellectual ancestry: the work of Vilfredo Pareto. 'Nothing is more instructive than the history of facts, doctrines, and economic thought. Whether it be economic systems, the evolution of real incomes, monetary phenomena, demography, international relations, ideology, or the interaction between these factors and their chains of cause and effect, nothing is more significant. I cannot but side with Schumpeter here. If, *in order to understand economics*, one had to choose between mastering economic history or mastering mathematics and statistics, there is no doubt that one must choose the former. But the best for an economist, of course, would be this dual mastery. This was the case for Vilfredo Pareto, the greatest economist the world has produced to date, who was able to bring together with penetrating intelligence a wide command of the mathematics of his time and a truly extraordinary command of the history of societies since Greco-Roman antiquity' (1989, 10).

inherent complexity, however, economic phenomena cannot be reduced to a single agreed-upon model. The quantum jump in method actually heightened the distinctive characteristics of economics as a social science. By narrowing the focus of analysis of complex structures, it increased the degree of excludability of hypotheses and, hence, the multiplicity of modelling strategies.

The history of economics, therefore, can foster the progress brought about by the formalist revolution, suggesting ideas to build new theories and helping the choice of models for efficacious policy design. Knowledge of the classics can support the advancement of economic theory, providing insights into novel aspects of economic analysis, hinting at alternative theoretical frameworks and broadening the economist's perspective. The heedful study of the great economists can contribute to innovative research and create a bridge between the past and the future of economics.

References

Allais, Maurice (1989) 'My Life Philosophy', *American Economist*, 33: 3–17.

Backhouse, Roger E. (1998) 'If Mathematics Is Informal, Then Perhaps We Should Accept That Economics Must Be Informal Too', *Economic Journal*, 108: 1848–58.

Barone, Enrico (1908) *Principi di Economia Politica*, 2nd edn. (1913), Rome: Athenaeum.

Baumol, William J. (1991) 'Toward a Newer Economics: The Future Lies Ahead!', *Economic Journal*, 101: 1–8.

Blaug, Mark (ed.) (1991) *The Historiography of Economics*, Aldershot: Edward Elgar.

—— (1999) 'The Formalist Revolution or What Happened to Orthodox Economics After World War II?', in Roger E. Backhouse and John Creedy (eds) *From Classical Economics to the Theory of the Firm: Essays in Honour of D.P. O'Brien*, 257–80, Cheltenham: Edward Elgar.

—— (2001) 'No History of Ideas, Please, We're Economists', *Journal of Economic Perspectives*, 15: 145–64.

Cesarano, Filippo (1983) 'On the Role of the History of Economic Analysis', *History of Political Economy*, 15: 63–82; reprinted in Blaug (1991), 151–70; Chapter 1 above.

—— (1997) 'Currency Areas and Equilibrium', *Open Economies Review*, 8: 51–9.

—— (1998) 'Hume's Specie-Flow Mechanism and Classical Monetary Theory: An Alternative Interpretation', *Journal of International Economics*, 45: 173–86; Chapter 5 above.

—— (2006a) 'The Equilibrium Approach to Optimum Currency Areas', *Banca Nazionale del Lavoro Quarterly Review*, 59: 193–209.

—— (2006b) *Monetary Theory and Bretton Woods: The Construction of an International Monetary Order*, Cambridge: Cambridge University Press.

—— (2006c) 'Economic History and Economic Theory', *Journal of Economic Methodology*, 13: 447–67.

—— (2006d) 'The Origins of the Theory of Optimum Currency Areas', *History of Political Economy*, 38: 711–31; Chapter 11 above.

Clower, Robert W. (1995) 'Axiomatics in Economics', *Southern Economic Journal*, 62: 307–19.

Cournot, Antoine A. (1838) *Researches Into the Mathematical Principles of the Theory of Wealth*; trans. N. T. Bacon (1929), New York: Macmillan.

Debreu, Gerard (1991) 'The Mathematization of Economic Theory', *American Economic Review*, 81: 1–7.

de Finetti, Bruno (1963) *L'apporto della matematica nell'evoluzione del pensiero economico*, Rome: Edizioni Ricerche.

Eichengreen, Barry (1992) *Golden Fetters: The Gold Standard and the Great Depression, 1919–1939*, Oxford: Oxford University Press.

Fisher, Irving (1934) *Are Booms and Depressions Transmitted Internationally Through Monetary Standards?*, New Haven, Conn.; reprinted in Robert W. Dimand (2003) 'Irving Fisher on the International Transmission of Booms and Depressions Through Monetary Standards', *Journal of Money, Credit and Banking*, 35: 49–90.

Frankel, Jeffrey A. and Rose, Andrew K. (1998) 'The Endogeneity of the Optimum Currency Area Criteria', *Economic Journal*, 108: 1009–25.

Friedman, Milton (1968) 'The Role of Monetary Policy', *American Economic Review*, 58: 1–17; reprinted in Milton Friedman (1969) *The Optimum Quantity of Money and Other Essays*, 95–110, Chicago: Aldine.

—— (1991) 'Old Wine in New Bottles', *Economic Journal*, 101: 33–40.

Giocoli, Nicola (2003) *Modeling Rational Agents: From Interwar Economics to Early Modern Game Theory*, Cheltenham: Edward Elgar.

Hahn, Frank (1991) 'The Next Hundred Years', *Economic Journal*, 101: 47–50.

—— (2005) 'General Equilibrium for Intellectual Historians', *Storia del Pensiero Economico*, 2: 5–12.

Harcourt, Geoffrey C. (1995) 'On Mathematics and Economics', in *Capitalism, Socialism and Post-Keynesianism: Selected Essays of G.C. Harcourt*, 201–17, Aldershot: Edward Elgar.

Hayek, Friedrich A. (1935) *Prices and Production*, 2nd edn, New York: Augustus M. Kelley.

—— (1989) 'The Pretence of Knowledge', *American Economic Review*, 79: 3–7.

Hicks, John R. (1976) '"Revolutions" in Economics', in Spiro J. Latsis (ed.) *Method and Appraisal in Economics*, 207–18, Cambridge: Cambridge University Press.

Keynes, John M. (1923) *A Tract on Monetary Reform*; reprinted in *The Collected Writings of John Maynard Keynes*, vol. 4 (1971), London: Macmillan.

—— (1931) 'Economic Possibilities for Our Grandchildren', in *Essays in Persuasion*; reprinted in *The Collected Writings of John Maynard Keynes*, vol. 9 (1972), 321–32, London: Macmillan.

—— (1936) *The General Theory of Employment, Interest and Money*, London: Macmillan.

—— (1939) 'Professor Tinbergen's Method' (a review of J. Tinbergen, *A Method and Its Application to Investment Activity*), *Economic Journal*, 49: 558–68.

Laidler, David (1991) *The Golden Age of the Quantity Theory: The Development of Neoclassical Monetary Economics, 1870–1914*, Hemel Hempstead, England: Philip Allan.

—— (2003) 'The Role of the History of Economic Thought in Modern Macroeconomics', in Paul Mizen (ed.) *Monetary History, Exchange Rates and Financial*

Markets: Essays in Honour of Charles Goodhart, vol. 2, 12–29, Cheltenham: Edward Elgar; reprinted in David Laidler (2004) *Macroeconomics in Retrospect*, 410–27, Cheltenham: Edward Elgar.

—— (2004) 'Monetary Policy after Bubbles Burst: The Zero Lower Bound, the Liquidity Trap and the Credit Deadlock', *Canadian Public Policy*, 30: 333–40.

Lakatos, Imre (1978) 'Falsification and the Methodology of Scientific Research Programmes', in Imre Lakatos, *The Methodology of Scientific Research Programmes: Philosophical Papers*, vol. 1, 8–101, Cambridge: Cambridge University Press.

Marshall, Alfred (1890) *Principles of Economics*, 9th variorum edn (1961), Cambridge: Macmillan.

McKinnon, Ronald I. (2006) 'China's Exchange Rate Trap: Japan Redux?', *American Economic Review: Papers and Proceedings*, 96: 427–31.

Mirowski, Phillip (2002) 'A Pall along the Watchtower: On Leaving the *HOPE* Conference', in E. Roy Weintraub (ed.) *The Future of the History of Economics*, Annual Supplement to Volume 34, *History of Political Economy*, 378–90, Durham and London: Duke University Press.

Morishima, Michio (1991) 'General Equilibrium Theory in the Twenty-First Century', *Economic Journal*, 101: 69–74.

Mundell, Robert A. (1961) 'A Theory of Optimum Currency Areas', *American Economic Review*, 51: 657–65.

Negishi, Takashi (1992) Comment to 'Breaking Away: History of Economics as History of Science' by Margaret Schabas, *History of Political Economy*, 24: 227–9.

Pareto, Vilfredo (1909) *Manual of Political Economy*; trans. Ann S. Schwier (1971), New York: Augustus M. Kelley.

Patinkin, Don (1956) *Money, Interest, and Prices: An Integration of Monetary and Value Theory*, Evanston, Ill.: Row, Peterson.

Ramsey, Frank P. (1928) 'A Mathematical Theory of Saving', *Economic Journal*, 38: 543–59.

Samuelson, Paul A. (1952) 'Economic Theory and Mathematics – An Appraisal', *American Economic Review: Papers and Proceedings*, 42: 56–66.

—— (1969) 'The Way of an Economist', in Paul A. Samuelson (ed.) *International Economic Relations*, 1–11, London: Macmillan.

—— (1987) 'Out of the Closet: A Program for the Whig History of Economic Science', *History of Economics Society Bulletin*, 9: 51–60; reprinted in Blaug (1991), 181–90.

Schabas, Margaret (1992) 'Breaking Away: History of Economics as History of Science', *History of Political Economy*, 24: 187–203.

Schumpeter, Joseph A. (1954) *History of Economic Analysis*, Oxford: Oxford University Press.

Stiglitz, Joseph E. (1991) 'Another Century of Economic Science', *Economic Journal*, 101: 134–41.

Taylor, Mark P. (1995) 'Exchange-Rate Behavior under Alternative Exchange-Rate Arrangements', in Peter B. Kenen (ed.) *Understanding Interdependence: The Macroeconomics of the Open Economy*, 34–83, Princeton: Princeton University Press.

Vaughn, Karen I. (1993) 'Why Teach the History of Economics?', *Journal of the History of Economic Thought*, 15: 174–83.

Ward, Benjamin (1972) *What's Wrong with Economics?*, London: Macmillan.

Watson, James D. (1980) *The Double Helix: A Personal Account of the Discovery of the Structure of DNA*, New York: Norton.

Wicksell, Knut (1898) *Interest and Prices: A Study of the Causes Regulating the Value of Money*, (1965), New York: Augustus M. Kelley.

Author index